WHOLE CHILD

PARENTING

Birth to Age Five

Concept by Claudia Sandor

WHOLE CHILD

HEALTH AND CARE
Hygiene
Diet
Routine
Yoga

COGNITIVE DEVELOPMENT
Problem-solving
Attention
Numbers

PHYSICAL DEVELOPMENT
Motor skills:
Sensory
Gross
Fine

SOCIAL-EMOTIONAL DEVELOPMENT
Self-control
Friendship
Feelings

CREATIVE DEVELOPMENT
Dramatic Play
Dance
Music
Arts

LANGUAGE DEVELOPMENT
Communication
Speaking
Literacy

WHOLE CHILD:
BIRTH TO AGE FIVE
Six Areas of Development

WHOLE CHILD

whole \hōl\ **child** \chi-əld\ *compound noun*
1 : a child who is completely developed in all six areas

A **whole child** grows up to reach his or her full potential.

A **whole child** is a **well-rounded** person and lifelong learner.

A **whole child** is ready to face the world with **confidence.**

A **whole child** has **self-esteem, knowledge,** and **creativity**.

A **whole child** will live a **happy** and **fulfilling life**.

Being a successful parent starts with understanding your child.

The Whole Child Parenting Program covers every aspect of a child's cognitive, social-emotional, language, creative, physical, and health and care development.

By using clear examples, color-coded stages, simple and logical steps, age-appropriate materials and toys, developmentally appropriate activities and workbooks, and core parenting books, the Whole Child Program will change the way you think about learning.

Welcome to parenting for the new millenium!

Published by Whole Child Parenting, Inc.
Whole Child Parenting books, activity books, toys, and materials are
available at special discounts when purchased in bulk for premiums
and sales promotions as well as for fundraising or educational use.
For details, please contact us at:
sales@wholechild.co

Whole Child is a registered trademark of Whole Child, LLC
Library of Congress Control Number: 2016905512
ISBN 978-1-944930-01-1

Created by the Whole Child Education Team with:
Early Childhood Education Specialist, Erin Weekes
Book design by Willabel Tong
Art direction by Dan Marmorstein
Editorial direction by Editorial Services of Los Angeles

Visit us on the web at: www.wholechild.co
Email us at: publishing@wholechild.co

Printed in the United States of America.
1 3 5 7 9 10 8 6 4 2

Contents

Chapter 3: Age Two

Chapter 4: Age Three

Chapter 5: Age Four

What Is Whole Child Parenting?

It Is Parenting from Head to Toe

Whole child parenting involves exposing your child to everything he needs to be happy, healthy, well adjusted, smart, and developing right on track. A whole child is a well-rounded person, someone whose innate talents have been developed in every major milestone category and who is ready to face the world with confidence. A whole child has the self-esteem and knowledge to develop his true potential.

Whole child parenting is you doing what you can, with our help, to get him there. The Whole Child Parenting Program is for busy people just like you. With interactive materials that support you at every step, using toys, workbooks, activities, videos, web support, and an app, the Whole Child Parenting Program takes into account the whole child and helps you, the parent or primary caregiver, do what is necessary and best for your child at every stage, every age from infancy to five years old. It helps you parent with a purpose, giving you practical advice and materials that explain the whys and how-tos and goals of each step you take to help your child grow.

Whole child parenting is a process that begins with you. It can be overwhelming to think about the responsibility you have to your child over the next 18 years, much less the next five years, which are the most important years of your child's life.

These first five years are crucial years because development, in both the body and brain, is happening at a rapid pace. These first five years will set the stage for how your child problem solves, communicates, socializes, and thinks for the rest of his life. And **your presence and influence will always matter the most in these first five years.** The world is constantly changing; Will your child be ready for the global economy years from now? Just by reading this book you are setting yourself along the right path for being the best parent you can be for your child.

HOW TO GET ON THE RIGHT TRACK NOW

Whole Child Parenting: Birth to Age Five has **five major sections: Infant, Toddler, Age Two, Age Three, and Age Four.** Each section is divided into six chapters for the six areas of development seen in the column at right. **Each area of development is assigned its own color.**

Each of the six chapters begins with a chart and summary to introduce you to the concepts and terminology in the pages ahead. Within each chapter, **you will also get real-life activities and insights that paint a picture of how your child demonstrates these developmental concepts** in everyday life. In addition to examples, there are tips and advice for parents and primary caregivers to use to support and guide you as

1 Cognitive
Development

2 Social-Emotional
Development

3 Language
Development

4 Creative
Development

5 Physical
Development

6 Health and Care

you and your child encounter and master each of the upcoming milestones.

The Whole Child Parenting Program has developed five smart, modern, easy steps to help you raise a happy, thriving child.

> ## The Whole Child Parenting Program involves:
>
> 1. **Committing yourself**
> 2. **Educating yourself**
> 3. **Creating the right environment**
> 4. **Using the right materials**
> 5. **Staying on track**

That's it. Five steps to making your experience with your child the most rewarding and productive experience in your life.

STEP ONE: COMMITTING YOURSELF

Let's start with commitment. As a parent you have already taken the huge step of accepting responsibility for the little person in front of you. What is next required might not even be a step that needs articulating for you, but it's worth stating here: **You need to commit quality time to raising your whole child.**

There is no formula or script when it comes to being successful in parenting. Many parents look to doctors, textbooks, and experts for the secrets to parenting success. And while all of these are great sources, none address the whole child. And the whole child needs your attention.

Each child is different and has a different temperament, dif-ferent interests, and a different personality. As a parent, you are also different. Every parent has different values that come from being a part of different cultures, socioeconomic classes, education levels, religions, and family sizes. The best way to be successful in parenting is to be involved with your child. By being involved and communicating with your child, you are better able to support her and her needs.

Many wonder what the real measures and outcomes of good parenting are. It does not involve your child having a high IQ, being talented in sports, or making a lot of money. Good parenting results in raising a child who grows up to give back to society, is independent, has a good work ethic, gets along well with others, and understands her identity and self-worth.

When it comes to measuring your success as a parent, it is important to look at the quality of the relationship you have with your child and not how effectively you can control your child. Just because your child listens and follows the rules does not mean she understands or respects them; it just means she is obedient.

The quality of your relation-ship has to do with your in-volvement and communication with your child. Know what guidelines are appropriate to set for your child, and explain them in a way that shows why these rules are necessary and important. As a parent, you need to meet your child's needs and help her feel respected. This can be done by explaining the reasons behind rules and discussing your child's feelings and opinions.

When your child feels like she is a valued member of the family and the community, she will then develop the confidence needed to begin moving toward being independent and making her own decisions.

Parents who are uninvolved with their children tend to make their children feel ignored and unvalued. At the same time, parents who are overly controlling and establish strict rules over all avenues of their children's lives tend to make their children feel stressed and have low self-esteem. It is important to find the middle ground between controlling your child and overlooking your child.

Your child is born naturally impulsive, immature, and ambitious, and she looks to you for guidance and support. This is why it is important to **make sure you communicate clear guidelines and expectations** for your child to alleviate stress and misunderstandings.

THE FOUR STYLES OF PARENTING

Whole Child Parenting: Birth to Age Five combines research, expert advice, and firsthand experience. In the past few decades, early childhood education has grown exponentially.

In the late 1950s, psychologist Erik Erikson organized development from birth to death into eight stages; according to Erikson, a person cannot successfully excel in the next stage of life without first completing the stage before.

Looking specifically at the first three stages, which cover ages birth to five, we see that a person's success lies first in his relationship with his parents. **Stage 1,** covering ages birth to two years old, focuses on a child's ability to develop **trust** with his parents. From there, children move on to **Stage 2** (for ages two to four years old), when the child is developing autonomy. **Autonomy** is your child's sense of self as an individual. Your child develops a sense of self by exploring the environment, learning about his own interests, and testing his limits. Moving forward to **Stage 3** (ages four to five years old), your child is **finding his purpose and place** within the family.

In the last 40 years, developmental psychologists have established **four styles of parenting.** The best parenting style is a combination of these four parenting styles—one in which you approach different situations with different solutions and always communicate with your child.

Authoritarian Parenting

The authoritarian parenting style can best be described as strict. Authoritarian parents tend to set rules that result in rewards or punishment if they are not followed. Rules are not explained and usually follow a reasoning of "because I said so." **These parents usually set high demands and expect obedience** but are not very responsive to their children. Children who grow up under the authoritarian parenting style tend to be obedient and usually well performing in school but socially exhibit signs of shame, low self-esteem, and lowered happiness levels.

Authoritative Parenting

The authoritative parenting style establishes rules and guidelines for children instead of just demands. Authoritative parents are more nurturing and forgiving, rather than simply punishing. They are responsive to their children and willing to listen and answer questions.

An important quality of authoritative parents is that they create clear standards for their children and adjust those standards based on their children's conduct.

Children who grow up under the authoritative parenting style tend to be capable and successful at learning new things. Socially and emotionally,

they feel accepted and tend to be happy.

Permissive Parenting

The permissive parenting style is one that has few demands or guidelines. Parents tend to have low expectations for their children's maturity and abilities. **Permissive parents are more lenient with rules, preferring to avoid confrontation.**

This parenting style is usually nurturing and communicative but leaves children looking at their parent as more of a friend. Children who grow up under the permissive parenting style tend to often have poor self-regulation skills and may experience problems with authority and have trouble in school.

Uninvolved Parenting

The uninvolved parenting style is one with even fewer demands as well as little communication and responsiveness. Uninvolved parents fulfill their children's basic needs but tend to be detached and unavailable for their children in all other areas.

Children who grow up under the uninvolved parenting style tend to have low self-esteem, a hard time regulating their emotions, and a hard time making friends.

Your child's personality and temperament play a major role in how you choose your parenting style.

Research shows correlations

between parenting styles and their impact on children. There is also evidence showing other factors, such as a child's personality and the outside environment, playing a role as well. Your larger environment—such as culture, religion, socio-economic class, and family style—can also affect how your child reacts to your parenting. School, friends, and personality play a significant role in how your child responds to your parenting style.

It is important to be consistent with your parenting style, especially when it comes to discipline and setting expectations for your child. Besides taking into account her environment, think about other people in your child's life, such as your spouse or partner or caregiver. Take time to talk to each other about parenting styles and how you will work together when raising your child. Talk about what you both value as important and how you were each raised; this is important for keeping your parenting style consistent.

At the end of the day, you need to remember to be present and realistic. **Be present both physically and mentally in order to be responsive to your child's needs.** Be realistic in your expectations and the guidelines you set for your child.

Committing quality time as a parent, whichever parenting style(s) you choose, is the single most important factor in your child's healthy development.

STEP TWO: EDUCATING YOURSELF

Addressing the whole child means knowing about the general developmental milestones your child will experience at each age. Milestones define peak stages of accomplishment when your child achieves the end of one stage before moving on to the next. **Milestones are exciting, because when a child reaches one you get to see how far she has come.** And you get to look forward to the next amazing stage your whole child will go through.

But how can you be aware of milestones without knowing the specific developmental categories the stages occur in? How can you have realistic expectations about what is age appropriate and what your whole child should or should not be doing?

Whole Child Parenting: Birth to Age Five **lays out six major developmental areas of your child's growth and follows them through the first five years of your child's development.**

Cognitive development

The first area of development is cognitive development. Cognitive development refers to the process of learning and the growth of intelligence and other mental capabilities, such as memory, reasoning, problem solving, and thinking. Memory and problem solving play a large role in your child's ability to engage in science, mathematical thinking, and logic.

Your involvement strengthens your child's cognitive abilities over these next years and plays a significant role in her school readiness and how she will learn and retain information later in life. At birth, your child's brain is only a quarter of the size of an adult brain; by age five, it has grown to be close to the same size and volume as yours.

Take advantage of these first five years to set the path and exercise the brain to its fullest potential. The Whole Child Parenting Program will very clearly define the stages of cognitive development and will help you be involved in your child's growth in this area.

Social-emotional development

Social-emotional skills reflect how effectively your child is able to interact in social settings. In order to interact well he must develop positive relationships. He must learn to recognize and regulate his emotions and reactions while communicating his feelings.

For young children, social-emotional skills provide a pivotal foundation upon which are built a range of other skills that are necessary in preschool as well as on play dates. Development in this category will help to determine how well your child succeeds with peer interaction throughout his life.

In order to interact well with others your child must develop positive relationships with others. He must also effectively coordinate his actions with communicating his feelings. As well, he must learn to recognize and regulate his emotions and reactions in many different social settings.

Your child needs to have good self-regulatory skills (i.e. the ability to calm himself down), keen emotional understanding (i.e. learning with help what made him feel the way he does), and growing communication skills that help him name how he feels and how he deals with those feelings.

Language development

Language development is how your child communicates, from basic sounds and gestures to the use of pictures in books and words for speaking. As she ages your child will be communicating more than her emotions and needs. She will begin to tell stories, ask questions, and describe people and objects.

Your child will use memory to remember words and past events when telling stories. At an early age, your child's memory will also play a role in symbolic play when she uses props and objects as symbols to represent her ideas. These symbols will later translate to letter recognition and emerging literacy.

The Whole Child Parenting Program identifies how to use sign language to support early literacy skills, and we also include signs in supplemental and supportive materials in the program. Sign language for communication plays a role in your child's social-emotional development because it makes her better able to convey her emotions and needs when she is largely preverbal.

Creative development

Creative development involves how your child uses music, art, movement, and dramatic play to express himself and build imaginative thinking. When doing art, let your child make a mess and indulge in all the different textures and materials you provide. Make a paintbrush or other tools available to your child and then let him explore the paint with his hands. **Creative development plays a big role in your child's physical development as well.** Music and movement build your child's gross motor skills (big muscles) by allowing your child to test balance and large body movements. Visual art builds your child's fine motor skills (small muscles) by allowing him to explore materials such as scissors, paintbrushes, and crayons.

Creative development can be used as an avenue for social-emotional development. Through art and dramatic play, your child can express and act out feelings, model behavior, or work through emotions.

Through activities, examples, and tips, *Whole Child Parenting: Birth to Age Five* shows how important creative development can be to your child's other areas of development as well.

Physical development

Physical development refers to your child's control over fine motor skills (small muscle movements of fingers, toes, and wrists) and gross motor skills (bigger movements that use the large muscles in the arms, legs, and torso). Between birth and five years old, your child's body and motor abilities make great strides.

Physical development has a lot to do with your child's self-esteem and sense of trust. Your child is more willing to test her physical skills of throwing, kicking, and balancing when she feels comfortable and confident within her environment.

Physical development is important because it plays a large role in children developing independence and self-help skills. Getting dressed, feeding themselves, and cleaning up are all skills that involve both fine and gross motor skills, which, when combined, develop sensory motor skills.

The Whole Child Parenting Program explains how your child's physical changes correlate with the development of motor abilities and overall physical growth and development.

Health and care

This section discusses safety, grooming, self-help, and the health of your child. As your child grows older, he will be more independent with his hygiene, from small achievements like brushing his own teeth to bigger accomplishments like potty training.

As he goes through each developmental stage, your child's body is changing and growing at a swift pace. He is growing taller, sprouting new teeth, and becoming more active, which will reflect in changes in his diet each year.

Whole child parenting also involves using yoga. Yoga is a great resource in which to engage your child from infancy through age four and beyond. Not only does it allow your child to explore his balance, but it also strengthens his social-emotional development by helping him find an avenue to calm himself. Yoga can also provide a bonding experience for parent and child.

Reaching Milestones

An important and exciting addition to our exploration of the six developmental categories is the Reaching Milestones section we provide at the end of the book. This assessment list will allow you to see everything your child should be doing and accomplishing developmentally around that age. Milestone assessments provide an exciting reflection of all that you are doing to support your whole child.

STEP THREE: CREATING THE RIGHT ENVIRONMENT

Now that you have committed your time and started educating yourself, it is time to follow through by setting up the right environment. Setting up an environment where your whole child will thrive plays a large role in all six areas of their development.

The importance of play

We are in a day and age in which there is an abundance of technology and information available to us. It is hard to remember a time when an answer to a question wasn't a mouse click away or we couldn't watch a video about how to fix something.

Technology has made our lives so much easier over the years, but that is not the case when it comes to our little ones. **Young children need to have the opportunity to make their own connections and discoveries within their environment.** Children between the ages of birth and three learn the most through play.

When setting up an environment that fosters **free play**, it is important to have child-sized furniture as well as incorporate baskets and trays for storing toys. Child-sized furniture and organizational materials such as bins and trays for different categories of toys help your child build independence and self-help skills. Being able to pick what he wants to play with from the shelf or bin will build upon your child's personal interests.

Just because your child is more in control of what activity and materials he is exploring in free play does not mean that you do not need to be involved in free play with your child. Setting up learning and play environments and making learning materials available is just part of encouraging free play. When watching your child explore materials in free play, it is important to interact with him.

The main aspect to remember about free play is that your child's interests guide it.

Structured play is also an important type of play and can help foster and build specific skills. Structured play differs from free play based on the fact that you are planning the activity and materials in which your child is engaging. You are leading the way with a specific activity that has a specific goal. Examples of structured activities can be doing a science experiment with your child or sorting different colored blocks. It is important to have both a combination of structured and free play activities available for your child.

Indoor environments

Incorporating child-sized furniture as well as baskets and trays for storing toys helps your child build independence and self-help skills.

Trays and baskets allow you to provide more manipulatives (age appropriate toys that foster growth) for your child and make it easier for your child to help care for and clean her environment. **When furniture and materials are at your child's eye level, she is able to have better control of her physical movements and be more aware of her environment.**

When setting up an environment that is beneficial for your child's language skills, it is important to have age-appropriate books available. Your child's interest in books both while reading with you as well as pretending to read on her own helps her relate words to pictures. Take your child's language learning to the next level and place labels like TABLE on your kitchen table. Your child will start making the connection between words and objects.

When doing art, let your child get messy and indulge in all the different textures and materials you provide. Investing in an easel, putting down a tarp, providing a smock, or buying washable paint can help you make your indoor environment fit for creative exploration. Having some paper and crayons out on a table that is child-sized makes expressing herself and her ideas easy. She can use the crayons to express herself creatively and create symbols that depict her feelings or needs.

Besides art materials, your child can express her thoughts and feelings through dramatic play by modeling roles and situations when dressing up or using props. Having a mirror in your child's room allows her to explore her self-concept skills. You will find your child making different faces in the mirror or watching herself stack blocks. Having a mirror that is at your child's eye level builds her self-concept by developing a better understanding of herself as an individual who has her own interests and ideas. Don't overwhelm your child with too many choices or structured activities, but instead follow your child's needs and interests to help encourage independence.

Your commitment to your child is very important when it comes to building attention span and memory skills. Having a rug or a chair that is child-sized will make your child more comfortable and thus want to spend longer on an activity. Your child's attention span is a cognitive skill, and it grows as your child grows older.

The Whole Child Parenting Program provides you with all the guidelines, furniture, educational books, activities, supplies, and toys for your whole child's stimulating environment.

Outdoor environments

Environments where your child can engage in free play allow him to develop self-identity and develop his own interests. He is able to learn more about himself by testing his cognitive and physical limits. There aren't always many opportunities for your child to fully engage in free play at home, which is why **outdoor environments provide beneficial play spaces for your child.**

By its nature, play is flexible, changeable, and multifaceted, so your child's play environment should reflect those criteria as well. Play is a core and vital component of how young children learn. Structured and unstructured play provide health benefits by allowing your child to be physically active as well as engaging in problem-solving and creative exploration.

Outdoor environments provide space and opportunities for structured activities that help children learn to communicate and work together, while unstructured activities in large, open areas help your child push limits and take risks.

Your child can make a mess, climb, shout, jump, and run as fast as he wants in open spaces. He can fully express himself and explore his body's movements. From this, your child will develop a sense of competence and confidence in his own physical abilities.

Large, open areas provide opportunities for your child to be creative and use his imagination. He can make connections and witness vivid colors, patterns, and textures in an outdoor environment.

Without material items, media, or structured rules, children can create their own games, engage in dramatic play, and entertain themselves through the use of their mighty imagination.

Nature provides an abundance of science and math opportunities that your child can explore and manipulate. Problem solving, learning cause and effect, and investigating use all of your child's senses. Your child will be exposed to nature and its elements and make connections by witnessing weather, ecology, growth, and natural life cycles. He can explore what happens when he throws a rock in a pond, adds water to dirt or sand, or watches snow melt.

It is not always easy to find a safe outdoor environment for your child. For families in the city, it may mean you need to travel a little farther, but the benefits are worth it. Outdoor environments can actually be considered cleaner than indoor environments, especially when it comes to germs.

By being in a large space with richly fresh air, germs and infectious agents are spread out. Indoor spaces tend to be more enclosed, which leaves bacteria to sit on surfaces and linger. Overall, the benefits of outdoor environments are enormous, and you need to take advantage of them.

How you set up your child's indoor and outdoor environments plays a large role in how he learns and develops. It is important to remember that you are a part of his environment and **in order for your child to thrive, he needs both a rich learning environment and your involvement.**

STEP FOUR: USING THE RIGHT MATERIALS

As parents, we frequently buy and invest in products and toys that are not age appropriate and serve no purpose developmentally, which is why the Whole Child Parenting Program has created developmentally appropriate tools and materials for the whole child that are both fun and educational.

When starting the Whole Child Parenting Program from infancy, you are able to build and adjust your child's environment and learning materials as she grows older. Many materials, such as toys and furniture, are able to grow with your child from infancy to kindergarten. Other materials, such as Whole Child Parenting activity books, toys, and parent resources, assist you with staying on track with your child's development while also helping you plan and measure your time and commitment to your child. The Whole Child Parenting Program is here to walk with you through these first five years.

A variety and quantity of materials are needed to accommodate young children's short attention spans. Children learn through concrete activities, and parents must be able to provide activities for both their physical, active needs and calm, quiet needs.

Having the right environment with both active and quiet play can help your child's social-emotional development by encouraging self-regulating skills. Having a quiet area to go to when your child feels overstimulated or needs a break is just as essential as having a safe area for her to be active and test her physical and creative limits.

A variety of materials is required

to stimulate the development of each age group. Some materials may fit into one or more categories; for example, an art activity can also serve as a fine motor exercise, and dramatic play can also act as a social-emotional tool.

It is important to remember that in order for your child to be able to explore and manipulate materials, she needs to have the materials made easily available to her at all times of the day. Setting up the right environment and investing in furniture that is both safe and easily accessible will play an important role in supporting your child's development.

STEP FIVE: STAYING ON TRACK

Once you have set up your environment, the Whole Child Parenting Program makes staying on track easier by providing you with activity books, toys, and learning materials. **Consistency and routine play a big role in your whole child's development,** so it is up to you to follow through and use these materials with your child.

Five years may seem far away, but time always has a way of sneaking up on us. In the blink of an eye, your child will be five years old and boarding the bus for school. This is a big milestone in your child's life, but you will be confident your child is ready for school because the Whole Child Parenting Program has helped you stay on track with your child's development. Your child is leaving for school a confident, happy, healthy learner.

In the end, all we want for our children is for them to be happy and confident because happiness and confidence set your child on the road to success. The Whole Child Parenting Program is here to get you to that point so you can take a deep breath and know your child is ready to face the world.

Through our *Whole Child Parenting: Birth to Age Five* book, educational materials, and workbooks, tips, and activities, apps, videos, and web support, you will have the tools to build a relationship with your child that allows him to confidently express himself through his creative and social-emotional skills, which in turn help him build his cognitive, language, and physical skills. You want your child to be healthy, happy, and complete, developing at or ahead of the curve. The Whole Child Parenting Program was developed for you, the committed and caring parent.

infant >

(Birth to 12 Months)

Milestones for an Infant

 **COGNITIVE** 1

- Develops vision
- Uses vision to focus on objects
- Explores with cause and effect
- Begins thinking and problem solving

 SOCIAL-EMOTIONAL 2

- Learns to develop trust and security
- Expresses and understands emotions

 LANGUAGE 3

- Develops an understanding of verbal communication
- Communicates wants and needs through smiles and cries
- Experiments with sounds

CREATIVE 4

- Creates music through playing with sound
- Develops spatial intelligence through art experiences
- Starts building the foundations for dramatic play

 PHYSICAL 5

- Uses senses to control large and small motor movements
- Learns to roll over, sit up, crawl, stand, and walk
- Uses touching and grasping for learning

 HEALTH AND CARE 6

- Uses self-soothing skills
- Starts solids at four to six months
- Begins to boost physical strength and skills

infant
(Birth to 12 Months)

Your baby has arrived! You've made it through the excitement of labor and delivery, and now you're ready to head home and begin life with your baby. This is a time to develop the bonds that will last a lifetime, providing your child a vital foundation influenced by the caring and nurturing relationship you build. This foundation will help your child develop self-esteem and the ability to relate positively with others.

1. Cognitive Development

> **> Cognitive development refers to the way your infant uses his brain to process information.**

Your baby processes information through problem-solving events, using his memory, and thinking, and reasoning through everyday experiences.

In your baby's brain, there are a hundred billion neurons, also known as brain cells. All of these brain cells connect together as your baby grows; this is what makes your baby smarter. Connections are formed by all of the wonderful experiences you provide for your baby to learn.

Your baby is born with a strong desire to soak up information and learn through the things he sees, hears, smells, tastes, and touches. He then stores the information, sorts it out, and uses it now and in the future.

In order for all this information to soak in, there are two very important things your baby must have; these two things stimulate learning so that connections can be made. These two important things are *relationships* and *emotional support*. Relationships provide your baby with a secure emotional base from which he can learn and explore. A secure emotional base enables your baby to feel safe, feel confident, engage with others, and seek support from you when needed as he takes in information.

The following chart provides you with an image that walks you through your child's stages of intellectual development.

Understanding these areas of cognitive development will help you learn how your child thinks, how to support learning, and how to teach new skills.

Cause and Effect

Paying Attention

Problem Solving

Mathematical Concepts

WHOLE CHILD: INFANT
Cognitive
Development Components

Paying Attention >
Vision

Visual development in your baby sets the stage for cognitive development as she uses her sense of sight.

What else can your baby see?

* Your baby can see 8 to 15 inches in front of her.

* At one month, she will pay attention to the hairline of a parent.

* At two months, your baby will give more attention to the eyes on a face.

* At three months, your baby will focus on your facial expressions.

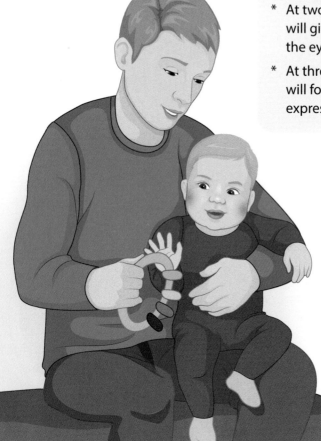

Visual Development

Your baby must have the ability to develop sight and focus her attention on you, other people, and objects. This occurs as your baby starts glancing around, looking at the faces of her parents, and seeing smiling responses. As her vision becomes more refined, your baby will use her eyes to focus on colors and respond to sounds by looking toward the sound.

Let's take a moment to talk about your baby's sense of sight during this age. Despite your baby's limited visual development, the moment you and your baby make eye contact for the first time she is developing her ability to focus her attention on you.

The more your baby makes eye contact during the first month after birth the more she will develop a preference for looking at your face.

It is very important for primary caregivers to keep their facial appearance unchanged after the baby is born. Limit your use of scarves and caps; don't get a new hair color or a drastic haircut after your baby is born; she does not care if your hair is done. She just wants to see your face and feel your touch; this is what makes her feel safe and comfortable.

In addition to having a preference for looking at their primary caregivers' faces, your baby is only able to see in black and white and shades of gray upon birth because the nerve cells in the back of her eyeballs are sensitive to light, but her vision is not fully developed.

Your baby will develop her ability to see color a few days after birth. At one week old, your baby will see red, orange, yellow, and green. These colors are more stimulating for your baby, so use them instead of pastels in your baby's room for mobiles, decorations, and curtains.

By six months, your baby's visual ability has grown tremendously; she is now able to see things more clearly and quickly. Your baby's vision is now 20/25, and she can see all the colors of the rainbow (red, yellow, orange, purple, blue, and green).

At six months of age your baby should have her first eye exam. Your pediatrician will check for nearsightedness (your baby can see closer objects) and farsightedness (closer objects are blurry); both are related to how light is focused as it enters your baby's eyes.

Your physician will also check for astigmatism, which occurs when your baby's eye is shaped more like an American football. If astigmatism is present, the light that is projected onto the retina is distorted, causing your baby to see a blurred or distorted image.

Support your baby's visual development by positioning yourself in her line of sight. Once she focuses, move your face so she follows you with her eyes. This will develop visual tracking skills.

During the period of 7 to 12 months of age, your baby is developing her ability to coordinate her vision with her attention span and to focus for two to three seconds on patterned objects of stripes and checks as opposed to solid-colored objects.

ACTIVITY

Dad is having some alone time with seven-month-old Ethan. He lays Ethan on his cloth ring on the floor, and then Dad takes his keys out of his pocket and slowly jingles them in front of Ethan's face. Ethan looks up at Dad and stares at the keys intently. Dad jingles and moves the keys from the left side to the right side and watches Ethan follow the keys with his eyes. Many times Ethan reaches up and attempts to grab the keys. As Dad sees this he lowers the keys a little bit so Ethan can touch them. Dad repeats this activity several times until Ethan is ready to move on to another activity.

INSIGHT

Because the keys are shiny and jingle, they reflect the light and catch Ethan's attention. The light shining on the keys is letting Ethan's eyes tell his brain that there is something interesting about these keys. This is what leads Ethan to explore the keys by reaching and touching them. Ethan is demonstrating his attention and hand-eye coordination skills. In the blink of an eye, he can reach out and touch an object, something that previously only happened by chance.

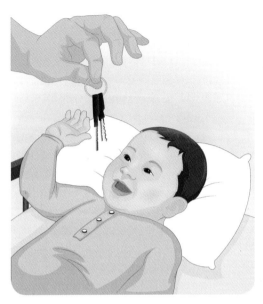

Visual development is important for your baby because to grow he needs to use the visual information his eyes send to his brain to understand the world around him and interact with it appropriately. You play an important role in helping your baby's eyes develop properly. To support your baby's visual skills, try the following activity.

ACTIVITY

 Make a tissue paper sun catcher. For the sun catcher, cut colored tissue paper into various sizes, lay a 4" x 5" sheet of waxed paper on a table, and brush the paper with white glue diluted with a few drops of water. Then place the tissue paper on top of the glue and let it dry (approximately 20 minutes). Make a hole at the top for yarn.

Using your sun catcher, hold it up in front of your baby's face. Give your baby a moment to see the sun catcher, then move it slowly from left to right, right to left, and up and down.

INSIGHT

When you see that your baby has stopped looking at it, stop and give him a moment to focus again on the object and repeat the process. Through this simple activity, you are giving your baby time to see color changes; develop tracking skills, attention, and focus; and use visual information.

Visual Attention

Visual attention is defined as your baby's ability to focus or concentrate on an object. This can only occur once your baby's vision has matured.

There is a link between cognitive development and visual attention with your baby. The duration of time your baby can focus on an object is related to an increase in her cognitive function.

As attention span increases with your baby, she also develops higher-order attention abilities or sustained attention that will be used throughout childhood and well into adolescence.

Let's visualize the timeline by which your infant develops focused attention. From birth to three months, your baby goes from sleeping all the time to developing periods of alertness and watching things in her environment (e.g. primary caregiver's hairline).

During the three- to four-month period, your baby combines alertness with her ability to visualize where objects are in her environment (e.g. colored objects with patterns). She can see if the object is in front of her or to the side or when the parent moves the object up or down, thus developing her peripheral vision (objects seen at the side edges of sight) and her ability to track where the object is.

Birth to 3 months	3 to 4 months	5-½ to 12 months
Your baby goes from sleeping all the time to developing periods of alertness and watching things in her environment.	Your baby combines alertness with her ability to visualize where objects are in her environment.	As you provide more interesting objects for your baby to see, she will develop her attention skills.

As you provide more interesting objects for your baby to see during the 5½ to 12-month period, she will develop her attention skills. More interesting objects include toys that are full of bright, primary colors, make noises (squeaking toys and electronic toys), and can be manipulated in a variety of ways (e.g. a mobile attached to the bar of a car seat).

Developing visual attention in your infant is important for three reasons:

1. It enables your baby to develop social skills because she must rely on you to provide visual stimulation and interaction opportunities.

2. Because your baby is restricted by her inability to move around on her own in those pre-crawling months, she needs toys on which she can focus in order to explore her environment and gain knowledge about the world around her.

3. Your baby's ability to visually focus her attention on her mother's or father's face leads to establishing a bond with her parents or other primary caregivers.

We have talked about why visual attention is important for your infant; we must also note an important skill developing in your three to nine month old.

This is attention control and refers to your baby's ability to choose what she pays attention to and what she ignores. This is what enables your infant to actively explore her environment despite what is going on around her.

As your baby matures, her ability to exercise attention control will continue to increase. This will play a critical role in your baby's cognitive and social-emotional development later in life. For instance, if your baby never forms quality emotional attachments with you as the parent or primary caregiver, she will experience periods of anxiety and uncertainty. This will lead to decreased attention control, thus preventing the development of your child's ability to stay on task, and affecting her ability to engage in social settings.

Mathematical Concepts >

Supporting Early Math Skills

Mathematical concepts are important components of rational and logical thinking.

As your infant interacts with his environment and with people in his world, he will use math concepts to make sense of the world in which he lives.

Infants develop math skills in the first year of life and are natural mathematicians. Your baby was born with an understanding of math concepts that involve quantities (e.g. when he cries because he wants more of his bottle or food).

Patterns provide another math concept for infants. Your infant's ability to experience patterns and routines enables him to become a logical thinker and to understand how his environment works in a predictable way. For instance, as

you care for your baby, he begins to recognize and anticipate a pattern of sequential activities that demonstrate how you will care for him on a daily basis.

You can play games with your infant, such as Pat-a-Cake or Peek-a-Boo to allow your baby to experience sequences and patterns.

As your infant recognizes patterns, he will also begin to understand **sequencing**. Sequencing is a particular order in which related events or things follow each other. Recognizing sequences helps your infant develop a sense of order, logic, and reasoning. Your baby sees the sequences of activities within his day and is able to predict what may happen next.

By age one, your child will become more involved with activities that require sequencing, such as waking up, eating breakfast, washing up, and brushing teeth. This is a sequence of events for your child.

Becoming aware of similarities and differences is awareness of **sorting** and **classifying**, which are mathematical concepts used in learning. As your infant approaches 11 months, he will learn the concepts of *more* and *enough*, which are two of the first number concepts that children develop.

ACTIVITY

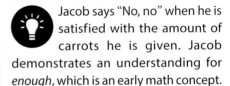 It is lunchtime, and Dad makes nine-month-old Jacob a lunch of carrots and soup. After Jacob finishes the tomato soup, Dad gives Jacob a carrot. Jacob eats the first carrot, but as Dad gives Jacob another one, he hears Jacob say "No, no" and shake his head.

INSIGHT

Jacob says "No, no" when he is satisfied with the amount of carrots he is given. Jacob demonstrates an understanding for *enough*, which is an early math concept.

ACTIVITY

Gently bouncing your infant on your lap as the other parent claps to the beat will demonstrate that beats are related to number concepts such as counting and one-to-one correspondence (e.g. one bounce for one beat).

INSIGHT

Math concepts can be introduced very early on. And music provides an enjoyable, entertaining way to learn, explore, and develop cognitive skills. It has been demonstrated that the parts of the brain that become active when music is played are the same ones that become active when math is practiced.

There are lots of opportunities during your baby's day to discover math concepts through play and to hear new math words.

At around a year of age, your infant will try to fit objects into various sizes of containers, which is the beginning of learning geometry (shapes and space). As your child approaches age two, he will learn how to do simple puzzles.

Even though your baby was born with a basic mathematical understanding, parents and other adults that interact with your infant have a very important role to play.

Your infant will develop and refine math concepts and skills through the routines, experiences, and interactions you have with him each day. By being aware of these early mathematical concepts, you can be more intentional in how you support your baby's math learning as well as school readiness as time goes on.

Math is everywhere; it is a way of thinking and problem solving. You use it more with your infant than you may realize. Think about the last time you played This Little Piggy with your infant's fingers or toes. As you take one finger or toe at a time to do the rhyme, you are showing your infant the math concept of sequential order.

Support your baby's development of mathematical concepts by using math talk, such as "You have two eyes and so does your bear. Let's count: one, two." You can also say, "You have two bottles. Let's start with the one that has more formula (or breast milk)."

Think about how many ways you are using math in your interactions with your baby. Remember, the key is to intentionally introduce math concepts every day with your baby.

The more you engage your infant in math play and math talk, the better chance he will have to develop the early math foundations necessary for learning math well into adulthood.

Activities to support mathematical development:

1 to 4 months:
Read board books that incorporate math concepts.

4 to 8 months:
Find materials with different textures (smooth satin, bumpy washcloths, soft cotton). Rub them over your baby's arms, legs, and bottoms of his feet and talk about how they feel. Fill empty water bottles with baby powder, cotton balls, or paper clips. Seal the top and let your infant explore them.

8 to 12 months:
Tie colored scarves together and put them in a paper towel tube with a little bit sticking out. Let your baby pull the scarves through the tube. Lay out boxes for your baby to crawl through, and talk about what your baby is doing as he crawls.

Cause and Effect >
Actions Bring Responses

Cause and effect refers to the relationship between an action and its outcome.

Understanding cause and effect starts with your baby interacting with her environment and then learning an action that will lead to an effect.

This is the beginning of her ability to understand cause and effect. For instance, each time your baby cries, she begins to learn that you will pick her up or use an object such as a rattle to distract her.

If your baby were to also shake the rattle, she would hear a sound; when she drops the rattle on the floor, she sees it disappear. Through play, your baby is learning that she can cause things to happen or change.

ACTIVITY

Mom shakes a rattle in front of Chelsea and says, "See the rattle?" As Chelsea is sitting in her high chair she reaches for the rattle and grabs hold of it with a fist grip.

Chelsea then drops the rattle. Mom picks up the rattle and hands it back to Chelsea. As soon as Chelsea gets ahold of the rattle again, she drops it on the left side of the high chair. Chelsea's eyes are fixed to the floor as she drops the rattle.

Mom picks up the rattle again, saying "Oops! The rattle fell on the floor!" Mom hands the rattle back to Chelsea. Chelsea takes the rattle in her hand, looks at it, and then drops it on the right side of the high chair, keeping her eyes fixed on the rattle that has fallen to the floor.

INSIGHT

Chelsea is experimenting with what happens when she drops the rattle. She watches it fall to the ground on both sides of her high chair. She will continue to drop the rattle (cause) and see it fall to the ground (effect). This activity will test your patience; however, it is an important way for your baby to learn about cause and effect and her ability to influence her environment.

As your baby grows older, her memory is developing. You'll start to see her absorbing information and applying it to her day-to-day activities.

During this period, one of the most important concepts she is using in cause-and-effect situations is her memory. We previously discussed your baby reaching toward an object that makes noise and dropping it on the floor. As your baby understands that she can cause these interesting reactions, she will continue to experiment with other ways to make things happen.

Think about each time you sing a particular song as you feed your baby; she will begin to anticipate the song and the feeding each time you begin the activity. The same goes for when your baby interacts with another family member and learns that by laughing she makes that person smile; she will then laugh again to get the same effect. These experiences with your infant will increase social skills and set the stage for symbolic and language learning.

Problem Solving >
Thinking

Your baby is learning how to get what she wants, when she wants it; this is also called thinking and problem solving.

During the first year of your baby's life, she is making great strides in her ability to think, solve problems, and communicate with you. These are critical cognitive skills.

For instance, your baby thinks to herself, *I want that rattle!* Your baby solves the problem by deciding to roll over and reach for or crawl to the rattle. Maybe your baby is thinking, *I am hungry!* She solves the problem by communicating through cries, grunts, or pointing until you feed her.

Once you are sure your infant's basic needs have been met and she is not in any danger, it is important to give your baby time to work on problem-solving skills.

Think about times you have just put your baby in the crib, and she immediately begins to cry as you turn to leave the room. Even though you may want to pick her up again and rock her longer, this is a great opportunity to let your infant work on her problem-solving skills, namely the skill of being able to self-soothe and see what she can do to make herself comfortable enough to go to sleep. It is certainly hard to listen to the cries, especially when it is your first baby, but as your baby matures, she will need to be able to put herself to sleep.

It is also very important to support problem-solving skills when your baby is learning to feed herself a bottle or use a spoon. Infants as young as six months have been known to feed themselves; they won't get all the food on the spoon or even in their mouths, but they are developing self-help skills and problem-solving skills. They are also developing their wrist muscles and fine motor skills (small muscle skills).

When you support problem-solving skills with your infant, you are supporting her brain development and giving her the power to think and constantly learn about the world around her.

Support your baby's problem-solving skills by responding to her efforts to communicate. Use words to describe what she is experiencing: "I see you looking at the toy on the floor. Let me get that for you." Talking to your child and explaining what you are doing when you do it also increases language development.

> ## Your infant's problem-solving development:
>
> **0 to 2 months**—Your infant is born with built-in problem-solving tools called *reflexes* (rooting and sucking for food).
>
> **2 to 4 months**—Your infant is more alert; she explores; hand-eye coordination begins to develop and bringing toys to mouth leads to problem solving.
>
> **8 months**—Your infant plays with toys to produce responses to actions by grasping, shaking, and banging.
>
> **12 months**—Your baby uses more purposeful levels of problem solving and is no longer limited to what is immediately in front of her. She can now push a toy aside to choose another one.

Remember, the Whole Child Parenting Program offers appropriate developmental products and monthly activity books that walk you through supporting your child's skills. Using these in conjunction with the recommended age-appropriate room materials ensures faster development.

2. Social-Emotional Development

> **Social-emotional development begins in infancy and involves your baby bonding with you and developing a trusting, secure, and safe relationship with you.**

When your baby is soothed by a parent's voice it sets her on the right path emotionally. Reading your baby's cues and attending to her needs from the day she is born starts off her social-emotional development on the right track. When your baby is born, she has no idea who you are; she doesn't know what role you will play in her life. Fear overcomes her initially; she cries because she has been taken out of her warm, safe environment (the womb).

For this reason, it is important to hold your baby as soon as you can when she is born. Lock eyes with her, hold her, and speak softly to give comfort, letting your baby know that you are here and she is safe.

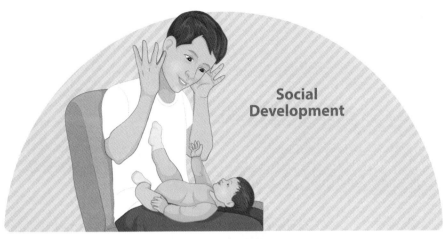

WHOLE CHILD: INFANT
Social-Emotional
Development Components

Babies are not born with social skills; they develop as the baby grows. Your role as the parent or primary caregiver is to teach and encourage these abilities. By doing so, you give your baby a sense of who she is in the world. By helping her learn who she is, you affect how she will learn and how she will develop relationships with others; you also start her on the path to having positive self-esteem.

1. Social Development

Social development is the process through which your baby learns how to interact and express herself with others. This process is taught by you. The way you react to your baby's needs and cues helps build social connections.

2. Emotional Development

Emotional development is the process in which your baby learns to recognize and express her feelings and to establish a personal identity independent from you. Parents and primary caregivers play a big role in their baby's emotional development when they help babies learn to express their feelings.

Parents, family, and caregivers interacting with the baby from the very start helps the child form bonds that later will encourage her to build other satisfying relationships.

Remember, the Whole Child Parenting Program offers appropriate developmental products and monthly activity books that walk you through supporting your child's skills. Using these in conjunction with the recommended age-appropriate room materials ensures faster development.

Social Development >
Forming Relationships

Social development reflects your baby's growing trust in you and how secure she will feel in the world.

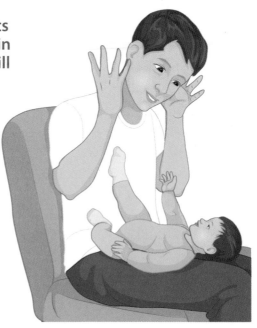

More awareness is being placed on the foundation of social development during the first three years of life. This foundation will be reflected in your child's ability to be successful in relationships, with the additional belief in her ability to achieve any goal she puts her mind to.

ACTIVITY

Four-month-old Holly is sitting with Dad in the chair. Dad holds his hands over his face and then swings his hands out and says, "Peek-a-boo, Holly! I see you!" Each time Dad shows his face, Holly laughs. When Dad tries to stop the game Holly kicks her arms and legs to let Dad know she wants to keep playing the game. Dad decides to continue to play the game until Holly loses focus and wants to move on to something else.

INSIGHT

Holly is discovering that relationships with people in her environment are fun and satisfying. Through this experience Holly demonstrates her ability to follow Dad in whatever he is doing. As well, Holly is letting Dad know that wherever Dad may go, she wants to interact and be with him.

When your baby is secure in her relationship with you, she then knows that no matter what happens you will be there emotionally, and you will show her how to form strong, positive relationships with others.

During the first three years of life your baby is working hard to develop trust and relationship skills. Your baby learns social skills first by using her eyes, next by turning her head to see you, and then by observing what you are doing around her. She finally ends with adding her body to the experience. This is why it is so important for your baby to stare into your eyes and fall in love with you shortly after birth. Your baby is learning who she is by how she is treated.

Parents play a big role in their babies' social development by sending messages like "I love you. You're such a smart baby. I love being with you. You are such a funny baby." Verbal messages like these will help form your baby's self-esteem.

Because the bond with you is becoming so strong there will be times during your baby's social development when she will have stranger and separation anxiety, which is apparent when a fear of unfamiliar people occurs and is expressed by your baby crying.

Separation anxiety is a normal part of social development; however, it does require your emotional support to let your infant know that the social encounter is a safe one, and she does not need to fear. This support can be given through touch; cuddles; a calm, soothing voice; and just taking the time to play an interactive game. For example, in the afternoons when your baby gets grumpy and it's not time for a nap, nothing works better than dancing with her. Put on some music and hold her in your arms. A good distraction is silly exaggerated movements like jazz hands (fingers splayed, wrists twisting), which are funny to your baby.

Parents have relationships with extended family and friends on a routine basis. Talk with these people when appropriate about your baby's likes and dislikes, what calms her and what upsets her. Working with extended family and others who may spend time with your baby helps to ensure that she will feel safe and secure with all relationships.

Social development is also learned through play experiences you provide for your baby. Your baby will learn about the world around her through play, and play builds all areas of her development.

Emotional Development >
Feelings

Emotional development is how your baby begins to develop the capability to experience, express, and understand emotions.

ACTIVITY

 Chad is in his crib sleeping when all of a sudden he breaks out in a very loud cry. Mom hears his cry on the baby monitor and goes into the nursery to see what is wrong. Mom says, "Chad, what's wrong, buddy? You were sleeping so well." Mom picks up Chad out of his crib, holding him close to her chest. Mom then discovers that he is wet straight through his diaper and his onesie.

INSIGHT

Crying is how Chad is expressing feelings, and he should be allowed to do so. Rather than using distractions to try to stop your baby from crying, try to figure out why the crying is occurring so that you are able to help. Here, Chad is signaling his discomfort to Mom through his cry, letting her know that something needs to be addressed so he can get back to enjoying his sleep.

Babies learn emotions through interaction with parents and caregivers. **Parents have a significant influence on how their children turn out, including their personalities, emotional development, and behavioral habits.** For instance, one important emotional reaction is crying, which is part of a baby's emotional development.

Before your baby is four months old, you must build trust and a sense of security by attending to his basic needs, which are feeding, comforting, and cleaning.

It is important for you to know the different types of cries your baby might have so that you can determine what type of comfort he needs. Understanding your baby's cry also includes understanding his temperament.

Your crying baby can be consoled with motion, cuddling, singing, massage, or a toy. But this will only last so long; at some point, these techniques will have to be added to the child's taking a more active role in feeling better. **Some babies self-soothe by sucking on a thumb or a pacifier, gazing at objects, or using other sensory experiences to calm down.** Your infant will learn to self-soothe if you give him a

> **An emotionally available parent will have the following characteristics:**
>
> **Sensitive**—is conscious of the infant's cues, understands those cues, and provides support;
>
> **Structured**—creates a sleep environment that is positive, quiet, and soothing on a consistent basis;
>
> **Nonintrusive**—recognizes that a baby needs quality sleep and does not create or allow distractions;
>
> **Nonhostile**—does not display frustration or anger when engaged in routines with the baby such as changing or going to sleep.

chance. The most important concept to understand is you must listen to your baby and learn to understand his cries to determine the root cause first, then move on to one of the techniques mentioned.

A crying baby can be emotionally draining for a parent. **It is important to understand that your baby is influenced by your emotions, tone and volume of voice, gestures, and facial expressions.** Your baby needs to feel affection and caring despite how you are feeling emotionally or physically.

Being physically present is not enough. When parents are just nearby and not emotionally invested in their babies or are not responsive, they are raising children who will be distressed and less engaged with their play or activities or other people. It is important for the overall development of your infant to be present enough to support him emotionally; this support will foster confidence and growth in all aspects of the whole child.

A critical time to be emotionally available is at bedtime. **Babies from one to 24 months sleep better when parents are emotionally available at bedtime.** When you are there to address needs it is easier for your baby to fall asleep and sleep through the night.

An emotionally available parent makes the baby feel safe.

As a parent, you need to adapt to your baby's temperament, because it is his unique emotional makeup. Take time to see what temperament your infant is developing; it will enable you to adapt to your baby's emotional makeup and support his needs.

A key aspect of emotional development in babies is learning how to regulate emotion. Your baby was born with little self-control, so he acts and reacts without the ability to stop himself.

When you have an understanding of the kind of temperament your baby has, you can provide better guidance to help him begin to manage his emotions. Furthermore, how you address the emotions of your infant and respond to him affects how expressive your baby will feel he can be later in life. The temperaments of parents and caregivers and the emotional climate of the home will influence emotional development. Therefore, make sure you have all the support you need to be emotionally present for the needs of your little one.

Let's explore some temperament traits your baby could have.

Intensity—Highly intense babies have powerful responses. They will cry loudly. Less intense babies tend to be calmer and quieter.

Persistence—Very persistent babies take on challenges. They do not like to be stopped in the middle of something (e.g. stopped during a feeding to get a diaper changed). Less persistent babies can be persuaded to move on and come back to an activity. Persistent babies can accept only a little modification in their schedule. They are bothered by surprises or changes in plans.

Sensitivity—Highly sensitive babies have their feelings hurt easily. Have you ever observed someone make a face at your baby, and he started to cry? You may think he was crying without a reason, but the sight obviously bothered him. Less sensitive babies are not as concerned when others act in an unusual or surprising fashion.

Perceptiveness—Highly perceptive babies get distracted easily. Less perceptive infants notice less of what is going on around them.

Feeding Your Baby

It is very important that you are emotionally present during your baby's feedings. This is a routine time for your baby, and it lends itself to bonding experiences between you and him. You can explore the many feeding options that are available to you: you can breastfeed, use formula, or do a combination of the two. Each has its own advantages and disadvantages when it comes to nutrients, cost, and convenience, but what is sometimes overlooked is the bonding parents and primary caregivers have when feeding their babies.

Bonding While Bottle Feeding

Emotional bonding will also occur if you are a parent who has chosen to bottle feed. Bonding actually occurs in many of the same ways as with nursing. **The simplest thing you can do when you feed your baby is engage in skin-to-skin contact.** By taking off your shirt and feeling your baby's skin against yours, you are boosting levels of the love hormone oxytocin between you and your baby.

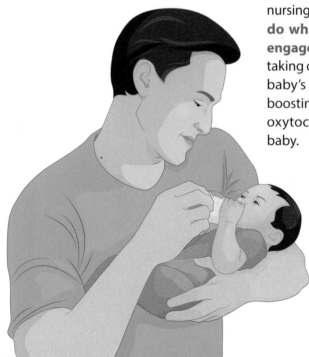

The most important thing to remember when bonding with your baby is to be present and in the moment while feeding him. Don't engage in distractions such as the TV, reading, or talking to another person. Make eye contact with your baby, and bring him close to you while you talk gently and smile at him.

3. Language Development

> **Language development is the effective way your baby combines cooing sounds, gurgling sounds, babbles, smiles, and cries to communicate different needs.**

Your baby is learning about language well before she will speak any words. Most babies have a natural head start from listening in utero; by the time your baby is born she will already show a response to her native language. Your baby even has the ability to use her sense of hearing to distinguish between nouns, verbs, and adjectives.

During the ages of three months to a year, a lot of language development is happening. You will hear her coo and laugh, play with sounds, and babble as she begins to communicate with gestures.

You are the most significant adult with whom your baby will interact and communicate. The way in which you respond to and engage your baby will support language development during these very important early years.

Cultivating Language

Receptive Language

Babbling

Nonverbal Language

WHOLE CHILD: INFANT
Language
Development Components

1.
Receptive Language

Receptive language is the ability to understand or comprehend speech that is heard or read. Productive language is speech that is produced. Infants are better with receptive language than productive language because infants understand verbal communication better than they can produce it.

2.
Nonverbal Language

Nonverbal communication includes facial expressions, the tone and pitch of the voice, and gestures displayed through body language. Nonverbal communication is especially important because your infant does not have the ability to communicate wants and needs through words.

3.
Babbling

Babbling is when your baby appears to be experimenting with uttering articulate sounds but not producing any recognizable words. Learning to talk occurs in stages, beginning with sighs and coos, which are followed by strung-together consonant-vowel sounds.

4.
Cultivating Language

Care for and encourage the growth of your infant's language development and explore specific ways you can prepare her for literacy development. Cultivating language involves your speaking to your child, reading to your child, and responding to her attempts to communicate with you. Engage your baby. That is how she will learn to engage with verbal and nonverbal language.

Even at the babbling stage, eye contact with your child helps him learn how to interact and to communicate with others effectively.

Receptive Language >
I Understand

Receptive language involves your baby's ability to listen and understand words.

ACTIVITY

 One simple way your baby is developing his receptive language skills is by listening and making meaning during routines. For instance, Mom walks into her son Aiden's room and says, "Good morning, Aiden!" as she picks him up from the crib. Then she proceeds with the morning or afternoon routine.

INSIGHT

Aiden's listening to Mom, along with experiencing the action of being lifted up, leads to his understanding that it is time to wake up. The sequential activities that follow reinforce this understanding.

Before your baby was born he was learning language. Even while in utero your baby was listening to the sounds and speech of your voice.

Listening leads to your baby eventually developing literacy skills that begin right from the start. Receptive language is very hard to see in action, as much of it is cerebral. When your baby responds to the sound of a nice voice, he is displaying the beginnings of receptive language. This is also a sign that your baby is beginning to learn that communication is important and useful in his life.

If your baby is crying and hears your voice this will quiet him down as it is a familiar sound. This is your baby demonstrating that he hears you and understands you're a support person.

While your baby is still learning to understand oral language he may appear to be comprehending what is being said because he is picking up key words (e.g. "Good morning, Aiden!") and getting visual information from the environment or from gestures by parents (e.g. experiencing Mom pick him up). This enables your baby to learn language in a relatively predictable pattern (listening leads to understanding).

Receptive language is important for your baby's development because it will help him communicate successfully. For instance, have you ever wondered why doctors want a baby to cry when he is born? A good vocal cry is a sign that the lungs are developed and that your infant has a voice. Your baby uses his voice to communicate that he needs you to help him feel safe and loved. This is the only way your baby knows how to communicate to you at birth.

Support the development of your baby's receptive language skills by making eye contact as you speak to your baby. He will be better able to see your lips move as he listens to your words.

Remember: Listening leads to understanding, and understanding leads to your baby's ability to follow directions during his toddler years and develop meaningful social experiences with others in his environment.

Milestones in baby's receptive language development include:

* smiling when he hears your voice;

* looking for the source of new sounds at four to six months;

* responding to requests ("Give it to Mommy") at seven months;

* pointing to a few body parts when asked (nose, eyes, tummy) between 12 and 24 months.

Nonverbal Language >
Communicating Wants and Needs

Nonverbal language involves sending and receiving messages, both intentionally and unintentionally, in a variety of ways without the use of words.

ACTIVITY

Six-month-old Anna is in her highchair having baby biscuits. She starts playing with her food as if wiping the highchair clean with her hands. Dad notices, saying, "Anna, it looks like you are telling me you are all done. Let me take off your highchair tray, and I will get you out."

INSIGHT

Through Anna's gesture of playing with her food, she is using nonverbal language to send a message to Dad: "I am done."

Messages can be sent through a touch or a glance, eye contact, a gesture or facial expression, or a sound made by your baby. Since communication during the first year of your baby's life tends to be nonverbal, communication is said to be paralinguistic, or before words.

Your baby will express himself literally within seconds of birth by using his voice. As we discussed earlier, the voice, which was used when your infant was crying at birth, demonstrated his ability to communicate with you from that very moment.

By the first month, your baby is able to discriminate between all of the different sounds that people vocalize in every language in the world. She is able to learn just about any language out there, but her ability to produce sounds is extremely limited. This is the prime opportunity to start teaching your infant a second language; you will be amazed to see her use the language once she begins to speak.

The first type of nonverbal language your baby displays is usually reflexive, as when he cried. Other reflexive communication made by your infant includes movements and facial expressions. Non-crying vocalization is heard when your baby coos. At first, cooing will be done by accident, but as your baby develops, it will be done with intentionality. Cooing includes basic speech sounds such as "ooooh" and "eeeeh."

As you talk with your baby, you give her the opportunity to practice her coos and continue to make sounds from her primary language, the language you speak to her most of the time.

Nonverbal language is one of the key aspects of communication and is used by every person from the time they are young. You will see your child use nonverbal language again when she repeats a verbal message (e.g. pointing in the direction of something) or when your child nods her head to mean "yes." Recall the famous proverb: "Actions speak louder than words." This is nonverbal language: action.

Sign Language

Sign language is a visual language that uses a method of facial expression (lips moving) and hand and body movements as a way to communicate.

Your baby can learn sign language at the same time she develops spoken language. When you give your baby access to sign language, you are enhancing the development of her linguistic, cognitive, social, and emotional abilities.

Sign language will give your baby a way to communicate several months earlier than babies who use only vocal communication. This will also help to ease frustration between the ages of nine to 12 months when babies are beginning to know what they want and need but lack the verbal skills to express themselves effectively.

As you teach your baby sign language, keep in mind the word **Ma.S.K.S.**

* **Ma**ke it interactive. Have your baby sit on your lap on the floor and hold her arms and hands to make the sign.
* **S**et practical expectations. Babies will not be able to communicate with sign language until eight months of age.
* **K**eep the signs simple and relatable for them, such as teaching *more*, *eat*, *daddy*, and *mommy*.
* **S**tay patient. Your baby will not do the signs correctly from the beginning; as she matures and with practice she will improve.

MOMMY

DADDY

GRANDMA

EAT

DRINK

GRANDPA

MORE

Remember, the Whole Child Parenting Program offers appropriate developmental products and monthly activity books that walk you through supporting your child's skills. Using these in conjunction with the recommended age-appropriate room materials ensures faster development.

Babbling >
Experimenting with Sound

As your baby hears vocalization by others, she is inspired to communicate back with her own vocalization patterns.

ACTIVITY

 Mom is staying home with her baby girl all day while her husband goes to work. One day, her husband comes home, and her seven-month-old daughter blurts out, "Dada!" Mom's heart sinks. She wonders how her baby says "Dada" first when she is the one caring for the baby every day.

Of course during this time, her husband is walking around the house like a proud peacock, texting everyone he knows; however, in reality, her daughter says "Dada" first because it was simply easier for her to say than "Mama."

INSIGHT

Babies will say words that are easier for them to form with their mouths because they are still learning to control their lips and mouth movements. In knowing this, Mom can now feel better about hearing the baby say "Dada" before "Mama." The most important thing about repetitive babbling is that your infant is practicing making deliberate and precise sounds.

Between three and six months, your baby will begin to babble. This is in response to sounds that you or other people make.

Think about a time you were so tired and you yawned in front of someone. That person then said, "Please don't yawn. You are making me yawn." Babbling is similarly contagious for your baby; she babbles, then you talk, then she wants to babble some more, and it keeps going until one of you gets tired.

Babbling will continue for several months. Around seven months, your baby will add repetitive babbling to her repertoire. In repetitive babbling, she will repeat the same speech sound over and over again; an example of this is "dadadada."

Repetitive babbling occurs because your infant is learning to control her lips and vocal cords and make them all work simultaneously.

During the seven- to ten-month period, babies begin to show a preference for speech, can distinguish intonations in the voice, and know how to take turns in conversations—all despite the fact that they still cannot speak.

In other words, the babbling really sounds like communication with pitch, pointing, and pauses that make statements and ask questions. It is a fascinating time to listen and respond to your infant engaging in reciprocal communication experiences.

Between 10 to 12 months, your baby will use protowords; these are words that are not exactly like the original word but close. You will hear "baba" for bottle or "Dada" and "Mama" for Dad and Mom. The differences between protowords and repetitive babbling are that now your infant is using two syllables as opposed to a string of sounds. Protowords move your infant even closer to the development of speech.

First words will usually occur between 10 and 13 months of age, and they will be nouns like "ball" and "Mama." There is nothing quite as exciting as hearing baby's first words.

The start of language communication is an exciting time for you and your baby. It is so important to make sure you are talking daily with your baby and speaking through routines such as diaper changes and feeding times.

Cultivating Language >
Build, Keep, Nurture

The best way to build your baby's language is to speak with him continuously.

ACTIVITY

Colby's dad is kneeling at the side of his crib ready to have some one-on-one time while he prepares for his child's afternoon nap. Dad begins to tell Colby a story his father told him when he was a little child. In a deep voice Dad says, "Once there was a furry rabbit" (Dad rubs Colby's blanket on his arm), "who lived with his father in the grass. His name was Snugglebug." (Dad tickles Colby's belly.) "And his mother's name was Rabbit . . ." Dad continues his story to the end, and then he asks Colby if he enjoyed the story as he gives him a kiss on his forehead.

INSIGHT

As Dad is talking to his son he is using shorter, simpler sentences, which he utters more slowly. Dad also provides an action to some of the words after he says them. This makes it easier for Colby to understand what Dad is saying. As Dad talks with Colby he is not only building his child's language skills, but he is also helping him develop his brain. Just like a baby needs food for physical growth, a baby also needs language for his brain development. The great thing is, language nutrition is free! You don't have to have fancy toys or expensive books. All you have to do is talk, interact, and engage with your baby in everyday conversations.

Speaking can include describing his feelings and expressing them out loud. Talk about the day and what he is eating. For instance, when you give him a bottle, you can say: "You are so hungry, and I have some warm milk for you. I will sing to you while you drink."

Tend to your infant's language development by paying attention to how you use language with him. One of the most common speaking techniques parents use with their infants is called "motherese."

In the above example with the bottle, Dad was using **motherese**, or baby talk. Motherese is "infant-directed talk," which is a non-standard form of English that is exaggerated and typically done in a high-pitched voice. Babies prefer motherese to adult-directed speech because motherese makes it easier for the baby to understand the structures of speech.

Motherese is important to use with your baby because it helps him learn to identify where words begin and end and gives clues needed to help in the development of his own language. Use correct grammar with your infant early on so as to not confuse him or teach bad habits.

Another simple method to develop your child's language skills is reading to your infant. In the beginning, your baby will not understand what is being read, but he will as time goes on; he will even want to participate. During infancy, reading enables you to look after your infant and have quality time with him.

Your baby has a desire for you to communicate with him, hear how he is doing, and babble together. Remember the yawning scenario: If you talk, your infant will talk back, and you can keep talking together.

Five simple ways to nurture your baby's language development:

1. Talk, talk, and talk. Your baby likes to hear a singsong speech, which means that the tone and pitch of the voice fluctuates a lot (as if you were singing) and is coupled with exaggerated facial expressions. Your infant prefers singsong speech because he likes the high-pitched sounds and watching your face when you talk to him. When your baby starts babbling, babble back with similar sounds. You will find that your baby babbles back to you.

2. Read, read, and read. It is never too early to read to your baby. It creates a perfect opportunity to bond with him. Your child will like listening to the sounds and rhythms of your voice. Pick stories that have lots of pictures and different textures; this will enable your baby to interact with you during the reading time.

3. Hold your baby's hand and let him touch the pictures. Name animals, colors, and other pictures in the book.

4. Follow your infant's lead. If your little one is giving more visual attention to a picture in a book, don't turn the page. Let him look at the picture as long as he wants.

5. Enjoy music together. Sing songs with your baby. He will love the rhythm and will be soothed by your voice. Songs like "Hush, Little Baby" will help your baby learn patterns and intonations of language. As your baby grows older, he will enjoy singing the songs with you. Music will lead to language learning as it allows your infant to watch your mouth, lips, and face as you form the words to the song.

Keep developing language with your infant by copying his sounds and encouraging him to imitate you. Put words to your child's sounds. Not only does your speech during this period help your baby learn to recognize speech sounds, but it is also how your infant will learn to take turns in a conversation and keep communication going as he grows.

4. Creative Development

> **Creative development reflects how your baby responds to colors, sounds, and movements. It occurs when he looks at different colors in books, interacts with puppets, or sways to music.**

From birth, your baby responds to contrast, colors, sounds, and movements. How your baby integrates these experiences will have an influence on her growth and development in many areas, not just creativity.

Creativity is developed through the various ways you interact with and respond to your baby. This can be seen in the ways that calm, soothe, comfort, engage, amuse, delight, and enthrall your baby. Playing creatively with your baby fosters many aspects of development. The physical skills creativity promotes become the primary way that your baby will learn about the world around her, thus giving her new ways of thinking, engaging, problem solving, and discovering.

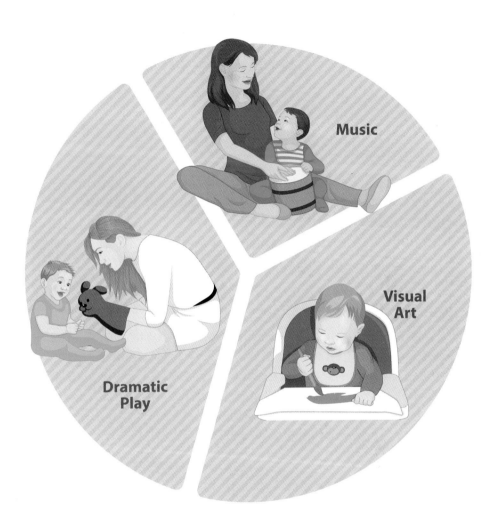

Music

Visual Art

Dramatic Play

WHOLE CHILD: INFANT
Creative
Development Components

Creativity is a process and not a product for babies; they are still developing the coordination to control and manipulate objects with intention; they are also still developing the cognitive ability to problem solve and organize their thinking.

1. Music

Music is creative play with sound; it occurs when sound meets imagination. Any experience—from the shaking of a rattle to the babbling noises from your baby—that involves the basic attributes of sound is potentially musical for your baby.

2. Visual Arts

Visual art development occurs when your baby is able to experiment with a variety of colors and drawing instruments (like paint brushes) to develop color awareness. During visual art experiences he will experiment with the marks that can be made on different surfaces by his hands with paint as he explores the relationship between how things feel and how they look.

3. Dramatic Play

Dramatic play encourages the development of babies' social and emotional skills (sharing, taking turns, conversing, understanding, and managing feelings). Creativity, problem solving, and language skills are developed through dramatic play, allowing your infant to learn that there are things she can control.

From the very start, dramatic play helps build creative skills and stimulates the imagination.

Remember, the Whole Child Parenting Program offers appropriate developmental products and monthly activity books that walk you through supporting your child's skills. Using these in conjunction with the recommended age-appropriate room materials ensures faster development.

Music >
Instrumental and Vocal Sounds

Music is very powerful for your baby as it opens doors for her to become more balanced and healthy, both physically and emotionally.

Engaging in music play with your baby will help build the bond between you and she. Think about a time when you sang a soft lullaby to your baby, and she locked eyes with you, listening to your voice and watching your facial expressions. It almost seemed as if she was instantly mesmerized and soothed.

Musical experiences for your baby will promote learning in other areas of development. Think about where your baby is developmentally. Is she grasping objects such as rattles and small toys? When you give your baby a rattle to grasp with her hand, you are helping your baby develop her physical abilities (fine motor skills) and encouraging her to shake and make music with the rattle.

By taking the time to talk to her during the experience of holding the rattle ("I see you are holding the rattle with a firm grasp. That is a good shake you did!"), you then promote physical development with praise in her burgeoning musical abilities (making noise by shaking).

Next, support her musical creativity by grabbing another rattle or maraca for yourself and shaking it to a beat. **Your baby will attempt to imitate you, thereby further developing her musical creativity**.

ACTIVITY

Once a week Nina and her mom attend a baby music class in the area. "Hello, everyone. We are going to play with drums today. Parents, place your baby in between your legs and the drum should go in front of your baby," says the teacher. She begins to hand a drum to Mom. Mom sets the drum in between Nina's legs and lets her bang on the drum any way she likes. She then gives it a try herself by tapping with a rhythm. Mom gives Nina praise and encouragement by saying, "You just made music, Nina! Hurray for Nina!"

INSIGHT

In this scenario, Mom is teaching rhythm to Nina. The wonderful thing is it does not look like Mom is teaching at all. As Mom is sitting on the floor with Nina tapping on the drum, she emphasizes the rhythms that a drum can make. Mom is amazed at the elation and joy that music brings to Nina. By bringing her baby to a group music class she is introducing the beginnings of music education.

"You just made music, Nina!"

Other activities you can do to develop your baby's musical skills include making it part of her bedtime routine. Play music while you give your baby a bath, or play a CD to help her relax and fall asleep independently. It does not always have to be classical music that you play; try some jazz or country. Sing to your baby, even if you think you can't do it so well!

Singing to your infant is the best way to expose her to music because she can watch your mouth movements and model your movements and facial expressions. You will see and hear your baby cooing and mimicking sounds heard in the song.

Avoid having your baby in the bouncy seat placed in front of the TV; instead, turn on your music player. Stereos are the next best thing to you singing and are much more beneficial for your baby's imagination and creativity than TV. Instead of watching characters dance or sing on the TV, your baby will use her imagination to begin to see how to move her body to music.

Take your baby to music in the park experiences in your neighborhood so she can see a live performance and hear how music is created. Also, invest in simple musical instruments such as rhythm sticks, shakers, jingle bells, a drum, and a xylophone. Let your baby explore the different sounds that each instrument makes. Have a concert with the two of you playing all the instruments you have. What fun!

Make sure to introduce songs and rhythmic chants that have actions your baby can watch or do with you, such as "Itsy Bitsy Spider" or "Pat-a-Cake." When parents expose their babies to music, they also support the development of good listening skills from an early age.

By making music a fundamental ingredient in your baby's everyday routine, you are not only solidifying the bond that you have with her, you are also encouraging your baby to experience the beauty and diversity of sounds from around the world.

ACTIVITY

Danielle and Ben are sitting on the blanket with Mom. Mom reads the story and starts to sing, "Old MacDonald had a farm, E-I-E-O. And on his farm he had a cow, E-I-E-O. With a moo moo here, and a moo moo there, here a moo, there a moo, everywhere a moo moo!" As Mom is singing Danielle begins to get on her hands and knees and is moving her head side to side almost as if she is moving to the beat of her mother's singing.

INSIGHT

As Mom starts singing Danielle begins to recognize that Mom's singing voice sounds different from the voice she uses to read the story. Your baby will recognize the melody of a song long before she understands the words and will react to the sound and beat of the music as she listens.

Visual Arts >
Born Sensory Learners

Your baby loves to experiment with different fabrics, textures, and visual objects in books.

ACTIVITY

 Mom is home with Levi on a cold and rainy Tuesday. Mom wants to have some bonding time with Levi, but she is unsure what else she can do besides read a book to him.

Mom remembers that she and her husband have just put together a photo album with pictures from the most recent family get together. Mom picks up Levi from the floor and takes him to the family room, where she removes the album from the shelf.

Together they sit and look at family photos as Mom describes each person to Levi. "Look, Levi, here is Grandpa with the fish he caught!" Levi reaches his arms out trying to grab the fish in the picture.

INSIGHT

When Mom brings out the photo album she shares a wide variety of photos of people with her son. Levi reaches out to the picture of Grandpa holding a fish, body language that shows that Levi is most interested in that photograph.

The visual art system in infants develops rapidly over the first few weeks after birth. **As early as nine minutes after birth, your baby will prefer to look at pictures and photos with color.** When parents look at pictures, they can verbalize what they like about it or what they would prefer to see. The point is to engage the baby.

A perfect way to introduce visual art to your baby is by simply looking at photos of people, especially familiar people. Introducing your baby to art early on promotes neuronal connections in his brain. You can watch your baby respond to large, colorful paintings and pictures via a visual fixation or a smile.

Visual art gives your baby the ability to learn about the world around him through hands-on learning experiences as well.

By the time your baby is between eight and 12 months, he can hold a large writing tool (crayon or chalk) using a fist grasp and feeling it between his hands. Tape a large piece of white paper to the table and watch your baby make marks and lines on paper; it is important to give writing materials to your baby and support him in their use. Let him draw whatever he likes.

You give your baby a sense of emotional satisfaction when he can make art. This comes from making the decision to make one mark or two on the paper, from the control he has over the materials he is using, and from the autonomy he has in the decision to pick up the tool.

Visual art experiences do not require fancy materials. Use basic materials such as crayons and washable baby markers. Visual art is an open-ended learning opportunity, and a recognizable picture is not necessary to have at the end of the experience. The goal of visual art for your baby is the process of discovery.

Visual art plays a role in all areas of your infant's development. Visual art for your infant will develop him as a whole child and promote learning and growth in the following ways:

* develops visual-spatial relationships like that of hand-eye coordination skills through making marks on paper,

* creates an opportunity for your infant to develop a nonverbal language to express his feelings,

* promotes self-awareness and individuality,

* heightens perceptual abilities,

* provides an important way for your infant to learn about his world!

Dramatic Play >
Pretending

Dramatic play is your baby engaging in pretend play as a way to explore his world.

It is hard to imagine how dramatic play coincides with your baby's development, but the foundations for dramatic play begin in infancy. Peek-a-boo games between you and your baby are an example of a dramatic play activity in which your baby enjoys the sudden appearance and disappearance of your face.

Dramatic play supports your baby in other areas of development:

Cognitive skills are developed as your baby comes to understand the environment through dramatic play opportunities.

Emotional development is supported as your baby uses pretend play to cope with fears and other emotions as he imitates you and your expression of feelings.

Social development is supported as your baby engages in pretend play with you. Babies imitate the social behaviors they see in their environment and then use these behaviors for future social interactions.

Motor skills are supported as your

ACTIVITY

 Tyler's aunt Olivia has made a sock puppet for Tyler. It is red, and she has glued big black buttons on it for eyes. Olivia decides that she will use her sock puppet to entertain her baby nephew by putting it on her hand and talking in a funny voice. Tyler absolutely loves it, letting out a belly laugh that can be heard by Mom in the kitchen.

INSIGHT

Olivia is showing Tyler a dramatic play experience. Even though Tyler cannot verbally join in, he participates in the pretend play by laughing and responding to his aunt. Olivia, using tools (the sock and her voice) to play act, helps her nephew better understand how he can communicate with his aunt.

baby walks to push the play grocery cart or stands to play with a spoon.

Language skills grow as you engage in parallel talk by giving your baby the words for what he is doing.

When you take a peek-a-boo game and enhance it with the use of your infant's familiar stuffed animals, making them disappear and reappear, this is a simple example of introducing dramatic play into your baby's environment. Adding animal sounds and changing the position where the animal disappears and reappears encourages visual tracing.

Parents can provide various play materials to support dramatic play:

From birth to three months, give your baby things to look at and listen to, such as hanging objects like lightweight scarves that are within view but not within reach. This will enable your infant to look, track, and identify objects in space.

When your baby is between two and six months, provide toys such as teethers and empty food cartons. You can allow your infant to follow his own interests with the toys or you can use them in responsive play with him.

During the three- to eight-month period, give small plastic wheeled toys, which will allow your baby to manipulate how the object moves.

Join in play with him by pretending to drive the wheeled toy to a destination.

For the 8- to 12-month stage, small rocking horses and push toys are also great; your baby will learn about cause and effect as well as learn how things function and are best used.

Your baby will prefer to play with objects that look like the real things you use. Most of all, he will participate in dramatic play with your support and engagement. As your baby matures in age, he will imitate you and practice your roles.

There are many things a parent can do to promote dramatic play with their baby that do not require purchasing fancy toys and materials. Do some of the following and watch how your infant responds as you build a stronger bond together.

* Using a pair of old keys, sit with your baby and pretend to start a car and make the "vroom, vroom" noise. Then watch and see how your infant responds. Look to see if he tries to make similar noises.

* Show your baby his reflection in the mirror. Place various hats on his head and watch his response, then place hats on your head. Is your baby laughing or smiling?

5. Physical Development

> **Physical development refers to how your baby develops head control, strengthens neck muscles, learns hand coordination skills, crawls, and later learns to walk.**

So much will happen during your baby's first year. Before you know it, your once tiny baby will be an independent person, able to move around and communicate.

Physical development occurs especially quickly during the first two years of your child's life. Your baby's birth weight generally doubles by six months and triples by his first birthday. You will see your baby grow between 10 and 12 inches in length (or height), and his body proportions will change during the first two years. When your baby was born, most of his body mass was in the head. As he gets older, the rest of his body catches up.

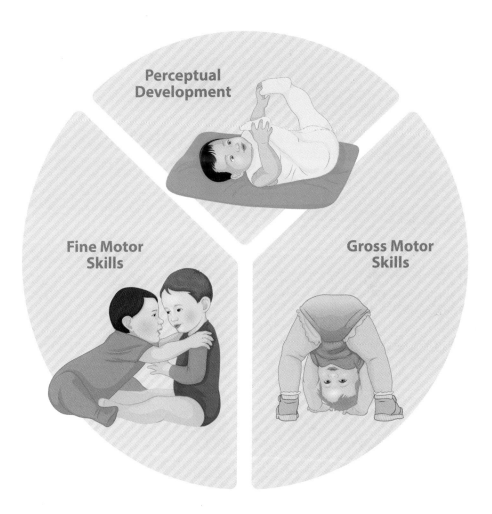

WHOLE CHILD: INFANT
Physical
Development Components

Infant motor development refers to changes in the capacity for voluntary physical movement. But before babies develop physical motor skills, they have simple reflexes. These reflexes facilitate babies' survival until they develop the ability to voluntarily control their own actions. This means that the first few weeks involve primarily reflexive movement; as growth occurs, your baby's reflexes turn into voluntary movements.

You will see some pretty important changes between birth and 12 months as your baby faces challenges that can only be solved by learning physical behaviors. It's all very exciting for a parent to observe baby's progress.

1. Perceptual Development

Perceptual development refers to the process of taking in, organizing, and interpreting sensory information. It is when multiple sensory inputs contribute to motor responses, i.e. when the senses tell the body what to do in response. For instance, when your baby turns his head in response to the visual and auditory cues he receives, he is exhibiting perceptual development.

2. Gross Motor Skills

Gross motor skills include the accomplishment of skills such as rolling over, sitting up, crawling, and walking. Gross motor skills enable your baby to move and gain different perspectives on his environment.

3. Fine Motor Skills

Fine motor skills involve the ability to hold writing tools (e.g. crayons), and participate in routines such as holding a bottle and eating. Touching, grasping, and manual manipulation give your baby experiences in learning about the features of people, objects, and the environment. Stacking rings and knob puzzles provide opportunities for your baby to practice fine motor skills.

The development of fine and gross motor skills happens rapidly in the early years, and it is important to provide your child with opportunities to build these skills.

Remember, the Whole Child Parenting Program offers appropriate developmental products and monthly activity books that walk you through supporting your child's skills. Using these in conjunction with the recommended age-appropriate room materials ensures faster development.

Perceptual Development >
Using the Senses

Perceptual development
involves your baby learning
to develop and use her five
senses (touch, taste, hearing,
smell, and sight) to explore
the world around her
through her developing
motor skills.

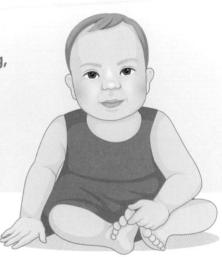

ACTIVITY

Mom takes Brooke to a baby gym class. Mom places Brooke on the floor in front of the infant climber. Brooke simply sits for a few moments looking straight ahead at the climber, then she begins to reach out her hand as if she is going to touch it.

INSIGHT

Brooke is using her perceptual information skills to make a choice about which motor action she will make (using eyes and hands to explore and observe equipment). Brooke is doing this before she decides if she even wants to crawl on the climber. Perceptual development combined with gross motor skills enable your baby to move and gain information and perspective on the environment she is in.

As a parent, it is easier for you to see gross motor skills than perceptual skills developing in your baby. For instance, you will see your baby start to raise her head during tummy time (gross motor skill), before you see how she is interpreting the world around her.

Think about when your baby turns her head toward you or reaches her arms out to you, you are not only seeing the gross motor skill, but you are also seeing how your baby uses her sense of touch and sight to connect with you. **In order for your infant to develop motor skills, she must see something in the environment that encourages her to act and then use her understanding to refine her movements so that she can interact with the world.**

Motor skills give your baby solutions to her goals of wanting to move and interact. For example, your baby will only learn to walk when the nervous system matures, allowing her to control certain leg muscles. This will occur when the legs have grown enough to support her weight and her desire to move. By working to develop your baby's perceptual motor skills, you enable her to move more effectively and with thought.

Typically, your baby will want to move when she is motivated by the challenge to cross the room; then she will initiate a few stumbling steps. Your baby will then refine those stumbling steps into smoother steps that are more effective for reaching the desired goal. Refining of steps happens through repeated trying and perception of the results obtained from that action.

It is important to note that even though the development chart in your physician's office may show motor development unfolding in a smooth, upward progression, this is not always the path your baby will take. Babies perceive things in their environment in different ways, and this will determine what motor path she takes. In fact, detours from the physician's chart will almost always occur as your baby develops at her own pace, and this is perfectly normal as long as she reaches the developmental milestone at the end within a few months of the suggested age.

ACTIVITY

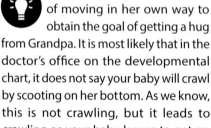 The entire family is over for Sunday dinner. Ashley is sitting on the carpet in the living room when Grandpa says, "Ashley, come to Grandpa. Come see Grandpa, and give me a great big hug." Ashley proceeds to bend her leg and put her other leg up in front of her, while she scoots on her hand and knee over to Grandpa.

INSIGHT

 Ashley puts together the skill of moving in her own way to obtain the goal of getting a hug from Grandpa. It is most likely that in the doctor's office on the developmental chart, it does not say your baby will crawl by scooting on her bottom. As we know, this is not crawling, but it leads to crawling as your baby learns to get on all fours and move. On the other hand, some scooters skip crawling altogether and move right away to walking.

Think about your baby right now. Does she crawl with hands and knees on the floor? Does she scoot on her bottom with one leg extended? Or does she scoot with both legs bent at the same time? **No matter the way she moves, your baby is just thinking about how to reach her goal.**

There are many things you can do to support perceptual development in your baby as she uses her motor skills. Do at least one of the activities listed on the next page with your baby, and see how her skills develop.

Everything that involves your baby's ability to move goes into the category of motor development. When you work with your baby to improve perceptual motor skills, you help her move more successfully and with intention. One day soon she'll get where she's going all by herself!

Auditory perception:

The best thing you can do is read stories with your baby from birth. You do not have to read the words on the page, but you can focus on describing the pictures. Play different genres of music with your baby. Watch her reactions. Does she try to shake her body or move her head in response? Does she ignore it? Does she listen very carefully?

Visual perception:

To help your baby improve this important sense, engage her in activities that sharpen her understanding of what she sees. Lay her down on the floor and place some colorful patterned and checkered toys in front of her. Give her an opportunity to look for the toy by placing a few to the right or left of her eyesight.

Oral perception:

Let your baby taste new foods that are not too spicy or too sweet or too sour or too salty, but that feature one of these characteristics. Watch her pucker her mouth or suck furiously or chew excitedly or even spit it out.

Olfactory perception:

Let your baby smell different objects. It is possible that she may not understand to sniff in, but you can pass an object under her nose and away to see if she smells it and how she responds. Does she like the flower smell and try to grab it away from you? Does she linger or scrunch her nose at the smell of a cut lemon? This exercise can be challenging, but your baby is smelling different scents all the time in her environment.

Tactile perception:

Give your baby objects with different textures. Give her corrugated cardboard to feel or a fabric with raised patterns or a squishy, slimy toy and watch how she interacts with it. Does she repeatedly run her fingers over the edges or the surface? Does she recoil and move away? Does she poke at it? Does she try to put it in her mouth?

Gross Motor Skills >
Large Muscles

Gross motor skills involve the ability to control the large muscles of the body. These are associated with arms, legs, and torso.

Your baby's gross motor skills will develop before her fine motor skills, because gross motor development is from head to toe. **The first gross motor skill your baby develops is her ability to gain control of her head.** Control of the head is vital for your infant to direct her attention.

At birth, your infant's head was so heavy she did not have the neck muscles to lift her head; however, from around four weeks up to five months, you observed your baby develop her first large muscle skill (controlling her head).

Another major large muscle skill that develops in your infant is reaching. At birth, your baby reached without intention. She reached with no coordination between reaching and grasping, resulting in your infant reaching for objects but not accomplishing the goal of getting them.

Reaching develops in a timeline for your baby; between three and five months, you will see intentional reaching take place.

Between five and seven months, your baby uses guided reaching techniques. Her ability to coordinate her vision and control of her reaching has improved. As a result, she becomes more accurate and deliberate when reaching for an object.

By 11 months, you will see success; your baby can now use both hands equally for reaching and grasping. Even though you see both hands engaged in this process at this time, between nine and 13 months you will also see your infant having a preference for one hand over the other.

Now we have come to one of the best parts of gross motor development in your infant: WALKING!

On average, it takes babies about 12 months to learn how to walk because they have so many other behaviors to learn beforehand. As we discussed above, they must first learn how to reach. This is necessary in order for them to grab onto an object and pull themselves to a standing position or to maintain balance. Even before this, your baby has to learn to sit up without support, which occurs between six and eight months.

Practice will develop your child's gross motor skills. If she doesn't practice, she won't learn. So give yourself a break and put the little one down; let her learn to spread her wings and walk. Once a week do one of the activities below with your baby.

Runway for crawlers—Gather a towel and a small baby blanket. Lay them out in a line. Sit at one end and encourage your baby to crawl by cheering her on (you could say, "Come on, Tyler, crawl to Mommy. You can do it.").

Grab and go for walkers—Put one of your baby's favorite objects just out of reach on the front end of the couch. Encourage your baby to grab it and then bring it to you. This will encourage muscle coordination, motor planning, and problem-solving skills.

You must consistently support your baby's gross motor development through simple activities that are not based on the purchase of a product. **The development of your infant's gross motor abilities will be determined by the interaction she has with you.**

ACTIVITY

Marcus is sitting in his bouncy seat while Mom gets dinner together. Marcus is cooing and making all kinds of noises while sitting in the seat; in fact, he is so loud that it causes Mom to pause for a moment and just watch. On Marcus's seat he has a bar with several toys dangling down from it. As Mom watches her son, she begins see him thrust his hand forward almost as though he is throwing his hands at the toys on the bar.

Mom watches, trying to figure out what Marcus is doing. Sometimes he will reach the toy and other times he misses it. When he is able to reach the toy, he tries to open up his little fingers. This is when Mom realizes Marcus is trying to grasp the toys and he cannot do it just yet.

INSIGHT

Marcus is demonstrating what is called *ballistic reaching skills*; this is when your baby gets his hands into the vicinity of the object reached for, but corrections need to be made to have a smooth grasp of the object.

Marcus is still learning to gain control over his reaching and grasping skills. As he matures these skills will improve and thus support better hand-eye coordination.

Fine Motor Skills >
Small Muscles

Fine motor skills involve the ability to use the small muscles of the body, specifically the hands and fingers.

Fine motor skills begin to develop at the same time as gross motor skills; however, because your baby has to put her body in place first, the fine motor skills usually lag behind the development of gross motor skills.

As we discussed before with reaching, grasping occurs as your baby gets older. Initially, however, grasping will only occur when she accidentally comes in contact with the object or you place it directly in her hand.

The first big milestone in fine motor skills occurs when your baby is about nine months old. At this time, she is able to hold small objects between her thumb and forefinger, which is what is called the *pincer grasp*. This is extremely important because it paves the way for other fine motor skills such as writing and buttoning clothing.

Fine motor development involves skills that require your baby to control her eyes and head, as well as other muscles. Babies learn the art of controlling several different parts of their bodies through trial and error.

It begins as your baby learns how to control her eyes through focus and attention, and then she has to learn how to use her eyes with her arms and hands to create a fine motor movement. It is very complex and takes time.

Between 10 and 12 months, you will observe your infant being able to hold a spoon and feed herself, even though her aim will not be right on target.

Because fine motor skills are vital to the success of writing skills later in life, it is very important for you to support your baby's development. During everyday routines, encourage your baby to grasp objects by putting them directly in her hands or tapping the top part of the hand with the object.

You can stimulate your baby's sense of touch with simple materials like a scarf. Put your baby in your lap and show her the scarf.

Talk about the color and texture. Tell your baby that you are going to rub the scarf on her arms, legs, and face.

Watch for her to reach for the object as you touch each area. Depending on her age, you will see her just wave her arms, reach for the scarf, or actually grab it and close her hand. Activities such as these not only help build a bond between you and your baby, but they also develop her fine motor and tactile sensation skills.

As you are supporting and encouraging your baby's physical development, remember that everything works together. Gross motor skills develop with fine motor skills. Skill building happens over time and builds on past developments.

ACTIVITY

Evan and his older brother are sitting together at the table. His brother is eating blueberry yogurt for an afternoon snack. Evan looks up at his brother with a big smile and then stretches his right arm out to reach and grab his brother's spoon.

Evan succeeds and is very proud that he is able to hold the spoon in his hand. Evan attempts to put the spoon in his mouth as he brings it up to his face. On his first attempt he only gets the side of his mouth. After trying a second time he gets some of his brother's yogurt in his mouth. Yummy!

INSIGHT

Evan is able to focus his attention on his brother's spoon and use his hand-eye coordination to grab it. Because he is still developing his fine motor skills he misses his mouth the first time, but after he tries again he succeeds.

6. Health and Care

> **Health and Care refers to the safety, grooming, self-help, and well-being of your child.**

Many parents do not understand some of the most common health procedures needed to care for their baby. The following pages cover health information that is easy to comprehend and can be applied to the routine care of your baby.

Whole Child: infant

Health and Care

Hygiene >
Bathing, Ears, Eyes, Nose, and Tooth Care

Bathing

Bathing is an excellent time for your baby to relax. **A couple of baths a week is generally all that is needed.** Bathing your baby every day will dry out his skin because it eliminates many natural oils.

Use a free-standing tub with a nonslip area for baby's back that is comfortable for your baby. Do not fill it with more than two or three inches of plain, warm water (not hot nor cold) and avoid soaps. Keep one hand on the baby and use a soft cloth to wash your baby with plain water and just a drop of mild baby wash.

Bath time for your baby is not only fun, but can also stimulate development. For instance, as your baby listens to you talk, he is also picking up speech patterns.

Ear Care

It may sound gross, but earwax is important in keeping the ear clean and healthy. Earwax is a substance that keeps dirt and foreign objects out of your infant's ear. **To clean your infant's ear, never use a cotton swab or insert anything into the ear canal. Your baby's middle ear is very short, and you could puncture the eardrum.** Use a damp washcloth to clean the outside of the ear if you see wax buildup.

Your baby's hearing

One to three months:
Your baby is born with fully developed hearing at birth.

Two months:
Your baby will begin to recognize and hear voices and respond to where the voice is coming from.

Three months:
Your baby will begin to coo and imitate high-pitched sounds and vowel sounds.

Four to six months:
Your baby will start to focus more on familiar voices and try to imitate sounds and words he hears. It is important to talk to your baby all the time and engage in two-way conversation when he babbles.

Seven to nine months:
Your baby begins to respond to familiar words and sounds, such as his name or the word "no."

His attention span is becoming more focused, and he begins to follow and search for familiar sounds and voices.

Ten to twelve months:
Your baby is beginning to make connections with the words and sounds he hears. He assigns simple words to objects such as ball, mama, etc. He points to familiar words or objects around him.

When engaging in sign language with your baby, mouth the word you are signing as well so he can imitate you.

Eye Care

Did you know your baby should have his first eye exam before he can walk? However, most children do not have an eye exam until they have reached the age of five. During your baby's first eye exam at preferably six months of age your pediatrician will simply check the basic working order (eye movement ability) and structure of his eyes to make sure everything is developing well. Your doctor will focus on your baby's eye movements and reaction to light or familiar objects. If your baby has clogged tear ducts, consult your pediatrician.

Cleaning

Your baby's eyes are very delicate and sensitive.

To clean your infant's eyes, use water and a soft cloth or cotton ball and wipe from the inside to the outside corners of the eyes. Make sure to wash your hands and use a different cotton ball or washcloth for each eye.

Taking photographs of your baby is so much fun. Have you ever wondered if the use of flash when taking photographs can cause harm to your baby's eyes?

No one can say for certain that a flash does or does not cause much harm; however, there are ways of taking a picture of your baby that do not require using the flash, and this is the safest way to get a picture of your little one. Take pictures in shady places and from directions that diffuse the light; you will get a better picture than one taken with one source of light (the flash) anyway.

Your baby's eyesight

One to three months:
Your baby can focus on objects 8–12 inches from his face and can track movement with his eyes.

You can help build your baby's eye muscles by locking eyes with him and moving from side to side as he follows your gaze.

He smiles as a response to seeing something familiar and begins to imitate gestures such as sticking out his tongue, licking his lips, spitting, and opening his mouth.

Two months:
Your baby can see color but not different tints and tones of colors. He focuses on primary colors and black and white.

Toys that are black and white with detailed designs or primary colors are best to buy for him at this age.

Four to six months:
Your baby can track objects as they move across the room. Infants begin to develop depth perception and understand that things exist even when they are not there. Peek-a-boo and toys that move in and out of view are great at this age. Your baby will start watching your mouth more and try to imitate the movements and sounds you make. His babbling will become more complex and include many "m" and "b" sounds.

Seven to nine months:
Your baby begins to respond to and imitate people's expressions and emotions.

Eight months:
Your baby's vision has developed to the point of being almost the same as an adult's, and he can see things farther away.

Nine months:
Your baby will recognize familiar people and objects, causing him to have heightened stranger anxiety when there are new people around or when he is in a new environment.

Ten to twelve months:
Babies can now judge distances fairly well and throw things with precision. Your baby will start testing depth perception through cause and effect by dropping things from the table or throwing them to see how far they will go.

Nose Care

With babies come a lot of mucus and drool. Mucus serves a number of purposes.

Mucus is a coating that both keeps germs from being ingested by your infant and acts as a thin layer of moisture that prevents tissues underneath from drying out.

However, it is important to keep track of your baby's comfort level and help her when she has too much mucus. When your child has a cold or allergies or there are drastic seasonal changes, your infant may produce more mucus as a response to the dry weather or to flush out more germs.

Avoid a nasal spray unless your doctor recommends one, and make sure the only nasal spray you use is a saline solution. Use a bulb syringe to help your baby "blow her nose" by sucking out excess mucus since she cannot do it herself.

Steaming in the bathroom as well as cool-air humidifiers are great ways to soften the mucus in your infant's nose before cleaning it. You can also raise the crib mattress so the baby's head is slightly elevated during sleep; however, never put a pillow or blanket under your infant's head when sleeping as it can cause suffocation; put an object under the mattress itself to elevate one end.

How to use bulb syringe with your baby

1. Squeeze the air out from the syringe and ensure that a vacuum is created.

2. Place your baby on the bed or changing table with her face toward you. Slightly tilt his chin.

3. Gently place the rubber tip of the bulb syringe in one of her nostrils and gently release the bulb to suction out the mucus.

4. Remove the syringe and make sure that the mucus is taken out in a tissue by squeezing the bulb with force.

5. Repeat the same process with the other nostril after cleaning the bulb syringe by wiping it.

6. Clean the inside of the bulb syringe using soapy water that can be filled in by squeezing and squeezed out.

Tooth Care

Average timeline of infant teeth developing:

6–10 months:
lower bottom two teeth

8–12 months:
top two teeth

9–13 months:
top lateral incisors

10–16 months:
two lower lateral incisors

Your baby will get her first teeth between four and seven months old, though some children wait as late as 12 months or so to sprout their first tooth. The front bottom teeth are the first to appear, and the last teeth to appear are the molars.

All babies are different, and their teeth emerge at different times and affect them differently. Teething can be painful and can cause irritability and fussiness. You will notice her drooling more because her gums are very sensitive and swollen. Drooling can cause face rashes due to irritation from the constant moisture.

Discomfort in her mouth can cause your infant to refuse food and change her sleep patterns. Diarrhea or fevers (about 100.4° F) are not uncommon when your infant is teething. Talk to your doctor about teething gels or medication to help your baby with the pain. Chewing cloths, refrigerated teethers, or cold food (if your baby is old enough) can also help with the pain.

If your teething baby is uncomfortable during teething, keep things cool!

Chill your baby's spoon, teething ring, or sippy cup by putting it in the fridge for a few hours. The coolness will help reduce tenderness in the gums.

Diet >
Hungry?

Most babies initially lose between five and nine percent of their birth weight but will regain it by the time they are two weeks old. In the first month, your baby should gain five to 10 ounces a week and in months two and three continue to gain five to eight ounces a week.

Up until four to six months, your baby should be fed only formula or breast milk. Parents have the option of breastfeeding or using bottles with either breast milk or formula. Solid food should not be introduced yet because your baby's digestive tract is still developing.

Reflexes such as the rooting reflex and sucking reflex can help you as a parent to pick up on hunger cues and feed your baby in response.

The rooting reflex is your baby's search reflex for feeding. This reflex is triggered when you touch or stroke your newborn baby's cheek, specifically along the side of his mouth. Your baby will turn his head toward the side being touched, open his mouth, and seek something to suck.

The sucking reflex comes when a finger, pacifier, or bottle touches the roof of your baby's mouth. The sucking reflex will last for about three to four months after birth. It is an automatic response that helps your baby eat.

What your baby should be eating

0–3 weeks—Your baby should be drinking between one to three ounces every two to three hours, totaling about 8–12 feedings a day. An average baby should consume two to three ounces of formula or breast milk for every pound of body weight.

3 weeks–3 months—Your baby should be drinking three to four ounces and have between six and eight feedings a day.

3 months–6 months—Your baby should be drinking four to eight ounces and have between four and six feedings a day. At this time, your baby is sleeping through the night, so he will eat more in the morning and before bed.

Allergies

Allergies can cause vomiting, diarrhea, rashes, coughing, and or sneezing. Food allergies are one of the most common ailments that can occur during this age. Pets and insects can also cause an allergic reaction in your baby. After giving your child a new food, wait three days before giving it to her again so you can better monitor her reaction to it and see if she is allergic.

Your baby will most likely be allergic to the same things as you are, so be cautious when giving those foods and be sure to monitor her reaction.

Enough nourishment?

When breastfeeding, it is not always clear how much your baby has had to eat. Some signs that your baby is getting enough nourishment are:

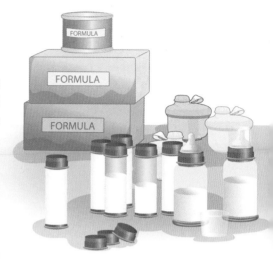

* Your breasts feel softer after nursing because they are less full of milk. After feeding, your baby seems relaxed and satisfied.

* Your baby has at least three bowel movements a day in the first month, and they are a yellowy mustard color.

Some signs that your baby is not getting enough nourishment are:

* Your baby is continuing to lose weight.

* Your baby does not reach his birth weight after five days of being born.

* After the first five days, your baby has small, dark stools.

* Your infant's urine is very dark and is the color of apple juice.

* Feedings take longer than an hour.

* Your baby is fussy and tired most of the time.

Formula makes it easier to measure how much your infant has eaten; however, it is important not to overfeed your infant. If your baby seems like he is still hungry, only give him only an ounce more to eat and do not assume that every cry or sucking reflex is an indication that he is hungry. A sign your baby may still be hungry is if he finishes the bottle quickly and starts looking around for more.

If your baby is overfed, vomiting may occur. Tummy pain or discomfort may also be a sign that your baby is overfed. **Infants show tummy pain by bringing their legs up to their tummies or tensing their bodies.** Check with your doctor if you feel your baby is overfed; your doctor can check your baby's weight.

Introducing Solid Foods

Between four and six months: you will start introducing solid foods.

At this age, you can start looking for cues that your infant is ready for solid foods. Most babies start solid foods around six months old. Solid foods at this age consist of semiliquid cereals or pureed foods such as squash, apples, carrots, and potatoes.

Begin gradually introducing solid food into your baby's diet. Start the first day with one teaspoon of pureed food or cereal that has been mixed with formula or breast milk. **If your child is resistant to solid foods, let him smell it or put a little on his lips and let him taste it and take a minute to think about it.**

Between six and nine months: your baby should be eating six to eight ounces about six times a day, totaling 32 ounces. Continue to give your baby formula or breast milk until he is a year old.

At this point, you can introduce a larger variety of solids such as pureed meats and other proteins. Increase solids at this point by ¼–½ cup total in two or three feedings.

Between nine and 12 months: your baby should be eating seven to eight ounces during each of three to five feedings a day, totaling 24 ounces. It is not uncommon for your baby to start drinking a little less formula or breast milk as more solids are introduced.

At this age, you can start introducing mashed foods and finger foods. Examples of finger foods include ripe bananas, peaches, and well-cooked pasta. It is also a good time to introduce O-shaped cereal, crackers, or small pieces of soft, cut-up bread to help with your child's teething. You should see your child start moving his jaw in a chewing motion at this age.

When your baby does not like something you offer him or is full, he will usually arch his back or turn his head away from you. If your infant does not like one of the solid foods he is offered, try again in a couple of days.

Bottle Storage

When feeding your baby using bottles, it is important to be safe and attentive. Because your baby is still working on holding up his own head, he will need a lot of support.

Your baby should be propped up at a 45-degree angle while feeding, and you should keep bottles out of cribs and especially away from changing tables. Holding your baby while feeding is not only a great way to reduce the amount of air your baby swallows while eating, but is also a perfect opportunity for bonding.

Formula Storage

Store unopened containers of formula at room temperature and always check the formula's care instructions and expiration dates. Prepared bottles should be used immediately or refrigerated and given to your baby within 24 hours. Discard formula that your baby has not consumed within one hour. Do not use any harsh chemicals when washing bottles and nipples; soap and water are just fine.

Breast Milk Storage

Your breast milk changes as your baby develops, and it is important to use it as soon as possible after pumping it. The antioxidants in your breast milk are the most beneficial to your baby when the breast milk is fresh. It is also important to keep bottles clean and sterile.

When pumping breast milk, make sure to wash your hands and storage materials, as well as keep all storage materials in a dry, clean place. Because your breast milk is a bodily fluid, it is important that after you pump it you keep it between 60° F and 85° F (16° C–29° C), but only keep it for between six and eight hours. If you want to keep breast milk for 24 hours, you need to keep it fresh in a cooler with ice at 59° F (15° C) or freeze it. **When thawing breast milk, run warm water over the container until the milk becomes slightly warm. Separation is normal and can be alleviated by gently shaking the container.**

Do not use a microwave to heat the milk because it can create hot spots and burn your infant's mouth and throat. It is important that you do not refreeze thawed milk or feed your infant breast milk that has been thawed for more than 24 hours.

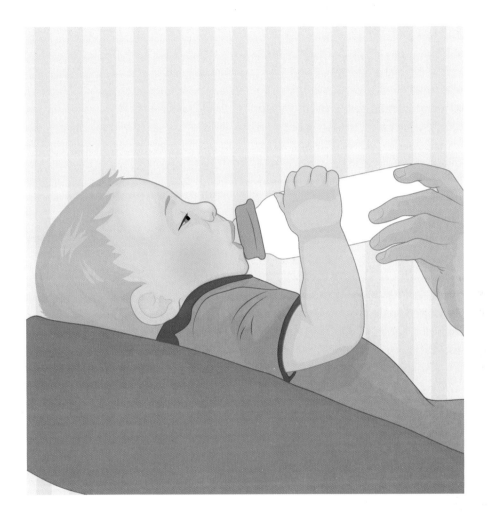

If you are worried about wasting breast milk, start with four ounces of breast milk in each bottle and heat up more if he is hungry so you won't have to throw away any unused breast milk.

Diaper Changing >

When it comes to diapering your baby, you can choose between disposable or cloth diapers. Also, while many parents purchase a changing table, there are other options such as changing mats or simply placing a towel down on a bed. **The most important thing to remember about your diapering area is that it should be easy to clean and have enough space for your baby to lie down safely.** Some changing tables come with a strap, but if you are changing your infant on a surface that does not, it is important to keep at least one hand on the baby at all times. Prepare your supplies before starting, and keep distractions to a minimum. Do not walk away from your baby at any time.

Preparation

* Make sure to wash and dry your hands before starting.

* Set up your diaper changing surface.

* Gather all of your supplies before you start:

  • clean diapers,
  • plenty of wipes or wet cloths,
  • diaper rash cream.

Diaper Changing Procedure

There are a variety of ways parents can change or prefer to change their baby's diapers; however, the following steps are important when it comes to the comfort, health, and safety of your baby when diaper changing.

1. Place the new, clean diaper under your baby while he is still in his dirty diaper. Placing the clean diaper down first keeps the diapering surface clean and protects it from getting dirty.

2. Unfasten the tabs of your baby's diaper and remove it. If there is poop on the diaper, use the front half of the diaper to wipe the bulk of it off your baby's bottom wiping from front to back, especially for girls, because if stool gets into the urethra, it can cause a urinary tract infection.

3. Fold the top half of the diaper under your baby so the clean diaper does not get dirty while you wipe your infant's bottom. Dispose of the dirty diaper in a trash receptacle that is specifically for diapers and bodily fluids and has a lid.

4. Lift up his bottom slightly by gently grasping his ankles to properly clean him. Wipe his bottom with a wipe or damp cloth from front to back (toward his bottom).

5. If your baby has pooped, make sure to clean all of his creases by his legs and bottom so that he will not get an infection or diaper rash.

6. Add any creams if needed and place the front of the clean diaper on your infant and tightly secure it.

Wet diapers are one way to get an idea of whether your baby is getting enough milk to drink. Within five days after birth your baby should have three stools daily and five soaking wet diapers per day, though infants can go through up to ten diapers daily.

Change your baby's diaper frequently to avoid diaper rash or chafing that can occur from the moisture locked in the diaper. **Avoid using baby powder because your baby can easily inhale tiny particles of it that are light enough to be carried into the air and can cause respiratory problems.** If your child has sensitive skin, try switching to just water and towels because some wipes have alcohol in them that can dry out your infant's skin or fragrance that can irritate his skin.

Wash your hands and your baby's hands after you're done changing the diaper. Feces can cause illnesses or infections such as pink eye. Clean and sanitize the diaper changing area between uses with a bleach sanitizer solution, leaving the bleach sanitizer on the surface for at least two minutes (wipe or let air dry before use). Alternatively, you can cover the changing table with a larger cloth and just change the cloth after each use, cleaning the surface of the changing area with cleanser every few days. Never give your baby a bottle or feed him on a diaper changing area.

Poop

Your baby is going through many changes, from his new surroundings to feedings, and his poop will reflect those changes.

One to two days old—Your infant's poop may consist of a dark blackish-greenish tarry substance that is a result of everything your baby ingested while in your uterus and that was left in his body after birth. Be gentle when cleaning this poop off your infant's body.

Two to four days old—Your infant's poop will be a mostly unscented, very dark shade of green almost black color because it is made up of ammonic fluid, skin cells, and other things ingested in utero.

After four days—Your infant's poop will start to lighten up and look greener.

Breastfed poop—will be a yellow, slightly green color with a thicker, mushier consistency, but it can be runny at times, especially in the beginning.

Formula fed poop—will be thicker like peanut butter and tend to stay more in the realm of tan, brown, or yellow coloring.

Solid food poop—will be thicker and a more distinct color of brown. Don't be alarmed if your infant's poop resembles colors of the food he ate or includes small pieces of food. This happens because your infant's food travels through his intestines quickly, and he may have swallowed some pieces before fully chewing them. Solid food poop also begins to smell more like adult poop.

Things to watch for:

* If your baby's poop is ever black (sign of digesting blood during breast feeding from a cracked nipple), contact your physician to make sure it is nothing more serious. Green,

yellow, or brown and runny poop can be a sign of an allergy or infection. Untreated, it may lead to dehydration.

* After you have started feeding foods, white poop could be a sign that your baby is not digesting food. All five colors (green, yellow or brown, red, and white) will require a call to your physician immediately. Also, as mentioned before, it is important to monitor your baby's poop when introducing new foods.

* Poop that has mucus in it can be due to your baby drooling; however, if you notice constant poops with mucus, it can be a sign of infection.

* Signs of constipation include poop that is hard and pebbly and often causes discomfort for your baby. Constipation can be due to introducing solid foods or even a lactose intolerance. Constipation can sometimes be accompanied by blood due to the hard poop irritating the anus on the way out.

* Diarrhea is very common and can come in the form of a "blow-out," which is usually very runny and made up of more water than solids. The color is very light and can occur in response to a new food. If your baby has been having diarrhea for more than a few days, contact your doctor.

Sleep >

Swaddling

Swaddling your infant is a great way to keep your infant comfortable and warm while sleeping. It is also a great way to keep your infant from being disturbed by the startle reflex.

To swaddle your baby:

Your baby should be snug but loose enough that his legs can move.

* First lay a blanket like a diamond on a flat surface and fold down the top corner about six inches, forming a straight edge.

* Then place your baby on his back so that the top of the fabric you folded over is at his shoulders.

* Bring your baby's arms down while you pull the left corner of the blanket over him.

* Pull the right corner of the blanket over your baby and tuck it in under his left arm.

* Then pull the bottom corner up, and finish by pulling the left corner of the blanket over your baby and tucking it gently under him. Some infants love the safety and security of being swaddled. Other infants may resist swaddling.

Sleeping Safety

There are a number of safety precautions to take when putting your little one to sleep. These precautions are especially important from birth to three months because of his inability to hold up his own head.

What to know:

* Your baby should be placed on his back to sleep, never on his stomach or side. When sleeping face down, your baby may overheat or rebreathe the air he just exhaled, causing a lack of oxygen.

* Avoid placing your baby on his side; he can accidently roll over on his tummy. **When your infant is about five or six months old, he will be able to roll over onto his tummy on his own.** If he is rolling over on his own, he may sleep on his tummy because your infant is demonstrating that he has enough arm strength to hold himself up and roll over again if needed.

* Do not have soft objects like toys, quilts, pillows, or crib liners in your infant's crib as they can cause suffocation. If your infant is chilly, dress him in warmer clothes when putting him to sleep instead of adding a blanket, but avoid overheating him.

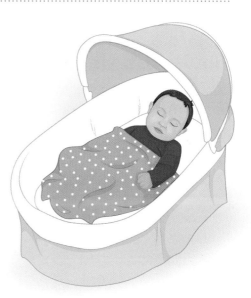

* Never cover your baby's face with a hood, hat, or blanket and make sure there is fresh air and proper ventilation in the room. Swaddling can help your baby sleep soundly on his back, but it is important to make sure the blanket is tight enough not to unravel but not so tight that your infant will overheat.

* Sleep in the same room as your infant for about the first 12 weeks so that you can hear him wake up when he is hungry, wet, or uncomfortable. It is okay to sleep with your infant in the room, but do not have him share a bed or sleep with another infant or sibling. Alternatively, you can use a sound or video monitor; just make sure it is close enough and acute enough to pick up all sounds your infant may make.

Warning: Infants can make strange noises all night long. Some sound like dolphins, others make grunts, and sometimes a baby will wail in his sleep—and they can do all this and not even wake up.

* Don't give your infant a bottle in his crib because he is not elevated enough to drink it safely; however, pacifiers are great when putting your infant to sleep because the sucking motion soothes and calms him as he falls asleep.

Create a Safe Environment

During the 7- to 12-month period, your baby will explore everything in her environment.

* Take time to check and baby proof the corners of all furniture and cabinets.

* Attach barriers or gates to the top and bottom of stairwells.

* Cover all electrical outlets.

* Use fasteners to "lock" all cabinets below waist level.

* Pull electrical cords out of reach.

* Doorknob covers can be added to close off rooms to children once they become walkers.

How much sleep?

Between birth and about four weeks:

Babies need about 16–17 hours of sleep every day. They tend to sleep between one to two hours at a time, and these sleep times are scheduled around their eating times, which are every two to four hours.

Four to six weeks old:

Your baby needs between 14–16 hours of sleep.

After eight weeks:

Your baby will begin to sleep more through the night and less during the day, but he will still wake up during the night to eat.

Between three and six months:

Your baby will begin to establish his own sleep schedule and be fairly consistent with it.

Around four months:

Infants need about five naps a day.

At four months:

Changes will occur in the usual sleep schedule as he is adapting to a schedule that now includes sleeping longer at night.

At six months:

Your baby will be taking three to four naps a day. Your baby is consuming enough calories that he can sleep comfortably through the night for about five to six hours without needing to wake for a feeding.

Remember that each child is different. Some babies will sleep through the night at six months, others will take a year.

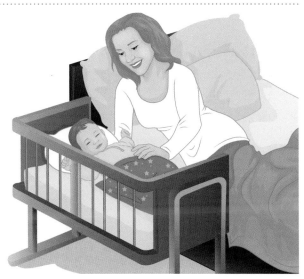

Sleep Training

Night weaning starts around six months as you start developing more of a routine for your infant with eating and sleeping schedules. As he wakes up in the night, try to soothe him back to sleep by patting his back or rocking him. **Do not force night weaning on your child. If he is crying for long periods of time, tend to him and attempt to night wean again in a couple of weeks.**

* At eight months old, your baby will begin to self-soothe back to sleep if he wakes up. Infants usually start moving toward a two-nap schedule at this age and will continue to follow that two-nap schedule until the infant reaches toddler age and switches to one nap.

* Remember that each child is differ-

ent, and there are a number of different ways to sleep train or night wean your infant. The most important thing to remember is to make your child comfortable and happy.

* Your infant will let you know if he is not ready, and you shouldn't push him. If your infant is having a hard time keeping a consistent sleeping schedule, try another approach or try again in a couple of weeks. Stressing out yourself and your infant will not make it easier for either of you to sleep.

* **Sleep training is important, but so is building trust with your child.** If he has not calmed down after two or three minutes, tend to his needs and comfort him. Happy baby equals happy parent.

Mind and Body >
Yoga

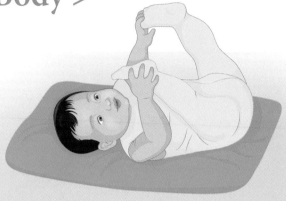

Babies benefit greatly from participating in yoga.

Yoga encompasses the whole body and is beneficial for both body and mind. It can set a foundation for your infant at birth for future exercise and movement while also promoting less stress and calm behavior, which can lead to better sleeping and a calmer temperament.

Through the movements of yoga (which you will have to simulate most likely as your child will not have the motor skills to accomplish the movements on his own), your baby's organs are being massaged and stimulated, specifically those organs in the digestive and nervous systems. Physically, you and your baby are exploring body movements more, which will make your baby more confident with his physical abilities and can build his self-esteem. Try lightly massaging his body, pushing his legs gently into his tummy and

stretching them out gently, and pulling his arms out gently and gently pushing them in.

Stimulation of the nervous system can calm babies between feedings and before going to sleep, which helps with the balance of their daily routine. Stimulation of the nervous system can also contribute to brain and cognitive development.

Yoga is another great opportunity to bond with your baby as you lie together and explore his body through nonverbal communication. By having this opportunity for calm, nonverbal communication, you are building the groundwork for his future social interactions.

Get into doing yoga and massage with your child on a regular basis to start him off on the right path for regular exercise.

While your infant is too young to imitate and practice poses with you, he will nonetheless benefit from physical activity with you.

Remember, the Whole Child Parenting Program offers appropriate developmental products and monthly activity books that walk you through supporting your child's skills. Using these in conjunction with the recommended age-appropriate room materials ensures faster development.

Reaching Milestones >

You will see your baby's development by how he plays, learns, and speaks (babbles). As a parent you play a critical role in his development. Providing a safe and loving home and spending time together—playing, singing, showing picture books, and even just talking—will make a big difference!

Although babies develop through a generally predictable sequence of steps and milestones, they may not proceed through these steps in the same way or at the same time as their peers. Your baby's development is also greatly influenced by factors in his environment and the experiences you provide him. The information below is a guide to explain what an average baby might achieve. These skills may not occur at the exact times listed; skills can occur within a six-month to a year range. Consider what you read in the context of your child's unique development.

COGNITIVE

- **Birth–3 months:** I will repeat movements to master them, this will stimulate my brain cell development.

- **4–5 months:** I am curious about my environment as I watch what is going on.

- **6–8 months:** I will explore my environment through trial and error tasks (drop the toy and watch you pick it up for me).

- **8–12 months:** I am a baby scientist. I want to explore during every waking moment so I can figure out how everything works around me. How can I get you to read my favorite book? How can I get the block out of the box?

SOCIAL-EMOTIONAL

- **Birth:** I am learning to trust my parents and other caregivers in my environment.

- **3–4 months:** I will settle down when my parents comfort me.

- **5 months:** I can smile, and you can smile back at me. I smile and gurgle when I am happy and excited.

- **6–9 months:** I can tell the difference between people I do and do not know. Sometimes you may see that I am afraid of strangers.

- **9–10 months:** I love to play games like peek-a-boo with my mommy and daddy, even others who will play with me. When I want you to keep playing with me I will signal by waving my arms and legs and make sounds to let you know I want to keep playing.

LANGUAGE

- **Birth–5 months:** I have different cries, facial expressions, and body movements to tell you I am sleepy, hungry, wet, uncomfortable, overwhelmed, or I want to play.

- **3–6 months:** I begin to babble to you.

- **7–9 months:** I'll begin with vowel sounds "oh" and "ah" then I will produce a full repertoire of sounds (*ma -ma -ma*).

- **8–10 months:** I can create long babbling sentences. I may be able to say a few words or say "baba" for bottle. I might push the cracker that I don't want off my high chair and say "nuh."

- **10–12 months:** I will point to pictures in books in response to verbal cues you will give me.

CREATIVE

5–12 months:

- I can clap my hands and move my body (head, arms) to a happy-sounding song.

- I can shake a maraca or mimic the sounds that you make.

- I like finger paints and will squeeze paint through my fingers.

- I like to squeeze slick dough because the texture feels good on my hands.

- I will play a game of peek-a-boo as I explore dramatic play concepts with you.

PHYSICAL

- **Birth:** I have random uncoordinated reflexive movements throughout the day. I will look for something to suck on, maybe my thumb or a pacifier you gave me.

- **3–5 months:** I can visually tracks objects with my eyes. I can kick my mobile and make it move with my feet. I can also shake a rattle and make a sound.

- **5–6 months:** I can reach and grasp for objects. If I can't reach it, I will roll over to get the object.

- **7–9 months:** I can sit in my high chair. Put me on the floor and I can push my head and torso up.

- **9–12 months:** I can go from a sitting position and get to another place by crawling or scooting. I can pull to a standing position when I want to see something. Sometimes I may stoop to get something or to help me poop. My hand-eye coordination skills are really improving.

HEALTH AND CARE

- I need a bedtime routine so I will know nighttime is for sleeping, not playing. Pick a reasonable time, such as around 7:00 P.M., and choose three or four things you'd like to do every night, such as bathing, drinking, reading a story.

- To prepare for my bath routine, gather everything you'll need: tub, hooded baby towel, diaper cream, diaper, lotion, and cup to rinse my hair.

- Sit down with me to give me a bottle or food so I can develop healthy eating habits and social skills.

Environment >
Infant's Room

Your baby's early learning and developmental experiences begin at birth and will continue through kindergarten.

Birth through age five is a distinct period of life for your child; the experiences she is exposed to now will set the foundation for her success in school and in other areas.

Environments that are stimulating for your baby are filled with safe objects to explore, allow freedom of movement, and provide a variety of experiences.

The most important aspect of a stimulating environment is how you create an inviting, challenging play space in which your baby can interact with you.

The key to achieving this goal is to organize all materials using your **Six Drawer Whole Child Color-Coded Organizer**; this will enable you to access materials easily. It will help you focus because you'll choose which of the **six categories of development— cognitive, social-emotional, language, creative, physical, and health**—you and your baby will interact in.

The following picture shows what the recommended infant room looks like. The objects and materials shown will support you in creating a stimulating environment for your baby, one that is filled with specific furniture and age-appropriate toys to give her opportunities to practice all her new skills.

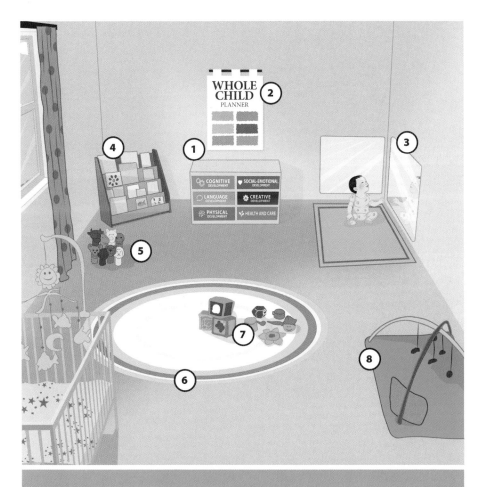

Whole Child: Infant's Room

The following list contains must-have items for your baby's room. These items will be used interchangeably with your other Whole Child Parenting materials.

1. Six Drawer Whole Child Color-Coded Organizer
2. Whole Child Wall Planner
3. Mirror
4. Bookshelf
5. Puppet/Pretend Play Materials
6. Carpet
7. Blocks and Soft Toys
8. Play Mat

toddler >
(12 to 24 Months)

Milestones for a Toddler

 **COGNITIVE** 1

- Begins to sort shapes and colors
- Matches pictures with objects
- Recognizes quantities of one to three

 **SOCIAL-EMOTIONAL** 2

- Shows defiant behavior
- Shows separation anxiety
- Recognizes themselves in mirror

 LANGUAGE 3

- Says between 10 to 20 words
- Uses two-word sentences
- Follows one-step instructions

 **CREATIVE** 4

- Can sing
- Explores art materials
- Dances to music

 PHYSICAL 5

- Runs with ease
- Rides a tricycle
- Holds markers and crayons

 HEALTH AND CARE 6

- Walks alone
- Uses cup and spoon
- Changes from two naps to one

toddler
(12 to 24 Months)

Between the ages of 12 to 24 months your child is embarking on some new milestones and going through very visible changes. You will see your toddler's arms and legs are becoming stronger, which makes it easier for him to pull himself up to stand and move around. He is able to reach and explore more of his environment. However, with emotions at a high, this can cause some challenging behaviors and tantrums when he does not get what he wants. In this year we will help you with some tips to work with your child and his often challenging (but interesting!) behavior.

1. Cognitive Development

> **Cognitive development refers to how your child's mind is working and his process of learning.**

Cognitive development also involves your child using his senses as well as his motor skills to learn and discover the world around him. Your toddler learns information by engaging in everyday routine activities such as playing, eating, taking trips, and getting dressed.

Your child is using the senses of touch and sight to interact with objects and make connections.

The following chart provides you with an image that walks you through the stages of your child's intellectual development.

Understanding these areas of cognitive development will help you learn how your child thinks, how to support learning, and how to teach new skills.

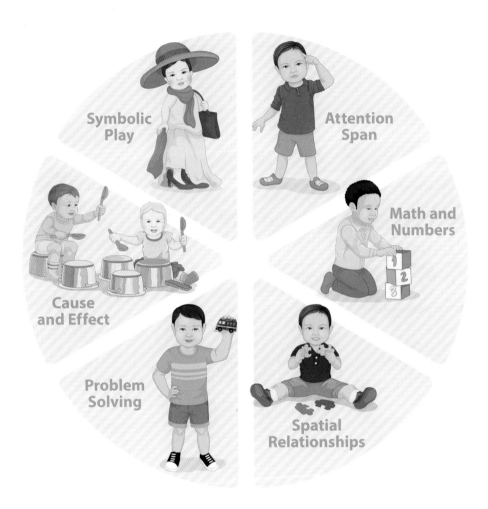

WHOLE CHILD: TODDLER
Cognitive
Development Components

Under each cognitive area, the chart below gives you specific skills you can expect to see as your toddler develops. This chart will allow you to have practical expectations for your child at this age.

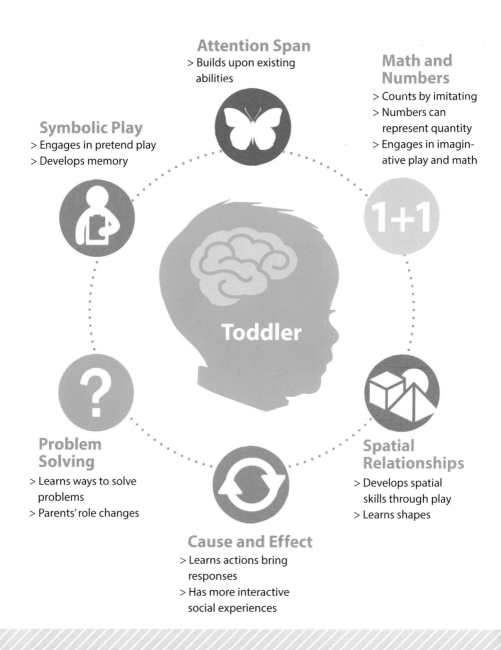

Attention Span
> Builds upon existing abilities

Math and Numbers
> Counts by imitating
> Numbers can represent quantity
> Engages in imaginative play and math

Symbolic Play
> Engages in pretend play
> Develops memory

Toddler

Problem Solving
> Learns ways to solve problems
> Parents' role changes

Spatial Relationships
> Develops spatial skills through play
> Learns shapes

Cause and Effect
> Learns actions bring responses
> Has more interactive social experiences

Your toddler has the ability to remember an experience that happened some hours prior, or even a day ago. This is demonstrated by watching your toddler repeat a prior experience he had. Take, for example, your child stacking one block on top of the other or using a toy as a phone and talking. Because his brain is expanding, your toddler is able to think in a more complex manner and is beginning to understand symbols during play by realizing those words can represent an object.

Perceptual cognition is a characteristic of cognitive development that enables your toddler to make sense of and understand all of the sensory information he is taking in. Toddlers engage in their world through their senses and learn more about what they taste, touch, smell, hear, and see.

This is why it is very important to allow your toddler to interact in a brain-boosting environment, enabling him to interact with everything around him. Making sure his environment is stimulating and age appropriate will be covered at the end of this chapter.

The subsequent chapters show you how your child acquires knowledge and demonstrates major development in brain growth.

Attention Span >
Concentration

Attention span involves your child being able to focus on an activity or learning experience for an average length of time consisting of two to six minutes.

While it is hard to gather a child's sustained attention at this age, your child will be able to pay attention in a structured activity lead by you. Make sure there are no verbal or visual interferences in your play space, and if your child gets restless, it's time to move on to some other activity.

ACTIVITY

 It is a beautiful sunny day, and Jack's parents want to take him to the zoo to see the new giraffe exhibit and watch feeding time. Jack is very excited, so off to the zoo they go!

Upon arriving at the zoo, Jack wants to go straight to see the giraffes. Jack says, "Hurry, Mommy!"

At the exhibit, Jack points to the baby and mommy giraffes and then walks back and forth between the left and right side of the exhibit to see the other giraffes that are standing under the trees.

After a few minutes Jack decides it is time to go and begins to pull on his dad's hand to see a different animal.

Jack's parents are very surprised that he wants to go so soon and before watching feeding time. They are also surprised to see Jack lose interest in the giraffes so quickly.

INSIGHT

In this example, Jack's parents think he has quickly lost his attention regarding the giraffes; however, for his age, Jack has stayed just the right amount of time.

Attention skills enable your child to observe, take in information, and learn. Focused attention increases memory, and this supports cognitive development.

This area of cognitive development is getting stronger every day as your child moves closer to two years of age. You will see your little one grow a great deal during the toddler years. It is important to understand that the change in your child's attention span will not occur overnight.

When your child was an infant, his attention span was only a few seconds at most. Now that he is a toddler, your child's attention span has expanded and lengthened. This now enables him to do more activities and engage in learning experiences for longer periods of time, thus maximizing learning potential; however, for a parent, the attention span will still feel very short.

An excellent way to build your child's attention span is to teach a new skill a little bit at a time.

Think back to the zoo experience with Jack. Imagine that this time the family visits the giraffes for a brief period. While at the giraffe exhibit Jack mentions that he sees a mommy and a baby giraffe and wants to move on to see something else. Next time when the family visits the zoo, they can extend the time and talk about how the mommy giraffe is bigger than the baby giraffe. By actively building on the experience, Jack's attention span will be extended, giving the opportunity for a new learning experience to take place.

Also, remember to have clear expectations and consider your child's emotional state before engaging in a learning activity that requires attention. Your child will be able to better focus if he is not tired or upset or hungry. With these things in mind, you can create a supportive environment for your child to learn.

Some ways that you can support focused attention include:

* Have your child repeat words after you. For example, when you say *giraffe*, *baby*, *mommy*, or *zoo*, have your child repeat the word. This will let you know how much attention your child pays to the conversation or activity.

* Read books with your child and point to pictures. Ask your child to look for certain pictures on the page.

Memory

As your child grows older, he will be able to retain information for longer periods of time.

Your child has the capacity to remember familiar faces, songs, words (*more, please, Mommy, Daddy, eat*, and other words that relate to his everyday world), and objects (e.g. pictures or toys) in his environment.

You will hear your child say the word *cat* when he sees one on an afternoon walk, or you will hear him sing the entire song of "Itsy Bitsy Spider" because he remembers all the words.

During memory development, your child is using what is called "working memory," which is your child's ability to keep immediate information in his mind to complete a task. You can see this when you give your toddler verbal instructions such as asking him to get his blanket and take it to his bed, an activity he has participated in time and again. You will also see working memory when your toddler can participate in routines and imitate an action or activity previously observed.

At times, you will notice that your toddler may not remember something. This is perfectly normal since your toddler has not completely mastered the ability to access all the information that is in his memory bank. As your toddler has more practice talking about and piecing together all the experiences he has in a day, his ability to remember and tell you things will increase. **Keeping predictable routines for your child supports his memory development.**

ACTIVITY

 Twins Justin and Mary are sitting on the kitchen floor together. Mom hands both of the children a cup with milk in it. While Mary is drinking her milk, Justin takes Mary's cup from her hand and tries to pour his milk into her cup.

Mary starts to cry because she now has milk all over her red shorts.

INSIGHT

Justin remembers seeing his mom pour milk into a cup for him and Mary, and he is trying to do the same thing. Justin is imitating an action that he has observed.

Each time toddlers practice basic skills, they are drawing from memory. Everyday experiences around the home develop children's cognitive skills.

Remember, the Whole Child Parenting Program offers appropriate developmental products and monthly activity books that walk you through supporting your child's skills. Using these in conjunction with the recommended age-appropriate room materials ensures faster development.

Math and Numbers >
Sense and Awareness

Count how many apples we have.

Math and number awareness are the foundations for learning more advanced math concepts.

ACTIVITY

Helena has just come home with Dad from a parent's day out activity. Helena says, "Daddy, I want apple." Dad begins to prepare an afternoon snack for her by getting two apples from the fruit bowl and washing them.

Dad says, "Let's count how many apples we have." Helena looks at the apples for a moment and together they begin to point and count each apple, "One, two . . ."

Then Dad cuts one apple in half and says, "Let's count how many pieces we have. One, two . . ."

Dad then says, "Good job! We have two pieces."

INSIGHT

With Dad's help Helena is able to count two objects. By pausing for a moment, Helena uses her mental ability to think about what she is looking at (apples) and about to do (I need to point as I count), and then she counts the apples before they are cut into pieces.

Math and **number awareness** involves your child recognizing numbers, counting, learning one-to-one correspondence, recognizing patterns, sorting, and classifying.

Number sense is seeing how numbers represent an amount. For example, how the symbol "2" is related to a quantity: two apples.

Number sense develops in stages. The first stage occurs during your child's toddler year when you must support your child by helping her learn to count objects out loud and assign each object a number. By assigning each object a number, you are helping your child see that there is a connection between the number and the amount of objects you are counting. As toddlers become older, they will also start to use relational words to indicate *more* or *same* in addition to number words.

During the toddler years, you and your child will count together because your child cannot yet count on her own and extra support is needed; however, as your child reaches the age of two, she will begin to count out loud independently from you. Counting is a huge milestone for your child, and it demonstrates that she understands the concept of number sense.

To support your child's number sense ability, count objects out loud that your child sees in her environment. Objects can include counting out loud how many blocks are on the floor or how many shoes are at the front door.

Just like in the example in which Dad is helping Helena count the pieces of apple for snack, you can also help develop your child's number sense through everyday routines (e.g. counting the number of cups at the table for dinner). By doing so, you are ensuring that your child will be able to succeed in early math and beyond.

Spatial Relationships >
Concepts

Spatial relationships are the relationships between the locations of objects to each other in a given space. This also includes the relationship between your child's own location and objects in a given space.

Spatial relationships can be explained using puzzles. For example, your child is working on a four-piece chunky shaped puzzle, and in order for the puzzle to fit together your child has to move around one puzzle piece to see how it fits next to another. Your child is moving the piece and changing its location within the given space that is the puzzle board. Your child will use trial and error to discover how things move and fit.

Toddlers learn about spatial relationships in a variety of ways, such as by spending time exploring toys in their environment. When playing with a ball, your child will see how the ball can roll into places that are small and that may make it difficult for her to reach with her hands. This is your child learning the relationship between her, an object (the ball), and the space around her.

There are so many simple things you can do to support your child's spatial development, such as giving her a ball to explore. **As your baby plays with her blocks or watches you roll a ball to her, she is learning about spatial relationships.** You can also ask your child to point to her nose, and then follow up by saying, "Your nose is on your face," and "Your nose is on the front of your head," and "Your nose is above your lips." Using words like *on* and *above* supports your child's use of spatial language. Some other examples of spatial language words you can use are *under*, *over*, *on top*, and *next to*.

For example, give your child opportunities to climb and jump so she'll learn how she can move up and down stairs. Set up an obstacle course using sheets and pillows; this will allow her to go *over*, *under*, *around*, and *through* different objects, and help her label how she is moving. Say, "You went under the table, and now you are going around the chair."

As your child continues to develop language skills, make sure to use spatial language words as part of your daily routine. **Supporting your child's understanding of spatial relationships will help your child be successful in a number of areas such as reading and math,** as well as aid her in following directions.

ACTIVITY

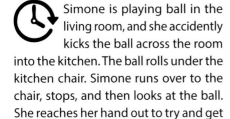

Simone is playing ball in the living room, and she accidentally kicks the ball across the room into the kitchen. The ball rolls under the kitchen chair. Simone runs over to the chair, stops, and then looks at the ball. She reaches her hand out to try and get the ball, but she cannot reach it.

Simone then realizes that in order to get to the ball she will need to bend down and crawl under the chair. As Simone bends down and begins to crawl she still does not feel confident that she will be able to crawl under the chair and reach the ball, so she stands up, pushes the chair over, and then bends down again on the floor.

On this second try, Simone is now able to reach the ball because she has moved an obstructing object in the space and can now access the object she seeks.

INSIGHT

When Simone stops to think, this demonstrates that she is using her problem-solving skills to help her understand the spatial relationship between her size and her ability to reach the ball (object) under the chair.

Cause and Effect >
Actions and Responses

Cause and effect is the relationship between an action and its outcome.

When your child presses a button on a toy and hears it go "beep, beep," he is engaging in cause and effect. The cause is your child pressing the button, and the effect is the sound the toy makes.

Through developing an understanding of cause and effect, your child will build his abilities to solve problems, to make predictions, and to understand the impact of his actions.

The concept of cause and effect is understood further as your child learns that certain actions bring a predictable response. He pushes the toy off the table, and you pick it up for him and place it back on the table. He pushes the toy off the table again. This exchange of cause (pushing the toy off the table) and effect (you pick up the toy) can go on and on to the endless delight of your toddler.

When your child is around 20 months old, you will notice how he experiments with cause and effect when playing with blocks. You will see your child stack one block on top of the other; as he places a third block (cause) on top of the tower, the tower falls down (effect). You will see your toddler try to place a large block on top of a small block (cause). When the large block falls over (effect), it will take your child a few tries before he realizes the small block should go on top.

However, when your child plays with blocks again, he will not remember exactly how the blocks stacked together and will begin to experiment with cause and effect all over again. This is because his memory skills are still developing. Give him time. These skills develop with age.

ACTIVITY

 Twins Catherine and Ian are excited because they are going to music class today. As the twins arrive at music class, the music teacher asks them to come sit on the floor.

The music teacher says, "Hello, everybody! Today you are going to play music with me using a pot and a spoon. This is a pot, and this is a spoon." She holds up each item to the class. "When I start to sing and play my guitar, you can start hitting your pot with the spoon. When I stop singing and playing my guitar, you should stop hitting your pot with the spoon. Watch and listen to me as I show you how."

Then she gives both children a different size pot and a wooden spoon. As she starts to play her guitar and sing, the twins begin to hit their pot with their spoon.

Catherine and Ian start by hitting the pot quietly and then each one gets louder and louder, hitting as hard as they can. The children get so loud they do not hear the teacher stop singing and playing her guitar. The music teacher has to remind the twins to stop.

INSIGHT

Even though Catherine and Ian do not stop hitting on the pot, each child is able to hear that by hitting on the pot they can make a noise. The harder each child hits the pot, the louder the noise gets. The causative action is hitting the pot with the spoon, and the effect is the noise it makes.

Problem Solving >
Thinking Skills

Problem solving is how your child comes up with solutions to complex challenges.

Your child may stand on a chair (solution) to reach a toy on the shelf (challenge).

Toddlers solve problems by various means: manipulating objects, imitating solutions found by others, using objects as tools, and participating in trial and error.

ACTIVITY

 Sixteen-month-old Lance is in his bedroom playing with his toy fire truck. He knows that his toy fire truck makes a sound, but he can't remember what he has to do to hear it.

Lance starts to shake the toy fire truck, turn it upside down, push the lights on the front, and even pull out the ladder trying hard to make the fire truck make a noise.

Finally, he presses the red circle (siren) button at the top of the truck and the fire truck makes a noise!

INSIGHT

 Lance is able to use trial and error to find a solution to the challenge he has, which is how to make the toy fire truck make a noise. The solution is pressing the red circle button on top of the fire truck.

As a parent, you play a key role in how your child develops problem-solving skills and how many times he will attempt to figure out a solution to a challenge. For example, your toddler has been attempting to open the closet door for a while. As he watches and studies you opening the closet door numerous times, he's finally able to open it himself. This is learning by imitating and observing problem solving in action.

Manipulating objects occurs when parents allow their toddlers to explore the object first. For example, Lance's mother could have pushed the button on the toy fire truck for him, but instead she allows time for her child to explore the toy and find the button so he can push it himself.

It is best to give your toddler the opportunity to solve the problem first before you intervene. If Lance continues to have a hard time, his mother can support him by turning the toy in a position that will allow him to notice and push the button himself. This will build your child's self-confidence and self-esteem as well as support the development of problem-solving skills.

Problem solving requires your child to use reasoning, decision-making, critical thinking, and creative thinking skills.

Your child will have so many problems to solve! As a parent, you can help by providing opportunities for open-ended exploration and by offering help. Give your child materials from around the house and let him make choices about how to use those materials. There are endless ways your child can explore plastic bowls, boxes, and scarves.

Sit back as you watch your child explore spatial relationships through problem solving by providing him with a spaghetti strainer and plastic straws as he tries to stick the straws through the holes of the strainer. Remember to keep your problem-solving activities simple. More complex problem solving will happen when your child grows older.

It is important to always encourage and praise your child when he engages in problem-solving tasks and activities. This will leave your child feeling confident in his accomplishments and excited about solving more challenges.

Symbolic Play >
Pretend Play

Pretend play is when your child uses objects in make-believe activities.

Symbolic play is when she imitates actions and sounds she encounters in everyday life and imagines scenarios that take familiar experiences in a new direction.

"I am Mommy."

ACTIVITY

 Rachel is in the closet of her mother's room. She finds some hats, shoes, purses, and a dress on the floor of the closet. Mom asks, "Rachel! What are you doing in the closet?" Mom does not hear a response.

Rachel begins to put her feet in her mom's shoes. She puts on her mom's dress by just putting her arms in any opening she can find, and then tops it all off with a hat. She comes out of the closet and stands in front of her parents. Rachel says, "I am Mommy," as she walks around the room.

INSIGHT

Rachel dresses up like her mother because these are clothes that she sees her mother wearing every day. Rachel is pretending to experiment with being Mommy. The clothing and accessories she puts on are all symbols she associates with Mom.

Pretend play allows your child to experiment with different experiences that have occurred in her environment. A child may push a block around the floor as a car or put it to her ear as a cell phone.

Pretend play supports creativity, language skills, and the understanding of social roles. Whether you have a girl or a boy, it is important for you to have dress up clothes for your child, as they provide one of the easiest forms of pretend play.

Since your child's daily routines are now more structured, you have to be intentional in exposing your child to pretend play opportunities. That is because pretend play is a crucial part of your child's development in all areas and will continue to evolve. As your child approaches 18 months, she will use more imagination during her play experiences, using a broom to row her boat made from a box she is sitting in. During this time you will see your child engaged in solitary pretend play experiences.

From ages three to five this pretend play will expand to include others and children assigning roles to one another. Pretend play provides a fun way for you to interact with your child. Get in on the fun and see what happens.

Why support pretend play?

* It exposes your child to new vocabulary, such as *dog*, *cat*, or *princess* and *king*.

* You will help her learn to play with others during group play experiences. This helps develop her ability to take others' perspectives into account and learn empathy.

Objects to support pretend play:

* play dishes and play food
* toy toolbox
* pretend doctor's kit
* dress-up clothing

Some of the best toys to support your child during pretend play should be everyday materials found around your home. A large cardboard box can expand your child's thinking to turn it into a rocket ship or a racecar. Providing a laundry basket will encourage your child to think about how it can be used as a cage for his stuffed animals.

2. Social-Emotional Development

> **Social-emotional development refers to your child's ability to understand the feelings of others, manage strong emotions and expressions in a positive way, and start and keep relationships.**

This stage of development for a toddler is unique and special. It starts with a loving relationship between you and your child; you give him a sense of comfort, safety, confidence, and encouragement. It can also be a difficult stage because toddlers see things in their own way and have strong feelings, which makes it difficult to understand what toddlers need from you.

Self-Awareness

Social Development

Self-Regulation

Emotional Development

WHOLE CHILD: TODDLER
Social-Emotional Development Components

1. Social Development

Social development involves playing and interacting with peers and having the desire to interact with other adults through story time, sharing, playing, and imitation. Imitation and pretending are used during social development to help toddlers understand social norms.

2. Emotional Development

Emotional development occurs when your child learns to use words to express feelings or thoughts. He is also learning about other people's feelings and how his behavior affects you.

3. Self-Regulation

Self-regulation includes a range of traits and abilities involving your child, especially being able to focus his attention, control emotions, and manage behavior and feelings.

4. Self-Awareness

Self-awareness is when your child realizes that he is a unique individual whose body, mind, and actions are separate from other people's. This is a very big milestone because it leads to the development of self-esteem.

Social-emotional development starts with parents, family, and caregivers lovingly interacting with a child.

Social Development >
Relationships with Others

Social development involves your child having the skills he needs to form positive relationships with peers and family members.

ACTIVITY

Nolan and his dad go to a family barbeque at the park on Sunday. During the drive in the car, Nolan is having a good time and singing along to the music.

When the two of them arrive at the park, Nolan becomes very quiet and stops singing.

"Nolan, we're here!" Dad says. Nolan puts his head down. "Nolan, look! Your cousin is here! Don't be sad, I'm here with you." Nolan jumps out of the car seat, climbs down and clings to his cousin, hugging her as tightly as he can.

"Nolan, play," says his cousin. Nolan still hugs his cousin tightly for a few more minutes until Dad comes over with a toy truck. "You can go play," says Dad. Nolan looks up at Dad again then lets go of his cousin and takes the truck with his cousin to the sand box.

INSIGHT

Nolan is given support when Dad tells him that his cousin is here and he is going to play with her. Because he feels supported and trusts that his dad is in close proximity, Nolan feels comfortable cementing a relationship with his cousin.

Social relationships help your child gain trust, confidence, and security—all of which are important for him to explore his environment, learn, interact, and build relationships with others.

Your child needs to learn to trust very early in life. When your child feels that he can trust you and other familiar people, then he will be more willing and open to meeting new people and peers. This is because your child understands that you will always be nearby to provide support when needed.

Relationships with your child first consist of meeting your child's basic needs through sensitive caregiving. **By responding in a warm, loving, and gentle way, you're helping your child learn about communication, behavior, and emotions,** making him feel safe and secure, and promoting a strong relationship between you and him.

Those relationships let children express themselves—a cry, a laugh, a question—and get something back: a cuddle, a smile, an answer.

If these needs are consistently met, trust develops. Secure attachment relationships provide your child with feelings of self-worth and confidence. What children "get back" gives them very important information about what the world is like and how to act in the world.

At this age, your child is happier playing next to rather than with a peer. He will imitate what he sees another child doing without interacting with him. Play at this stage of development is called "parallel play" in which toddlers will play next to each other but not with each other.

During this stage of development it is essential to make sure your child is encouraged (praised), loved (hugs and kisses), and can develop trust and security with you (needs being consistently met).

Playing with peers will help teach him key social skills such as how to be kind, to share, and to resolve conflict; however, it's too early to expect them to play together; this will not happen until around two and a half years of age.

Regarding Nolan's trip to the family barbeque, note that when he became quiet he was experiencing a bit of separation anxiety. Separation anxiety occurs when there is a physical separation between him or her and you. This is a normal experience for your child to have when he has formed positive social relationships with his parents and others he sees on a regular basis.

A securely attached child will miss his parents when separated and will welcome the parents' or caregiver's reappearance or staying in close proximity. **As your child grows older separation anxiety will lessen;** instead, he will use other skills such as language, eye contact, and gestures to stay connected to you. Yet even with these newest social skills, your child will continue to seek physical closeness to you.

Emotional Development >
Calming Emotions

Emotional development refers to your child's ability to control his feelings and the ways he reacts to the feelings he has.

ACTIVITY

 Sean's mom takes him to a playgroup at the local community center. Sean immediately heads toward the table with play dough. He sits down to play alongside his friend Zach.

Zach reaches out and grabs all of Sean's play dough. Sean quietly looks off into the distance, rests his head on his hand, and sits. The teacher asks Sean if everything is okay.

Sean, with a few tears rolling down his cheeks, points to the play dough in front of Zach. The teacher says to Sean, "I can see you are feeling sad. It is okay to feel sad when someone takes something from you."

INSIGHT

Zach knows it is not okay to take the play dough from his friend, but does not have the impulse control to stop his behavior. Sean is sad, but reacts quietly, while the teacher helps Sean identify that he is feeling sad, and validates his feelings.

It is important that you help your child name his feelings (happy, sad, frustrated) and express himself in a positive way. Your child's ability to express how he is feeling in a positive or appropriate way will have an impact on how relationships are formed with peers, family, and other people in his environment.

Toddlers haven't yet learned how to control their emotions, and mood swings can be alarmingly rapid and intense. But they are also—thankfully—short-lived, moving from screaming in frustration to smiling and playing within seconds. Staying calm, helping them with the source of frustration, and using distraction techniques ("Oh, look, a red leaf!") will help them. Don't expect miracles though—plenty of five year olds still have difficulty controlling their emotions.

Self-Regulation >
Self-Control

Self-regulation involves your child's ability to gain control of her bodily functions (e.g. mastering potty training), managing emotions (e.g. controlling tantrums), keeping focused (e.g. waiting for something she wants), and paying attention.

"Dolly, Mommy, dolly!"

You can support your child's ability to achieve a level of calmness and bring herself into a calm state by giving soft touches on the back or by providing a favorite soft blanket for her to cuddle and hold.

ACTIVITY

Lilly is at the store with her mom, and she sees a doll that she wants on the shelf. "Dolly, Mommy, dolly," Lilly says.

"No, Lilly we are not buying any dollies today," Mom replies. Lilly begins to have a tantrum in the store, screaming for the doll she can't have.

INSIGHT

Because Lilly has just turned 13 months old, she is still learning how to regulate her emotions and understand that she cannot have everything she wants. This kind of reaction is normal for a toddler. Mom knows that she is not going to buy the doll, but she also does not want Lilly to scream and cry in the store.

Mom has to take a deep breath and keep herself calm, even though she is embarrassed by the situation. By doing this, she can then focus on getting Lilly to calm down as well.

Tips

Support your child in times of difficulty. If your child has a hard time when you say "no" to something, remain compassionate and empathetic. When it comes to tantrums, the most common parenting advice given is to ignore the tantrums and they will go away. This is not the best advice because it can make your child feel undervalued or unsupported.

It is important to acknowledge your child's feelings by saying, "I understand you are sad" and waiting nearby for the difficult behavior to subside. Toddlers have a hard time because they are still trying to figure out who they are and develop their sense of identity in the world.

Offer emotional support to help your child work through his challenges. Arrange plenty of downtime between activities.

Offer a five-minute warning, then a two-minute warning, then a ten-second warning to help your child transition between one activity to another. These are simple actions that can help your child cope and calm down.

When your toddler has a tantrum, the following coping mechanisms will help you:

* See the tantrum from your child's point of view. Tantrums can occur because your child is tired or hungry, causing her not to feel well or to be irritated. As you see the situation from your toddler's point of view, you will have compassion to be able to deal with her tantrums.

* Remember, you always have options. If a tantrum begins somewhere in public, you don't have to stay. Feel comfortable picking up your child and going home. Sometimes a good nap will help, and you can try again another day.

* Consider whether saying "no" is absolutely necessary. What alternatives are there? You may be saying "no" to candy at the store, but perhaps you could say "yes" to fruit, some crackers, or another healthful treat.

ACTIVITY

Caleb comes out of his bedroom and goes to the kitchen to see his mom. "Hungry, Mommy!" says Caleb.

Mom replies, "I am making dinner now, Caleb." She rubs his back. "It will be a few minutes." Caleb goes back to his room.

A few minutes pass and Mom says, "Caleb! It's time for dinner. Come eat!"

Caleb runs into the kitchen. He stops right in front of Mom who is standing two feet away from his highchair. She hands Caleb his plate of food, he walks slowly while holding the plate with two hands to his highchair. He then puts the plate of food on the tray of his chair and climbs in. Mom pushes the tray so it locks on the highchair and says, "I hope you like it!"

INSIGHT

Through a structured routine (having set times for activities and events, like meals) Mom is supporting Caleb's self-regulation skills. Caleb is learning how to control his natural reaction of distress when he is hungry by being gently encouraged to wait a few short minutes for his mom to finish preparing his food.

Caleb's mom is also encouraging Caleb's independence by letting him put his plate of food on his highchair tray.

Encouraging your child's independence is not an easy job; it takes patience. But the long-term benefits are worth it. Your patience with and support of your child will help him gain mastery over self-regulation skills and become more independent.

The good news is that your child is at the age when he wants to have more independence and learn how to do things himself (putting on socks or carrying his plate to his chair). At first the desire and need for greater independence can lead to a struggle between your desires and the desires of your child. This can lead to screams, tears, and frustration. This age period is commonly described as the "terrible twos" (even though these types of independence-seeking behaviors start when your child is a toddler). Tantrums can be extremely difficult to manage. Your child will stomp his feet, kick his legs, yell, and throw things.

Realistic expectations, patience, and sensitive guidance on your part are important for your child and can help make the "terrible twos" pretty terrific!

Allowing your toddler to exercise independence will give him confidence and build self-esteem.

Remember, the Whole Child Parenting Program offers appropriate developmental products and monthly activity books that walk you through supporting your child's skills. Using these in conjunction with the recommended age-appropriate room materials ensures faster development.

Self-Awareness >
Self-Perception

Self-awareness involves your child learning about herself, such as how her body moves, what she likes and dislikes, as well as what she can and cannot do.

Self-awareness is the physical realization that your child is separated from you. She may have similar features as you (hands, hair, feet) but her features look different from yours. A lot of these physical realizations occur when your child looks at herself in the mirror and in pictures, and when she learns to identify her own name.

During this age, your child will demonstrate self-awareness skills by using words such as *I* and *mine*. You will hear your child describe her own interests ("I paint") and skills ("I jump"). This differentiation is one of the developments that will lead your child to developing self-esteem.

It then becomes your responsibility as a parent to support your child with verbal feedback and praise. You can say things like, "Yes, you can jump!" and "Yes, you can paint."

Building self-esteem supports your child's emotional health because it makes your child feel good about herself and understand she can do something on her own. This is critical in developing relationships with others and having the "I can do it" spirit.

As your child matures and reaches two, she will begin to see that even though she has features similar to those around her, she is an individual with her own personality and identity. With your support, your child will feel good about who she is as she becomes more aware of herself and the world around her. **Celebrate your child's personality as she grows day by day.**

There are several activities that will encourage self-awareness in your child:

* Have photos of your child next to pictures that he draws and display his artwork on your refrigerator door or wall.

* Hold a mirror in front of him and have him point to his eyes, nose, mouth, and ears. Talk about the color of his hair and the color of your hair. You can even sing the song and play "Head and Shoulders, Knees and Toes."

ACTIVITY

 Ethan is in the living room while his dad is watching TV. Ethan sees a man dancing on TV and decides he wants to try to do some of the same moves. Ethan starts to wiggle his fingers and clap his hands. As Ethan watches the man on TV, he sees the man move a finger in a way Ethan has never tried before to a song Ethan has never heard before.

Ethan looks at his hand and starts moving his finger up and down like the man on TV.

INSIGHT

By watching the man on TV, Ethan learns about the parts of his own body and how they move.

3. Language Development

> **Language development occurs when toddlers add new words to their growing vocabulary. From age one to three, children will learn 1,000 to 2,000 new words.**

Your child can learn language easily; this is also a critical time to acquire language before this ability gets less acute with age.

As your child approaches age three, his language skills will become more fluent. Therefore, it is very important for parents to engage in continuous language exchanges with their toddlers. For example, talk while doing things and going places, and expand on basic words your toddler says. If he says "car," you should respond, "Yes, that is a red car." These types of activities and reinforcement build your toddler's language skills.

Listening and Understanding

Communication and Speaking

Emerging Literacy

WHOLE CHILD: TODDLER
Language
Development Components

You will often hear your child say "wawa" for water. Focus on the effort your child is making at being understood, not how he is saying the word. You can then engage in a language experience by saying, "Yes, this is water." No matter what stage of language development your toddler is in, remember to help build his language skills by using simple language yourself. But don't use "baby" language when communicating with your child. You want to help him learn language correctly.

1. Listening and Understanding	Listening leads to your child becoming a good reader, good speaker, and understanding what you and other adults are saying. Teaching listening skills will help your child develop language and social skills.
2. Communication and Speaking	Communication involves the use of single words in combination with gestures. Toddlers speak using two- to three-word sentences to communicate with a specific purpose.
3. Emerging Literacy	Emerging literacy at this age develops from learning book-handling skills, having books read aloud, listening and talking, observing parents reading and writing, storytelling, and experiencing rich literacy environments.

Interacting with the world around her by identifying and naming objects and images will help her build her language skills faster.

Listening and Understanding >

Hearing

Listening and understanding is when attention is given to the things that we hear and how we subsequently make meaning and comprehend what we have heard.

"My toes!"

ACTIVITY

Bella is on the floor playing a game with Mom. Mom asks, "Bella, where are your toes?" Bella lifts up her foot and with her hand on her toes she says, "Here Bella's toes."

Mom then asks Bella, "Can you find the toes on your other foot?" Bella starts to lift up the same foot to show her mom her toes again. Bella says, "My toes!"

Mom then points to Bella's other foot to show Bella what she is asking and asks the question again.

INSIGHT

Bella is listening to her mom each time, but she does not respond correctly both times. The first time she is asked to find her toes, Bella understands the question. The second time Bella does not understand that the question has changed, and that she is being asked to find the toes on her other foot. When a parent can rephrase a question or use gestures to show alternate meaning, she is giving her child the chance to understand and act on her own.

The more opportunities your child has to listen to lots of people talking—verbal communication between people in her environment—the better chance she has of understanding what she hears.

Because Bella is still developing her listening and understanding skills, Mom needs to provide more support to her by using a gesture to help clarify her question and asking the question again.

Sometimes it seems like your child is not listening to you. That is because listening requires attention and focus, and these are skills your child is still developing. This is why making eye contact with your child when speaking becomes so important. It will help him listen better and understand what you are saying when you are able to grab his attention.

There are several techniques you can use when supporting your child's listening and understanding skills.

Like Bella's mom in the example, give your child a visual cue by pointing to the object or area you are talking about. Also, when giving one-step directions ("Bring your shoes, please.") reinforce what you asked ("What did Mommy ask you to bring?"). This will let you know if your child understands what you are saying or if you need to give a visual cue by pointing to the object.

With your support as your child matures, his ability to listen and understand will increase. Remember, listening and understanding lead to greater cognitive development.

Communication and Speaking >
Speaking

Communication and speaking reflect your child's abilities to give a message to another person through nonverbal cues (or sign language) and spoken words.

Communication and speaking also build self esteem in your child as she learns that her voice can be heard.

The ability of your child to communicate is important in relationships they will form with adults and peers. Communication in all its forms plays a key role in increasing her ability to use language effectively.

Keep in mind that you won't understand all of your toddler's words, at least at first. She still has trouble producing many sounds, so she may substitute the sound of "b" for "d," and so on. Your toddler might say, "Dat otay," and that is appropriate at this age. What's important, and worth celebrating, is her effort at being understood.

Just as your child needs nourishing food to build physical strength, she also needs linguistic nutrition (words for her vocabulary bank) for strong development of language, communication, and cognitive skills. The more you speak with your child the more she will learn to communicate with you.

Talk during daily routines about how you prepare the apple for snack by cutting it in half and how you clean up by wiping off the counter with a kitchen towel when you are done. Speak clearly, making face-to-face contact with your child.

Remember that every toddler is different; some develop their language skills at a steady pace and others do so in spurts.

ACTIVITY

Ava is sitting on the floor of her living room with Dad. Dad says, "Ava, it is time for your nap. Nap time for Ava."

Ava replies, "No rib!" for crib. "Ava, no ap!" for nap.

INSIGHT

With these simple words Ava demonstrates to her dad that she is building her word bank (*crib, nap, no*) to communicate that she does not want to take a nap right now.

Sign Language

Sign language uses facial, hand, and body movements as a way to communicate with others and helps your child develop her social and emotional skills by giving her another way to communicate, especially when she becomes frustrated.

The biggest benefit to teaching your child sign language, especially if she is a visual learner (because it uses both hearing and seeing), is that it boosts your child's cognitive development as she develops language and reasoning skills.

As you teach your child sign language, it is important not to focus on whether your child is producing the precise sign (exactly how it should look). The focus must be on celebrating that your child is communicating her needs to you when she otherwise would have used only verbal language, which is often not developed enough for her to communicate exactly what she wants.

ACTIVITY

Mom notices Sophia is not using many words when interacting with others. For this reason Mom decides to learn about baby sign language so that she can start teaching Sophia.

Mom starts learning and teaching simple signs to Sophia, ones she can use to say things that she wants or needs. Mom is looking forward to the time when she can see Sophia use the signs independently.

Mom and Sophia arrive home from a birthday party at her cousin's house on the other side of town. Mom gets Sophia out of the car seat, and they walk through the door. Once home, Sophia sits on the floor and does the sign for *sleep*. Then she follows by saying, "Seepy."

Mom is so excited that Sophia has used both the sign and the spoken word that she scoops up Sophia to give her a great big hug.

INSIGHT

Through a modified from of the sign for *sleep* and the use of the spoken word, Sophia communicates to Mom so that she can get her needs met.

Sleepy.

Emergent Literacy >
I Can "Read"!

Emergent or emerging literacy involves how your child interacts with books and when reading and writing, even though your child cannot yet read and write in the standard sense.

Emerging literacy refers to your child's knowledge of reading and writing skills before he actually learns how to read and write words. Emergent literacy involves the process of being literate.

Nursery rhymes are short and have a repetition of sounds and words in attractive, easy-to-copy rhythms. **Rhymes are important because parents and children can say them at any time and in any place.** Rhymes need no toys or even a book; they depend on the sound of the voice. And you can practice them in the car, at the store, or on the playground.

By playing with rhymes, your child will discover how language works and become familiar with the relationship between sounds and letters, which helps when he begins to read.

The good news is that adults can have fun with rhymes and rhyming stories as well.

ACTIVITY

 Take a moment and have your child sit with you on the couch. Get comfy. Read this little rhyme to your child while you wiggle each one of his fingers or toes.

"This Little Piggy"

This little piggy went to market.
This little piggy stayed home.
This piggy had roast beef.
This little piggy had none.
And this little piggy cried,
   "Wee! Wee! Wee!" all
   the way home.

INSIGHT

The rhyme "This Little Piggy" allows your child to play with repetition and language sounds such as "wee." Sharing "This Little Piggy" and other nursery rhymes and nursery songs supports emergent literacy.

When introducing rhymes, use popular rhyming books, then let your child explore the pages. Use exaggerated speech to make the words come alive. Add music if you have it, and you can sing rhyming songs together.

Remember, the Whole Child Parenting Program offers appropriate developmental products and monthly activity books that walk you through supporting your child's skills. Using these in conjunction with the recommended age-appropriate room materials ensures faster development.

4. Creative Development

> **Creative play and creative activities are important to your child's overall development. They help grow imagination and also develop problem-solving, thinking, and motor skills.**

Drama, music, dance, and visual arts promote the development of creativity and imagination in toddlers. These activities also help toddlers develop their senses through exploration and discovery.

Your child can use creative play to communicate his feelings. He might not always be able to explain verbally why he's feeling angry, sad, happy, or frightened, but in an encouraging environment, he might be able to express these feelings using paint, color, movement, or music. Toddlers often use both hands equally when they're painting or drawing, so you cannot yet tell whether your toddler is right handed or left handed. This usually becomes more obvious at about three or four years of age, though a preference can emerge as early as 13 months. The most important issue is that you provide as many opportunities as possible for your child to develop his creativity.

Dramatic Play

Music

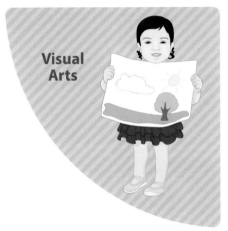

Visual Arts

Dance

WHOLE CHILD: TODDLER
Creative
Development Components

1. Music

Toddlers are continuously moving, so incorporate free dance while exposing your child to different styles of music. Start to observe your child's favorite song or genre of music. Play with different percussion instruments and start to teach your child about *loud* and *soft*.

2. Dance

Dance with your child in your arms or separately. Take time to imitate your child's movements so he knows you are present. At this age, your child can recognize his hands and feet. Play games by waving your hands or stomping your feet.

3. Visual Arts

Art is messy. Expect to see your child scribble, smash paint, and explore materials like paper and paint brushes. Art supports self-confidence as your child is allowed to create anything his mind can think of. These projects also engage fine motor skills so that your child will develop the skills needed for writing.

4. Dramatic Play

This is the age when your child starts to show preferences. Have props such as puppets, hats, and clothes from Mom or Dad. Encouragement in creativity is key at this stage as your child is taking cues from the adults around him.

Your home can provide innumerable opportunities for children to experiment and play, encouraging them to express their creativity and imagination.

Remember, the Whole Child Parenting Program offers appropriate developmental products and monthly activity books that walk you through supporting your child's skills. Using these in conjunction with the recommended age-appropriate room materials ensures faster development.

Music >
Vocal or Instrumental Sounds

Music is sound made by instruments or vocals or a combination of both.

As your child listens to or creates music, you will see her express her physical abilities and emotions by how she moves her body. Music is appealing to your child as well because it is something she can do independently. By showing her independence and expressing her creativity, your child is able to learn more about herself.

Developing a personal preference for different types of music starts when you are young. When children listen to certain styles of music repeatedly, they learn to like or prefer one style to another. This preference carries through to adulthood. Based upon this, it is very important to expose your toddler to many different types of music so that her repertoire will not be limited to only one genre.

Music will enable your child to develop physically as well. This can be observed when you see your child shaking her hips from side to side or when dancing with her legs slightly bent and apart. Your child is developing her large muscles in the hip area, strengthening her leg muscles, and continuing to develop her balancing skills.

You can encourage your child to move to the rhythm of the music by counting with her as she shakes side to side ("One and shake, two and shake, shake, shake, shake."). By doing this, you encourage math skills as well.

ACTIVITY

 Mom takes Harper to a mommy and me music class. They are running a little late, so when they arrive, Harper is anxious to go in.

Class has already started and the song playing is "The Ants Go Marching." Harper and Mom are each given a yellow and green scarf to wave around during the song.

Everyone in the class is encouraged to wave their scarves and march around the room to the sound of the beat expressed in the song as "Boom! Boom! Boom!"

All of a sudden the song starts to get slower and slower. Harper sees her mom start to march slower and slower, so she follows along; however, the pace is too slow for Harper, so she begins to march fast again, saying "Boom! Boom! Boom!"

INSIGHT

Through this activity Harper gets to interact with music that makes her move fast then slowly. She also gets to develop her physical skills by waving the scarf around and moving her legs up and down. The song brings out emotions of happiness as Harper gets excited and wants to keep marching fast.

Music really does open the mind and stimulate the body.

Dance >
Moving Lively

Dance is an excellent way for toddlers to develop gross motor skills as they move and thinking skills as they consider the move they will make next.

Activities like dancing will cause your child to think about balancing, moving, and shaking all at the same time. Often you will notice your child having difficulty and wanting to focus on one thing (like shaking the hips). This is okay because he is still building up his dance skills.

When your child hears music, it makes him want to dance without any prompting from you. Dance moves may only consist of him bobbing up and down with his feet planted on the ground. Your child is just enjoying the fact that he can bob up and down, shake, and move his feet without falling down. **As your child matures, you will see him combine moving side to side with circling around. As he moves into age two, you will notice that the arms are incorporated in his moves.** He's having fun, too!

Your child loves having a dance

partner. Set a time during the day to dance with your child to different genres of music. You may be surprised by how much rhythm you have!

As you encourage dancing in your child, you also encourage him to express himself and be creative. This will help him later in life as he learns to improve his coordination, build his spatial awareness skills, and think through ways of how to move his body.

ACTIVITY

It is a rainy day and Jaxon cannot go outside. Mom thinks it is a great time to turn up the music and let her little dancer twist and shout.

Jaxon loves to listen to very fast music, so Mom picks a playlist or CD with fast music. As soon as the music starts, Jaxon quickly throws out his arms, stands with his legs apart, and starts twisting his body and shaking his hips, legs, and arms as fast as he can.

From time to time Mom will join Jaxon and move with him to the song. On this occasion, Mom just wants to sit back and watch him let loose.

INSIGHT

When Jaxon was an infant he responded to dance and music by smiling and perhaps even clapping his hands. Now that he is walking on his own two feet, he has enough control over his body to do some more complex toddler dancing that involves more body parts.

Visual Arts >
Art I Can See

Visual arts for young children include anything they can see and create.

Visual arts can include scribbles on a piece of paper, a painting, her hand- or footprint, as well as coloring a picture, just to name a few options. **Visual arts reflect the world your child is in.**

Engaging in visual art supports your child's experience with different textures (e.g. crinkled paper or glue on paper) as well as developing fine motor skills, because so many art creations are done using hands (painting and coloring). **Your child is able to express herself by making choices such as what colors of paint to use or by combining different mediums.** When you give your child visual art experiences, you will help her gain a better understanding of her creative abilities.

Give your child experiences that are focused on the exploration of materials and textures.

Experiences should include some of the following examples:

*   Finger painting, which supports not only the development of visual arts but also understanding cause and effect.

*   Shaving cream painting on a cookie sheet to support the development of the senses when she experiments with the texture of the shaving cream.

*   Taping a large piece of paper to the table and leaving it there for a couple days. This gives your child the opportunity to engage in visual arts any time by being able to come and go as she pleases.

ACTIVITY

Traci and Mom have just come home from a new art exhibit at the children's museum. Mom wants to give Traci an opportunity to create her own art, so she goes into her office and comes out with a very large piece of white paper. Mom places the paper on the highchair in front of Traci and tapes down each of the four corners so the paper will be secure. Next Mom gives Traci a bit of yellow paint in a cup and puts the cup on the tray of the highchair next to the paper.

Traci begins to dip her hands in the cup and then slaps her hands down on the paper. Then after Traci puts her hands in the yellow paint again, she starts to touch her clothes and her face. By the time Traci is done, everything is yellow.

INSIGHT

Mom does not mind that Traci gets so messy. She is more excited that Traci is able to explore the paint and experiment with all the different places she can put it.

Visual art includes not only things that your child creates, but also art your child can see in a museum or outside at the park. Take a trip with your child to your local art museum. Seeing the works of other artists will open up your child's creative thinking. Support those skills by talking about the different art you see together at the museum (e.g. "Do you see the bird in the picture? It looks so shiny and like it is flying.")

Remember, no matter what your child does on paper, you do not need to insist on calling the image something or identifying it in any way. At this stage, she is only exploring, and the picture is not meant to represent something. When your child is finished creating a picture, talk about the colors she used (e.g. "I see you used yellow paint. It is very bright like the sun."). You can also talk about the different marks that were made on the paper (e.g. "I love your circles. Did you see you made a circle shape?").

At this age your child may not verbally say much about her creation, but by talking to her about her art, you are supporting her self-confidence and encouraging her to believe that she has the ability to create anything and do it well.

Dramatic Play >
Pretending

Your child will go to a place that allows him to pretend to be someone or something else.

"Meow, meow."

ACTIVITY

Justin is looking out the window of his family room when he sees a black cat walking by. As the cat stops and comes up to the window, Justin begins to say, "Meow, meow." Then Justin begins to bang on the window, which makes the cat run away.

Justin runs out of the family room to his bedroom and opens his toy chest. He pulls out a cat costume he has from Halloween. Justin brings the cat suit to his mom so that she can help him put it on. Once Justin has the suit on, he gets on his hands and knees and begins to crawl back to the family room window saying, "Meow, meow."

INSIGHT

Justin loves to pretend to be something that he sees in his environment. Mom supports Justin's imagination by letting him put on the cat suit and reenact being a cat. Mom can make this dramatic play opportunity even more fun if she also pretends to be a cat with Justin.

Dramatic play is when your child recreates the world of home through pretend play scenarios (e.g. pretends to sip warm tea from a cup at the dinner table).

Dramatic play supports the development of language and words as well as thinking skills when your child considers what he wants to be. **Dramatic play also builds social skills as your child interacts with others.**

Your child loves to engage in dramatic play experiences because it includes social interactions with you and his peers. Social interaction really starts at birth; however, during this time, your infant wanted to engage in role play only with you. Now he may want to include interactions with peers. Dramatic play is unique in that it includes imitation and can take place individually or in a social setting.

Make sure you provide a space and opportunities for dramatic play in your home. One example of how you can do this is by building a cave or tunnel for your child using boxes or sheets. You can take a sheet and simply lay it over the couch and loveseat or over four chairs. Your child will love to crawl under the

> **For your child, dramatic play will be brief; however, as your toddler matures, you will see him engage in longer dramatic play experiences with more details and accompanying language or even storytelling.**

sheet while pretending to be a bear in the woods saying, "Grrrr!"

Dramatic play does not have to occur in only one part of your home; it can take place anywhere (outside, kitchen area, bathtub, or the living room). The only requirement is that it should be spontaneous, safe, and fun. **For extra fun, participate in pretend play with your child—a sure opportunity for laughter and bonding.**

Toddlers love dramatic play. If you see your child mimicking a cat, pretend to be a cat, too. Scurry around the house trying to chase a mouse.

5. Physical Development

> Physical development includes your child's large muscle and small muscle skills.

Walking is the main skill that most parents think about in this area as they look forward to the day their child starts to walk.

Your child will begin to demonstrate more advanced skills as he matures—such as pushing his feet on a ride-on toy, tossing a ball (you will be amazed by how far he can toss a ball), and jumping up and down in one place and landing on both feet. His ability to roll back and forth and go from a prone position to a standing position with no support makes this an exciting time.

You will also see your little one stacking blocks, pillows, and even books when he wants to climb on something.

He can use a spoon to feed himself and hold a drinking cup. Until you see all of these things, you do not realize just how much your toddler has grown from infancy to now.

Because of all of the advances your child has made, you will see that he has a greater desire for independence and will become more and more determined to do things his own way (e.g. attempt to climb up onto a picnic table).

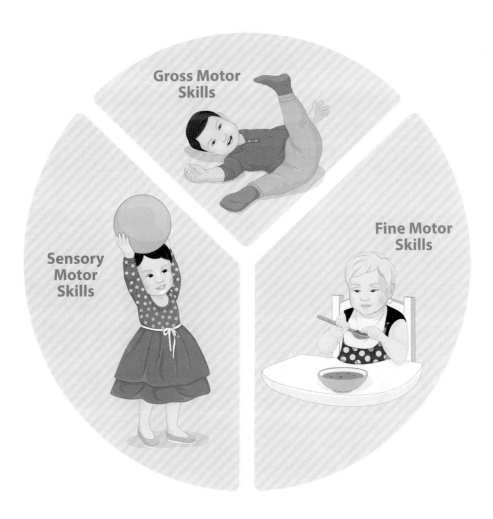

WHOLE CHILD: TODDLER
Physical
Development Components

1.
Gross Motor Skills

A gross motor skill involves your child's ability to control arm and leg movements. This includes climbing, walking up and down stairs, kicking a ball, carrying large items, running short distances, and standing on tiptoes.

2.
Fine Motor Skills

Fine motor development applies to small movements of the hands, wrists, fingers, feet, and toes. Fine motor development also includes the smaller actions of grasping an object between the thumb and a finger or using the lips and the tongue to taste an object.

3.
Sensory Motor Skills

Sensory motor skills include the five areas of taste, touch, hearing, smelling, and seeing and how they interact with objects and actions in the child's environment. Touch involves games that use the muscles; sight can be used to complete a maze or dot-to-dot puzzle; hearing might include playing listening games; smell can be used to go on a smell walk; and taste can involve trying frozen versus hot foods.

Parents and children spending time playing physical games and doing activities together is one of the best ways to help children develop gross and fine motor skills.

Remember, the Whole Child Parenting Program offers appropriate developmental products and monthly activity books that walk you through supporting your child's skills. Using these in conjunction with the recommended age-appropriate room materials ensures faster development.

Gross Motor Skills >
Large Muscles

Gross motor skills are movements that help your child develop large muscle control in the arms and legs.

Your child will use his body to learn how to interact with large objects in his environment (e.g. stairs on a jungle gym).

Gross motor development plays a role in making sure that your child remains healthy as he keeps his body moving. Physical abilities that are examples of gross motor development include crawling, walking, jumping, and rolling. An example of a jumping activity you can do with your child at home is hopping up and down like a frog.

ACTIVITY

 Mom and Brandon are on the floor of the living room doing some stretches and exercises together. Mom lies down on the floor like a log and rolls toward the couch.

"Your turn," Mom says to Brandon. Mom helps Brandon lie down on the floor to stretch his arms up and keep his legs straight like a log. Then Mom gives Brandon a little push so that he rolls along the floor.

As Brandon begins to roll over, he immediately puts his feet up and arm out, causing him to stop. Brandon then continues to rock back and forth from one side to the other with his feet in the air.

INSIGHT

With this simple movement, Brandon is demonstrating his gross motor skills. His waist and legs are moving together; however, at this age, Brandon is unaware that keeping his legs in the air stops his ability to roll over completely. Brandon wants to put his arms and legs out because he thinks that he will keep rolling and not stop. When Brandon gets older and has more control over his gross motor movements he will feel more comfortable letting himself roll.

Your toddler is still exploring his gross motor movements and experimenting with using different parts of his body in new ways. Because your child is still developing his balance and coordination it is important that you provide support by letting your child know that you are present to help him safely test his physical limits. This will build trust between you and your toddler and make him feel more confident in further practicing and developing his gross motor movements.

Fine Motor Skills >
Small Muscles

Fine motor development occurs when your child uses her small muscles (fingers and hands) to engage in activities.

ACTIVITY

 Dana is sitting with her parents at the dinner table. Mom gives Dana a spoon to eat her yogurt. At first Dana ignores the spoon and puts her hand in the bowl of yogurt, scooping the yogurt and bringing her hand to her mouth to lick her fingers.

"Dana, here is your spoon," Mom says as she gets up from the table and stands behind Dana. Mom then puts the spoon in Dana's hand, and with her hand on top of Dana's hand helps Dana bring the spoon to the bowl to scoop the yogurt. Then while still having her hand on Dana's hand, Mom brings the spoon to Dana's mouth so she can eat the yogurt. After Dana eats the spoonful of yogurt, Mom says, "You did it, Dana! Good job!"

Mom sits back down at the table and watches to see if Dana will use the spoon on her own. Dana takes the spoon and holds it with her fist. With her fist toward the base of the spoon, Dana dips the spoon in the yogurt and brings it to her mouth. Mom claps and says, "Good job!"

INSIGHT

Mom supports Dana by showing her how to use the spoon. Mom reinforces her encouragement of Dana by giving her praise, which entices Dana to want to continue to explore and try to use the spoon herself.

Fine motor development includes smiling, grasping, opening and closing hands, waving, and picking up an eating utensil or pencil. As your child grows so do her fine motor skills. You will see your child learning to do more with her hands. There are several things that your child should accomplish by the age of two in this area; one of those is being able to eat using utensils.

At this time your child is exploring her ability to feed herself with the use of a spoon. She will have some spilling, may miss her mouth from time to time, and may even use her hand to scoop food into her spoon. These are all age-appropriate examples of how your child is still developing grasping and scooping, and testing wrist movements and finger strength.

Many times parents do not give their toddlers a utensil because they feel like their child will be messy; however for a child to master eating with utensils, you must provide opportunities for self-feeding during daily meal times. The more practice you give the better your child will get.

There are many other ways parents can support fine motor skills. One way is by reading books together. Let your child use her pointer finger to point to pictures in the book and turn the pages. If she is not pointing to pictures, you can model first and then have her imitate you.

Give your child opportunities to work on fine motor skills during routines like taking off her socks. Your toddler will be able to grasp her socks and pull them off; this skill requires hand-eye coordination. You will observe your child grasp the sock with her whole hand; this is normal as her pincer grasp is still developing. **The pincer grasp involves using the thumb and pointer finger or the thumb and middle fingers to pick up and hold.**

When your child reaches age two she has developed more finger strength and will start to grasp writing utensils and eating utensils in a pincer grasp. When your child develops more finger strength, she no longer needs to use her whole fist to control the movement of a writing utensil, such as a crayon, and can begin making more detailed and precise marks when drawing. **It is important to remember that fine motor skills do not develop overnight,** and it is crucial that you support your child by providing fine motor skill development opportunities as part of your daily routines.

Sensory Motor Skills >
Seeing and Moving

Sensory motor skills involve your child combining his senses with large and small muscle movements.

> ### We know there are five senses:
>
> 1. taste (gustatory),
> 2. touch (tactile),
> 3. hearing (auditory),
> 4. sight (visual),
> 5. smell (olfactory).
>
> Some example of how these five senses play a role in the development of gross motor and fine motor skills are:
>
> * Touch: touches a ball and throws it;
>
> * Hearing: listens to your request to jump up and down or sit down;
>
> * Sight: sees where to kick the ball or how to grasp the paintbrush.

The first two years of your child's life are known as the sensorimotor stage. Your child needs to move his body and actively interact with his environment. Try to limit TV, electronic time, and other passive media sources. Interact with your child physically by playing games like kicking and throwing a ball together.

In addition to those five senses there are two more senses that are associated specifically with movement. They are **spatial sense** and **balance sense**.

Spatial sense lets your child know where his body is in relation to things around him. This sense can be observed when you see your toddler turn around and sit in a chair without falling down. It also contributes to your toddler's coordination skills. Without spatial sense, your toddler would be clumsy during movements and would move like a robot.

Balance sense is the movement of one part of the body while the rest stays in one place (lifting up one leg). Your child will stumble and fall sometimes; however, you should not see a pattern of this.

Pushing, pulling, twisting, turning, sitting, and rising are examples of the type of movements that develop balance and coordination skills in your toddler.
Encourage your child to use all of his senses to develop his motor skills by joining in the experience with him. Play games that require your child to listen and have physical contact with objects. Remember: What your child learns today will support his developmental successes in the future.

Based on your child's age, we know he will try the following as he discovers his gross motor abilities:

* try to balance himself with one foot up and hands in the air;

* attempt to climb objects (e.g. furniture, steps, simple climbing structures);

* hold objects or toys while walking (e.g. pulling a car by a string while walking around the room);

* ride a toy by using his hands or feet.

6. Health and Care

> Your toddler is developing more teeth, growing longer hair, and adjusting to a new diet.

Your child is on the move! She is pulling herself up, walking, reaching, and eating with her hands. Her daily schedules are changing along with her body. Your child is becoming more vocal and independent, which can come with some defiant and challenging behavior. There are a number of things you can do to help keep her clean and healthy from head to toe while avoiding big fights, struggles, and confrontations.

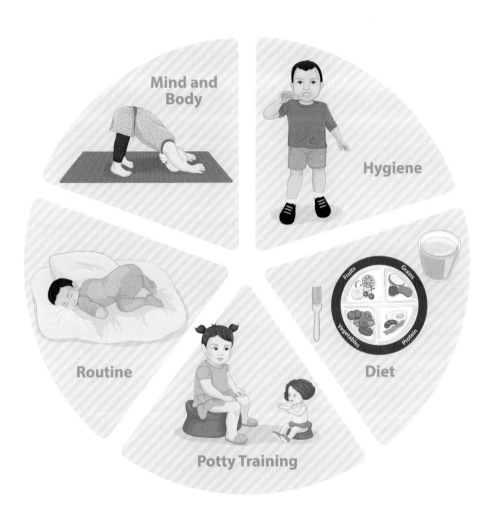

WHOLE CHILD: TODDLER

Health and Care

Hygiene >
Hair, Skin, Eyes, Nails, Ears, and Tooth Care

Hair Care

Your two year old's oil glands on her scalp and body don't become fully functional until puberty, so shampoo only as needed. Once a week is usually plenty.

Brushing

Brushing hair can help bring oils to the surface of the scalp. When trying to get out knots and tangles, try using a detangling spray and a wide-toothed comb or a brush with round-tipped bristles. Start combing or brushing out the ends and then work your way up to the scalp to avoid tugging and pulling.

Working Together

* Let your child use the comb in her hair or on a doll before combing her hair yourself.

* When in the bath, let her run her fingers in the shampoo just like you would.

* Let her wash her doll's hair in the tub.

* Let your child watch you wash her hair by propping up a mirror in the bathtub.

* While rinsing, have your child tilt her head back and use a bucket to avoid getting shampoo in her sensitive eyes.

Skin Care

Dry skin and dehydration can occur due to the weather.

When cleaning dry skin:

* Pat down skin and make sure not to wipe rough, chapped skin (especially face and cheeks).
* Apply sunscreen when going outside because toddlers' sensitive skin can burn easily.

Caring for dry skin:

* Try cutting back on bath time and sticking to 10-minute baths.
* Using the moisturizer within minutes of taking your child out of the tub will seal in the water that's still in her skin from the bath.
* Choose a non-alcohol-based moisturizer, such as Aquaphor® Baby Healing Ointment or Cetaphil® Moisturizing Cream.
* Reapply moisturizers at least two or three times a day.
* Offer your child plenty of water year round to replace the moisture that's evaporating from her skin.
* Add more fatty foods to her diet, such as avocados, flax seed, and olive oil.

Eye Care

Provide sun protection when outdoors by getting in the habit of using UV coated kid's sunglasses. This is especially important if your child's eyes are lighter in color.

The presence of eye and vision problems is rare. Most little ones begin life with healthy eyes and start developing visual abilities with no problems.

You will see that your child's hand-eye coordination and depth perception are well developed by this time. Remember: Consult your pediatrician if you see any of the signs listed below.

Check your child's eyes regularly to see if:

* your child's eyes are crossed,
* they are sensitive to light,
* one eye is wandering,
* both eyes cannot follow an object as it moves back and forth in front of her.

Conjunctivitis (Pink Eye)

Conjunctivitis, commonly known as pink eye, is the swelling of the white part of the eye and the inner surface of the eyelid.

Conjunctivitis can cause parents to worry because the eye looks extremely red. It does spread very quickly and is fairly common. It does not cause long-term damage to the eye or your toddler's vision. Some types of pink eye will go away without treatment, but other types will need medical attention.

Symptoms usually include:
* watery discharge,
* veiny redness in the white area of an eye,
* itchy and swollen eyes,
* stringy discharge that causes eyelids to stick together, especially after sleeping.

Conjunctivitis has three forms: allergic, viral, or bacterial.

Allergic conjunctivitis is not contagious and is usually connected to seasonal allergies, irritation, or intolerance to medication or anything topical put on the face that comes in contact with your child's eyes.

Viral and bacterial conjunctivitis are contagious and usually occur from an upper respiratory tract infection, sore throat, or cold. These types require antibiotic drops or ointment from a doctor. A cold compress can also help relieve discomfort.

Nail Care

Your child is constantly playing and exploring, so it is not uncommon for her to get play dough, food, or dirt in her fingernails. **Try to keep her fingernails short so that they can collect the least amount of dirt.** Wash your child's hands frequently, especially after activities or outside time. You can use a nail brush or toothbrush to help clean under your toddler's fingernails.

Trimming

Trim your child's fingernails after a bath. Water softens the nails, making them easier to trim and cut. Sing a song or count her fingers to keep her engaged and patient while you finish.

Ear Care

At bath time, clean the outside crevices of your child's ear with a damp, soft cloth.

DO NOT probe the inside of the ear. The middle ear is not fully developed, and you could end up puncturing the eardrum.

Ear Infections

Ear infections are most common in the middle ear because the Eustachian tube, which is a small passage leading from the nose and mouth (connecting the esophagus) to the area of the middle ear, does not fully develop until age three. Because it is so small, the Eustachian tube gets clogged after a cold.

Signs that your child has an ear infection may be your child pulling on her ear or seeing drainage come from her ear. Go see your pediatrician. Ear infections can get painful.

Tooth Care

By the time she is three years old, your child will develop 20 primary teeth. By 15 months, your child's molars will start coming in. These can be extremely painful for your toddler. Offer your toddler teething toys or frozen fruits to gnaw on to soothe teething pains. Topical ointments for teething can numb gum areas inside the mouth. Consult your pediatrician before administering any medication orally.

Brushing Teeth

Try to get your child in the habit of brushing his teeth. Get a small-head toothbrush with soft, round bristles and brush your child's teeth in a circular motion along the sides and along the outer gum lines.

Brushing can help clean any food stuck in teeth and massage your child's gums while he is teething. **Let him brush his own teeth for a little while before you brush them.**

Teething and Biting

During the teething stage, toddlers also enter a biting stage. Children tend to bite because of a combination of teething and a lack of language skills. They are still learning to communicate what they want or need. Because toddlers are teething at this age, they are orally stimulated by the introduction to solid and crunchy foods. They begin to test the waters and see what will happen if they bite you or their friends.

Sometimes it is to see if they can bite through the skin and other times it is to see how the friend will react. Toddlers also tend to bite due to a lack of language skills that are necessary for them to express feelings like anger, frustration, joy, and excitement.

Toddlers turn to biting as a substitute message for "I am mad at you!" or "I am very excited!"

What can you do about biting?

* Have teething toys around for your toddler when he is teething so he has something else to bite.

* Build his language skills through sign language. Encourage him to use signs for words like *more*, *no*, and *up* so that he can communicate to you what he wants without getting frustrated.

* Mouth the words and say them slowly as you sign to help your toddler learn how to say the words as he signs them, too.

* Let your toddler know that teeth are for biting food and not friends. Redirect him to another activity so he can focus on something else.

Diet >
Calories, Allergies, Safety, and Tummy Troubles

Children (12 months to 24 months) need:

* 3 ounces of grains (one slice of bread or ½ cup of cooked rice or pasta),
* ½–1 cup of fruits (¾ cups juice, ½ cup canned fruit, ¼ cup dried fruit, 1 piece of fruit or melon wedge),
* ½ cup of vegetables (½ cup chopped raw or cooked vegetables, 1 cup raw leafy greens),
* 1–1 ½ cup cups of milk or other dairy products,
* 2 ounces of high-protein foods (meat, poultry, eggs, and legumes)—1 ounce meat, 1 egg, ¼ cup legumes such as beans, 2 tablespoons of peanut butter,
* 3–4 teaspoons of healthy oils such as canola oil, olive oil, or tub margarine,
* Fats and sweets are empty calories and should be avoided.

Calories

Your child needs about 1,000 calories a day to meet her growth, energy, and nutrition needs.

She has a small stomach and will need to eat every two and half to three hours. A typical eating schedule for a toddler is three meals and two snacks a day. The food groups that make up a balanced diet are proteins, carbohydrates, fruits, and dairy.

Allow your child to pick from a variety of healthful foods and vary the foods she eats because her tastes and preferences change frequently. Based on the activity level of a given day or an increase in her growth rate, her appetite may change as well.

Babies and toddlers should be getting at least half of their calories from fat. When they turn two and their rate of growth slows, gradually lower the percentage of calories from fat, eventually changing it to one-third of her daily calories when she reaches four or five years old.

Avoid adding too many flavors or spices to your toddler's food because she is still developing her taste buds and is more sensitive to flavorings than adults. Making foods that are too salty, spicy, sour, or sweet will prevent your child from experiencing the natural tastes of foods.

Cutting your child's food into bite-size pieces can also encourage her to start feeding herself. She can easily pick up her food and put it into her mouth.

Switching to Cow's Milk

At 12 months, your child is finally ready to switch to cow's milk.

It is important to wait until 12 months for your child to switch to cow's milk because of a variety of internal developments still happening in her body. At 12 months, your child now needs the calcium and vitamin D that whole milk supplies.

You should be giving your child whole milk until the age of two unless your physician tells you otherwise.

Only give your child between 16 and 20 ounces of milk a day; too much milk can affect her diet and make her too full to eat other meals and foods.

Trouble adjusting to whole milk?

* Mix cow's milk with your child's formula or breast milk so she can adjust to the taste.

* Try adding cow's milk to foods such as hot or cold cereal in the morning.

* If your child is really putting up a fight, try adding other calcium-rich foods to her diet, such as yogurts and cheeses.

Allergies

With the introduction of more varieties of food starting now and continuing throughout her life, your child can develop allergies.

Indications of allergies include sneezing, itching, swelling in the face, and skin rashes (small bumps).

Food allergies: Are usually quite rare and follow your child's genetic background. If you have a food allergy that runs in your family, be careful when giving your child that food. Food allergies in young children typically go away with age.

Hay fever:

Can happen with environmental or seasonal allergies when your child is allergic to pollen, grass, dust, or animal dander. Symptoms include watery eyes, sneezing, and a runny nose.

Because children this age cannot yet blow their noses to clear their nasal passages, mucus drips down their throats, causing them to cough.

Safety

Have your child sit at the table with you to eat so you can monitor her feeding herself to ensure that she does not put too much food in her mouth at one time. Keep adding to her plate as she finishes to encourage your child to take her time.

Because your toddler is teething, she may be very attracted to crunchy or hard foods at one point and then not like them later. Keep trying a variety of kid-friendly and safe foods; something she didn't like today can be her new favorite tomorrow. Let her choose what she wants to eat from the healthful choices you provide (e.g. a piece of fruit, carrot sticks, or wheat crackers with hummus) so that you are ultimately in charge of the choices.

Highchairs

What to look for in a highchair:

Safety:

* Does the highchair have buckles to secure your toddler?
* Does it have the JPMA (Juvenile Products Manufacturers Association) stamp of approval?
* Is it easy to get your child in and out of the highchair?

Comfort:

* Is the chair big enough for your toddler?
* Is it comfortable for your toddler to sit through a whole meal?
* Is there a footrest to help with posture?
* What type of material is it made of? Is it easy to clean?

Sippy Cups

Most children at 12 months are ready to give up the bottle. Sippy cups have spouts that help your child switch from sucking to sipping, and they are mess free.

Things to look for in a sippy cup:

* no handles—this makes it easier to transition to a cup later;
* removable top—for easy cleaning;
* weighted bottom—some sippy cups come with a weighted bottom, which is a great way to control messy leaks;
* types of plastic—stay away from any plastic cups or utensils that contain BPA or say Recycle 7 or have the letters PC on the product. These are not safe for your young one.

Tummy Troubles

Constipation

Constipation is not always a sign of illness but can make your child uncomfortable. Constipation is usually accompanied by hard or painful stools.

What to do:

* Increase fluids: Give your child more water to drink.
* Diet: Make sure you are giving your child correct portion sizes when it comes to food and also change the variety of foods you offer. Introduce more fruits and vegetables.
* Try prunes, dried fruits (raisins and apricots), oatmeal, or green vegetables.
* Stay away from cow's milk, yogurt, cheese, cooked carrots, and bananas.

Diarrhea

Diarrhea is the opposite of constipation and involves very loose or too many bowel movements. Diarrhea can cause your child pain as well as make him become dehydrated and lethargic. Diarrhea can be caused by a virus or contaminated food or can be a side effect of medication.

If diarrhea starts quickly but ends by the next meal your child eats and isn't accompanied by fever, you probably should not be concerned.

Avoid:

* Drinks with sugar like soda or ginger ale; sugar may upset the stomach.

Vomiting

Vomiting is a virus caused by bacteria or a parasite. It can sometimes be followed by diarrhea.

Signs your child may be dehydrated include:

* not urinating,
* dry lips and mouth,
* looks pale.

What to do:

If your child is having trouble holding down liquids or food, try to rehydrate her with an oral rehydration solution.

Examples of oral rehydration solutions include:

* water,
* Pedialyte®,
* watered-down juice,
* chicken broth.

When administering oral rehydration solutions:

1. Give your child only a teaspoon of fluid every five minutes to help her keep it down.
2. If your child is able to keep the liquid down, keep increasing the amount of fluid you give her.
3. Keep giving your child fluids until your child stops vomiting.
4. If your child is ready to eat again, try to stick to these foods:

* dry toast,
* small amount of pasta (no sauce),
* hard-boiled egg,
* rice,
* bananas.

Potty Training >
Are We Ready?

Eighteen months to three years old is the average age to show interest in and start trying to potty train.

Signs your child may be ready for potty training:

* begins to communicate having a dirty diaper—your child may verbally tell you or draw your attention to her diaper by patting it or pointing to it;

* begins to show discomfort when wet or soiled—your child may walk with a wide stride or begin to pull and take off her soiled diaper;

* shows interest in the potty—models potty training with toys, dolls, or even herself;

* displays independence—starts to pull her pants on and off and follows basic one- and two-step directions.

Regularity

* is able to stay dry for up to two hours between diaper changes—shows that the bladder is maturing, and she is able to hold it longer;

* starts to have regular bowel movements at the same time every day.

Ready to Start?

* Stay close to home.

* Try no underpants or underwear.

* Try to encourage the most tries as possible so your child can get used to the feeling of going.

* Give your child plenty of salty snacks that make her thirsty. Diluting juice to drink will encourage peeing and support potty training quickly.

* Have all materials present at the potty (toilet paper, underwear or pullup, change of clothing if necessary).

* **Let her bring her favorite toy or stuffed animal to model potty training.**

Verbal Praise:

Be excited about your child using the potty!

* Sing a song, do a dance, clap your hands, and tell her with a smile you are proud of her.

* Don't be upset or annoyed when she has an accident. Remind her that pee goes in the potty. Have her help you clean up, do laundry, or get clean clothes together.

Follow Through

Potty on the go:

Invest in a travel potty to encourage consistency. It is important to keep up with your routine even when at Grandma's house, with your babysitter, or at school.

* The more days you get into potty training, the more consistent your child's potty times will become. Having a routine with nap and eating times adds to consistency.

* Have all your materials with you, such as wipes, clean underwear, and plastic bags for soiled clothes.

Potty time doesn't mean missing play time!

Don't make your child feel like going potty means she is missing out on an activity.

* Move the potty to the activity. If everyone is outside, let your child use the potty while she is outside so she doesn't put up a fight.

* Encourage your child to try before you start an activity or before you go somewhere. Have her try before and after lunch, as well as before you start a game or put out a new set of toys.

Routine >
Two Naps to One

Napping is important for your toddler and for you. She needs an opportunity to refuel her body with energy; otherwise, everyone in the house will feel the effects.

It is important to stay attuned to your child's cues for needing a nap. You may notice her staring into space, rubbing her eyes, or crying to signal it is time. Usually around 12 months, you will notice changes in your child's sleep schedule. Before turning 12 months old, most infants are on a two-nap schedule. Seventeen percent of children have already transitioned to a one-nap schedule by 12 months. At around 15 or 16 months, almost 60% of children have fully transitioned to a one-nap schedule.

It is common for children to change nap schedules from time to time. If your child has been showing you these signs, then it could be time for a change:

* crying or fighting nap times,

* waking up tired after too short a nap,

* not taking a nap at all,

* waking up in the middle of the night.

What is the best way to transition from two naps to one? Like many milestones in your child's life, moving from two naps to one is a gradual process that takes routine and consistency.

It can take anywhere from a few weeks to a few months for your child to transition to a one-nap schedule.

Put your child in the same place for nap each day. Don't let her nap in the stroller one day and in your bed the next. It is important for the nap place and environment to be consistent so your child will develop a routine for sleeping.

If your child wakes up early from her one afternoon nap, try soothing her back to sleep and see if she will sleep longer. Play some music or pat her back to see if she will fall back asleep.

One nap does not mean less sleep. Most toddlers need between 12 and 14 hours of sleep a day until they reach the age of three.

Tips for a smooth transition:

Adjusting your child's schedule
Try pushing his morning nap back by 15 minutes every day or two. You can also try to decrease the morning nap by 15 minutes every few days to shorten your child's morning rest and better preserve the afternoon naptime.

Winding down
Try finding activities that are calm and help your child relax before she goes down for a nap. Establish a naptime routine of reading a book or listening to calming music. Sound machines offer soothing sounds such as beach waves or rain falling that can help signal naptime.

Things to keep in mind
Many children are fine with one-nap schedules during the week but vary on the weekends. Try to be as consistent as possible on the weekends, but let your child take an extra nap if needed.

Mind and Body >

Aggressive Behavior

It is not uncommon for little ones to engage in some aggressive behavior, such as hitting and biting. Aggressive behavior is their form of communicating when they are frustrated because they have not yet learned the words to express their feelings; however, if your child is exhibiting numerous aggressive behaviors every day, he may need some help from you.

There are many ways to deal with aggressive behavior in a child. Before getting frustrated with your child's aggressive behaviors, try to observe when these behaviors happen. Look for patterns such as where, when, with whom, and what time the aggressive behaviors happen most.

If they happen around the same time every day, your toddler may be tired or hungry. Try to adjust his schedule.

If the aggressive behavior happens more often in public places than at home, think about the possible stimulation and who is around. Your child may be having a hard time getting your attention or feel a lack of control if he is in a place with which he is not familiar.

Always look at outside factors as well. Changes in routine or in the family can cause your child to act out for attention or out of frustration.

It is important to let your caregivers know if there are any changes at home and to make activities and routines as normal as possible.

Lastly, think of your child's temperament. Each child is different and has a different comfort level. Some children have a hard time meeting new people; others have difficulty communicating. Brainstorm ways to help your child, such as communicating through sign language or talking about an event before it occurs.

Yoga

Having your toddler participate in yoga can help an aggressive child funnel that energy into physical movement. Better still, yoga gives her the ability to exercise both her body and mind. Yoga encompasses the whole child by both strengthening children's bodies and calming their minds to better shape focus and build self-confidence. Through yoga, children are able to develop and foster more than just physical skills.

Yoga helps your toddler develop social-emotional skills such as self-regulation. Yoga is a great tool to help your child redirect her energy and emotions and better calm herself.

Physically, your toddler is learning how to manipulate her body and better maximize her mobility. She is exploring different ways of using her muscles to pull herself up, climb, and move from place to place.

Yoga is a great tool to build creativity and imagination. Your child can express herself through different movements. As a parent, you can incorporate different music, relatable animal or nature poses, and dance. Remember: Healthful habits started young will help with developmental successes as she grows.

Remember, the Whole Child Parenting Program offers appropriate developmental products and monthly activity books that walk you through supporting your child's skills. Using these in conjunction with the recommended age-appropriate room materials ensures faster development.

Reaching Milestones >

As your child continues to grow and mature you will see that she is unique. Growth and developmental stages are sequential, variable, and individual. The stages can occur in the same order as other children and the differences in how long the stages last will vary from child to child. You are an important component to the success of your child's development. Providing a caring and loving home and spending time with your toddler—playing, singing, reading books, and even just talking—will put her on the path to success!

The information below is a guide to explain some of the developmental milestones an average toddler will achieve. These skills may not all occur between the 13–24-month period; skills can develop within a six-month to a year range. Consider what you read in the context of your child's unique development.

COGNITIVE

- Builds a tower of at least 2–3 blocks and then knocks them over. Around 18 months can build a tower of 3 blocks, perhaps independently.

- Learns to explore objects and toys in a more complex way. Can organize toys, e.g. putting all the blocks the same color in a spot.

- Might be restless, but is able to sustain attention to one structured activity for 2–3 minutes; external noises and distractions may hamper this.

- Knows objects are used for specific purposes, e.g. using a toy key to put in a door.

- Will be able to complete simple chunky puzzles (ones with knobs will be easier to hold) of 2–4 pieces.

SOCIAL-EMOTIONAL

- Wants to be more independent and do things without your help.

- Can recognize distress in others (like when she sees a friend cry)—beginning of empathy.

- Gets frustrated trying to express herself. It is a time your toddler will need you to listen patiently and put into words what you think she is trying to say. This will help your child feel understood.

- She is learning how to care for others by the way you care for her. She may rub your back or comfort you when you look sad.

- Likes to play alone. Is emotionally attached to her toys or objects for security reasons.

LANGUAGE

- By the end of the toddler years, will say at least 35 words on her own—without imitating you.
- Understands and responds to words or questions such as, "Do you want water?"
- Shows desires by pointing or using vocalization of words.
- Loves to hear and read stories with you, especially about things she knows: animals, families, and other toddlers that look like her.
- Will use social words (*bye-bye*); requesting words (*more*); early pronouns (such as *me, mine*); location words (*up, down*); adjectives and adverbs (*yucky, fast*).

CREATIVE

- Begins to pretend and imitate in play.
- Shakes bells, likes songs, finger plays like "Itsy Bitsy Spider" and rhymes with nonsense words.
- Scribbles with crayons, finger paints on paper, makes crayon dots on paper.
- Uses fingers to swirl finger paint or shaving cream, squeezes oily molding dough.
- Holds and pats a baby doll, sits stuffed animals at a table.

PHYSICAL

- Walks with feet slightly apart.
- Climbs. Is beginning to manage corners and obstacles better. Curiosity will lead to her to explore "off-limit" territories. You will need to take extra steps to keep your child safe and help her learn right from wrong.
- Climbs up stairs with support from others in her environment.
- Holds a crayon with a fist grip and scribbles using preferred hand.
- Can hold a cup and use a spoon to eat.

HEALTH AND CARE

- Drinks from a cup, picks up finger food, and feeds self with spoon.
- Puts clothes in a hamper if asked and directed.
- Washes hands with help.
- Attempts to put on shoes, socks, and jacket.

Environment >
Toddler's Room

When you give your toddler toys and furnish her room you are supporting learning in a natural environment: your home.

It is the place where she will learn to master all **six areas of development: cognitive, social-emotional, language, creative, physical, and health.**

It might look like just child's play, but your toddler is hard at work learning important skills. Each new skill lets her progress to the next one, building on a foundation that leads to more complicated tasks.

In order for all of this to occur your toddler needs just the right learning environment.

There are several steps you will take to set up your home for learning. First you eliminate items in your child's room that make it look and feel cluttered.

Then you create a space in which your child feels free to make messes and play with few restrictions. You begin to achieve mindful organization by placing all skill-developing materials in your **Six Drawer Whole Child Color-Coded Organizer**.

The following picture shows what the recommended toddler room looks like. Many of the activities you will do with your toddler will occur in this space, an environment filled with furniture that has a purpose and age-appropriate toys.

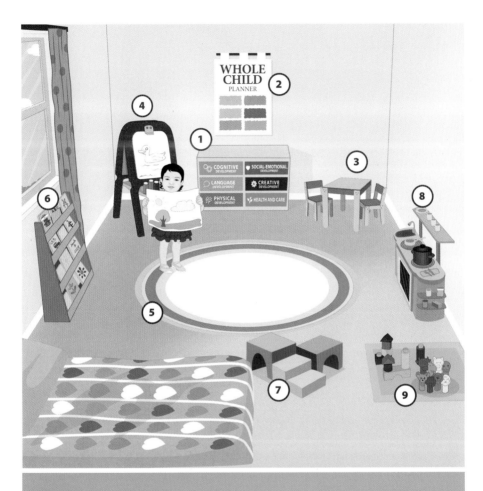

Whole Child: Toddler's Room

The following list contains must-have items for your toddler's room. These items will be used interchangeably with your other Whole Child Parenting materials.

1. Six Drawer Whole Child Color-Coded Organizer
2. Whole Child Wall Planner
3. Table and Chairs
4. Easel
5. Carpet
6. Bookshelf
7. Step Climber
8. Kitchen Set
9. Puppet/Pretend Play Materials

two >

Milestones for a Two Year Old

 COGNITIVE 1

- Can do simple sorting
- Recognizes and names colors
- Sings parts of simple songs
- Recalls past experiences

SOCIAL-EMOTIONAL 2

- Shows independence and awareness of body parts
- Identifies and talks about personal feelings
- Shows interest in helping with basic tasks

 LANGUAGE 3

- Shows interest in books
- Puts together simple sentences
- Can talk about books
- Can tell own age
- Knows first and last name

 CREATIVE 4

- Believes stuffed animals are friends
- Plays with rhyming words
- Moves to music

 **PHYSICAL** 5

- Runs with ease
- Bends over easily
- Rides a tricycle
- Holds markers and crayons

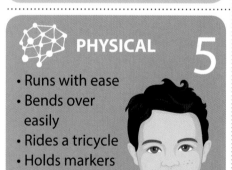

HEALTH AND CARE 6

- Almost all teeth in place
- Controls motor behaviors
- Body looks more proportional, longer legs and arms
- Potty trains, able to stay dry between potty times

two

Two year olds are thirsty for knowledge and are constantly exploring their environment and asking the question "Why?" They are starting to problem solve on their own, make connections, and categorize things based on color, shape, and size. This is an exciting time for your child in which you can introduce them to new lanugages, skills, and environments. Let's look at these milestones and more in the six areas of a two year old's development.

1. Cognitive Development

> **Cognitive development refers to how your child's mind is working and his process of learning.**

At two years old, your child's brain grows so fast that 250,000 nerve cells are added every minute. Your child's brain continues to grow after birth; by two years of age, your child's brain will be about 80% of the size of an adult brain.

In this year, your child's learning process is becoming more thoughtful and is greatly influenced by his environment. Your child is naturally curious and inquisitive and through his play investigates to make sense of the world around him.

During this stage of development, two year olds demonstrate how their minds are making more connections. Your child is moving past just observing and manipulating objects in his environment and is now beginning to understand the relationship between objects and ideas.

The following chart provides you with an image that walks you through the stages of your child's intellectual development.

Understanding these areas of cognitive development will help you learn how your child thinks, how to support learning, and how to teach new skills.

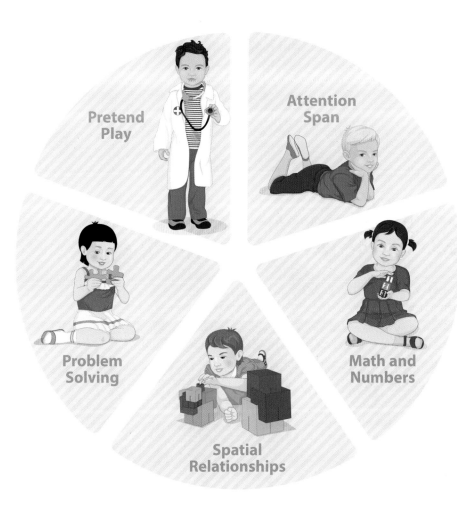

WHOLE CHILD: AGE TWO
Cognitive
Development Components

Under each cognitive area, the chart below gives you specific skills you can expect to see as your two year old develops. This chart will allow you to have practical expectations for your child at this age.

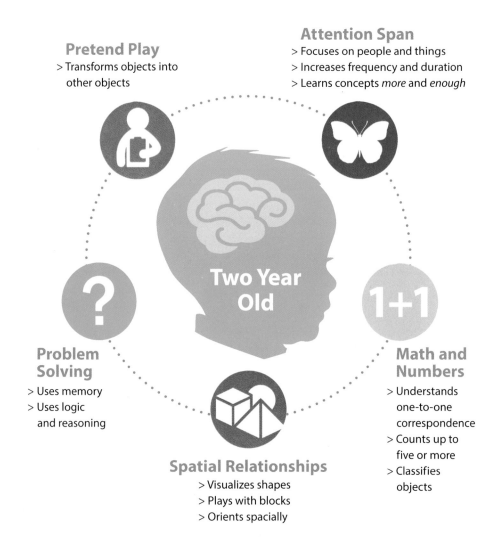

Pretend Play
> Transforms objects into
  other objects

Attention Span
> Focuses on people and things
> Increases frequency and duration
> Learns concepts *more* and *enough*

Problem Solving
> Uses memory
> Uses logic
  and reasoning

Two Year Old

Math and Numbers
> Understands
  one-to-one
  correspondence
> Counts up to
  five or more
> Classifies
  objects

Spatial Relationships
> Visualizes shapes
> Plays with blocks
> Orients spatially

Through his senses and developing motor skills, your child will use cause and effect and reasoning to explore unfamiliar objects. You will see your child start making connections between items and then begin organizing them into groups and categories.

Some of these connections can be seen through simple tasks such as sorting toys by color as well as through symbolic play, in which your child may use one object to represent another based on its physical features such as shape or size.

As parents, it is important to provide everyday activities that tap into your child's curiosity to help nourish the brain, which, in turn, will increase your child's learning efficiency and brain capacity. Any mental stimulation provided to your child will activate his mind and protect against cognitive decline.

You are preparing your child for the Olympics, and you have about five years to do it. This will feel like a lot of time, but in actuality, five years go by very quickly. Similar to the training of an athlete in the Olympics, the brain gets activated (warms up) and develops (refines skills) through repeated experience (workouts), interactions (team play), and environmental exposure (proper equipment and practice area), leading to greater performance.

Your child's brain is preparing for the Olympics as well, and in this case, the first five years are the most crucial for starting on the right path to developing your child's full potential.

The subsequent chapters show you how your child acquires knowledge and demonstrates major development in brain growth.

Attention Span >
All Eyes on You

Attention span refers to your child's ability to focus on a person and activity while ignoring other distracting things in the environment.

ACTIVITY

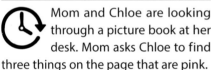 Mom and Chloe are looking through a picture book at her desk. Mom asks Chloe to find three things on the page that are pink.

Chloe points to a pink dress on the page and says, "Look, a pink dress!" but then loses focus and interest when it comes to finding two other pink items.

Mom notices this and says, "Chloe, why don't we find two more pink items before we turn the page?"

Chloe then looks at the page again and finds another pink item. "Good job!" Mom says as they turn to read the next page.

INSIGHT

 With Mom's help, Chloe is able to focus on the activity of finding three pink items longer than if she had done the activity alone. Mom is realistic in offering Chloe a simple activity when she asks her to find the pink items and does not force her to pay attention longer than two minutes.

In order for your child to learn about or remember something, she must stop and pay attention.

You will see your child's attention span grow tremendously over this year of her life. At the beginning of age two your child's attention span for one single activity is only about 30–60 seconds, but with your encouragement and involvement can soon last between two to three minutes.

By two and a half, your child is becoming more independent, and you will see her able to focus on an activity independently for up to two minutes if the activity is of interest to her.

By doing the following as a parent you will support developing your child's attention skills so she can engage in focused play activities:

1.	2.	3.	4.
Be mindful of how your child is feeling and what mood she is in, because when your child is sad, unhappy, tired, cranky, or just not ready to do an activity, her ability to focus decreases and paying attention becomes more difficult.	Set up the environment in which your activity will take place.	Make sure the area is not disturbed by loud noises or distractions from a TV or other electronic devices.	Be mindful of frequent interruptions by others as this can cause your child to lose focus on the activity in front of her.

Following these four steps, coupled with having an activity that is of interest to your child will enable your child to develop better attention skills.

If your child becomes distracted, provide support by making face-to-face contact and saying your child's name out loud, then remind your child of the activity you are working on. Keep in mind that speaking slowly and calmly and praising your child for her efforts at paying attention is most effective for keeping her engaged.

Attention is a very important skill for your two year old to have, because it is the groundwork for future development of memory and intelligence; however, attention is a difficult skill for your child to acquire, so give her time.

By playing with your two year old and asking her questions about the activity, you are helping her apply and build her attention skills.

Math and Numbers >
Numbers Game

Math and number awareness involves your child recognizing numbers, counting, learning one-to-one correspondence, identifying patterns, and engaging in sorting and classifying.

Can you find all the spoons and put them together in one spot?

Math and number awareness is the foundation for learning more advanced math concepts.

Classification is putting together things that are the same. Your child demonstrates early classification skills by sorting items based on how they look, sound, and feel.

ACTIVITY

 Dad places a few plastic cups and spoons mixed together on the floor in front of Eric. Dad asks, "Eric, can you find all the spoons and put them together in one spot?" Eric begins to pick up one spoon at a time and place them next to each other. Next Dad asks, "Eric, can you now put all the cups together in one spot?" Eric begins to pick up a cup and put it next to another cup until they are all in one spot.

INSIGHT

Dad supports Eric's math awareness by having him find and classify objects that are the same. Once the child has mastered classification skills, you must then expand his mathematical thinking by talking about the differences between the groups of objects.

Your child is aware that things belong together because of what the object does or how objects are used. For example, when your child thinks about a birthday cake he will also think about having candles with the cake to celebrate. This is because both items are used when celebrating a birthday, even though a cake and candles do not look alike. This is classification.

Your child is able to identify when there is one object as well as when there is more than one object; however, while your child understands that there is more than one cracker on his plate, he will not yet be able to tell you if there are four or six crackers on that plate.

Your child can count up to three and maybe higher but not yet in the correct order. Your child will most likely count items in groups larger than two like this: "One, two, three, five, seven ..." This is because your child understands through the skill of one-to-one correspondence that he can assign only one number to one object; however, he does not yet understand that the number he is assigning is related to the quantities of objects that he is naming.

Classifying skills are easy to support by doing activities as in the example with Eric, in which Dad uses simple materials found around the home, which Eric sees every day in his environment, or by helping the child see how items can be classified based upon how they are used, as in the example of the birthday cake.

Classifying objects is an important part of developing early math skills because it will help your child identify and describe relationships between objects. Your child's ability to classify objects he is playing with supports math skills such as understanding one-to-one correspondence.

It is important that your child can touch the items while counting so that each item represents a number. Children learn math skills best through hands-on play and the use of concrete examples using blocks, toys, or other household items.

Understanding number relationships and the purpose of numbers in counting leads your child to later be able to recognize patterns in materials and objects around him as well as patterns in his daily routine, such as the notion that naptime comes after lunch time. Patterns, routines, daily activities all lead to building math skills.

ACTIVITY

Ben is playing with blocks on the floor of his bedroom. He starts to count out the amount of blocks he has in front of him by grabbing and moving one block at a time toward his body.

Ben says, "One block" and then moves one block. Then he says, "Two blocks" and moves another block. When Ben moves a third block next to the others he says, "Three blocks."

"One block.
Two blocks.
Three blocks."

INSIGHT

By counting and moving the blocks toward him, Ben is learning one-to-one correspondence, which is when each block represents a number. Later he will learn the symbol for the numbers: 1, 2, and 3.

Counting skills are best learned when the child has an opportunity to touch and feel, sort and categorize objects or toys.

Remember, the Whole Child Parenting Program offers appropriate developmental products and monthly activity books that walk you through supporting your child's skills. Using these in conjunction with the recommended age-appropriate room materials ensures faster development.

Spatial Relationships >
Shape, Size, Distance

Spatial relationships refer to location and where things are in the environment (*on top*, *under*, *beside*, *next to*, *inside*, *outside*). When she understands these concepts she can better understand the concepts of distance and directions she is given.

Two year olds are more independent compared to toddlers, and their use of spatial skills has improved and will continue to improve as they grow. This is demonstrated by your child's ability to maintain her body in relation to her surrounding environment. Parents must support their child's spatial development by giving **spatial cues**.

ACTIVITY

Tommy's mom places a large refrigerator box on the living room floor. Tommy and Laura begin to move around inside the box, turning their bodies in different directions until they both are able to fit inside.

INSIGHT

Children understand and develop the concept of *inside* by moving around within the confines of the rectangular shape and work together to use available space in a fun, entertaining, and satisfying way.

*Which shape
is a circle?*

ACTIVITY

Jasmine is having a picnic lunch outside with her mom. Mom places an O-shaped cereal piece and a cracker in front of Jasmine and asks her what shapes she can see.

Jasmine is able to point to the O-shaped cereal and say it is a circle and that the cracker is a square.

INSIGHT

Jasmine is able to identify the circle and the square shapes based on their visual qualities, such as curved and straight lines. When Jasmine gets closer to age three, she will be able to articulate to Mom how many sides a square has and see that a circle does not have any sides. This skill forms an early basis for understanding simple geometry (identifying angles and shapes).

Spatial cues might include parents asking their child to find two of the same things in the environment, such as asking your two year old to "Get the ball under the table" (spatial cue of where the ball is located), as opposed to "Get the ball" (no cue is given as to where the ball is located). Spatial cues encourage your child to use primarily the sense of sight to focus on the sizes and shapes of the objects she is looking for in the environment (e.g. ball [shape], under table [size]).

Your child's spatial ability with shapes is purely visual. Children visualize and can see similarities and differences in shapes (straight, curved, zig-zagged, looped, thick, thin, circle, triangle, square, rectangle, flat, and pointy). Spatial abilities develop with time and experience.

Shapes are everywhere. As in the example with Jasmine, you are able to see how your child has shapes all around her. Therefore, the more you engage your child in spatial play by talking about shapes, the better chance your child will have of building the foundations necessary for other early math skills.

Problem Solving >
Keep Trying

Your child is naturally curious. Through active exploration he will use trial and error to figure out a problem.

When you think about the role memory plays in problem solving for your child, you will see him observe, think about a problem, and then later remember what he saw someone else do and imitate it.

Through everyday routines, parents can provide opportunities for their children's memories to improve. When getting ready for the bath, encourage your child to recall what is needed to take a bath. This will encourage your child to think about what to do if he doesn't have items necessary for taking a bath.

Your child is also starting to understand the relationship between objects, and you will see your child exploring this through cause and effect. As your child's understanding

---

ACTIVITY

Max is given two toy connectors to play with. He sits for a moment looking at both connectors, trying to figure out how they fit together to make a tower. After a few minutes, Max remembers that he can put one connector on top of the other, and he continues that process with other connectors to make a tower.

INSIGHT

In this example, Max uses trial and error to figure out how to fit the connectors together and then uses his memory to follow the same process with the rest of the connectors.

As he learns new information his brain will reorganize itself and store knowledge in the memory bank for later use with solving problems that occur through other play activities.

of cause and effect develops, he will express interest in pushing buttons and turning light switches on and off to see what happens.

You will see your child explore cause and effect situations all around him. One example is your child interacting with a family cat using a cat toy, a ball attached at one end to a string.

To see a cause, your child needs to think about how to produce the action needed to get a response from the cat (should he move the cat toy up or down, fast or slowly?). Your child will see the effect of bouncing the toy in front of the cat's face.

Activities like simple interactions with a family pet enable your child's brain to absorb knowledge and grow. It is important to expose your two year old to a variety of stimuli and

allow him to have hands-on inter-action with different materials.

In other words, two year olds need sensory rich activities because when your child is able to both see and touch the objects he is exploring, he will make a deeper connection and develop a better understanding of concepts like cause and effect.

Your child's learning process has become more thoughtful and goes beyond just manipulating objects physically. This is why it is important to provide your child with the high-quality toys (which does not have to mean expensive) that are important to his learning processes.

As you think about buying toys, here are some examples that encourage a two year old's problem solving abilities:

- **Wood puzzles** (with four to twelve pieces) are excellent because your child has to really think about where the pieces fit.

- Find **blocks** that snap together encourage your two year old to think about how to fit them.

- Use **objects that can be sorted** (by size, shape, color, smell) and things with hooks, buttons, buckles, and snaps.

Pretend Play >
Model Behavior

Your two year old will begin to engage in more complex forms of pretend play.

ACTIVITY

Lila finds a banana in the kitchen and decides that she will go sit by her dad on the floor and pretend to talk, using the banana as a phone.

Because your child is now beginning to form mental images of objects, actions, and concepts he is able to put together and act out more elaborate sequences of pretend play.

One form of pretend play you will see your child engage in is symbolic play. **Symbolic play is your child's ability to use objects, actions, or ideas to represent other objects, actions, or ideas.**

Another form of pretend play your child engages in is socio-dramatic play. **Socio-dramatic play** appears at the time your child begins looking for the company of others. Socio-dramatic play includes elements of

INSIGHT

This is an example of symbolic play because Lila is using an object, the banana, to represent a real object, which is a phone. Lily is also able to understand that a phone is used to communicate and talk to others.

Your child is showing you how she is categorizing objects based on how they look. The banana has a similar shape to a phone. Another example is a pot being used as a hat because both items have a similar shape and features.

Symbolic play is important because through play your child will express and represent his ideas, thoughts, and feelings.

"How do you feel?"

symbolic play; however, socio-dramatic play differs from symbolic play because it requires verbal interaction between two or more children.

Socio-dramatic play contributes to your child's ability to play with other children his age. As your child is engaged in play he is growing his vocabulary and developing conversation skills needed to engage in role playing events during play (e.g. you be the doctor, and I will be the one who is sick).

Socio-dramatic play gives your child something to talk about with another child or family member. Think about a play exchange your child had with you in which you were the patient and he was the doctor. You were asked by your child, "How do you feel?" and "Are you sick?" These types of experiences require listening and talking as well as giving a response.

A shared experience like this through socio-dramatic play supports the development of skills needed for the social interactions your child will encounter each and every day.

ACTIVITY

Teach your child to engage in make-believe play by setting up an environment that enables you to become your child's play partner. Play a game of doctor with your child, and have your child act out an experience he had with the doctor. Then switch roles so that he is the doctor and you are the patient.

INSIGHT

With your support, your child can overcome the anxiety he may have been experiencing regarding a doctor's visit. Practicing or rehearsing the sequence of events experienced on a typical visit to the doctor or other potentially stressful situations helps two year olds feel more comfortable and learn coping strategies (e.g. familiarity) for managing the situation.

2. Social-Emotional Development

> **Social-emotional development is the start of a two year old's knowledge, understanding, expression, and management of her emotions.**

Your two year old is building an understanding of herself as an individual, which increases her confidence in interacting with people, objects, and experiences in the world around her.

Healthy social and emotional development begins with your child having an attachment to other human beings. It is important that your two year old feels loved, important, and worthy. Because of that bond with you, she trusts that the world is a good place. These early relationships form the basis for all other relationships and interactions that she will have.

You will see your child develop an interest in playing with other children. Through interactions with other children, your child will begin to learn about empathy and others' feelings. Developing empathy enables her to cooperate and negotiate with her peers.

At this age your child has better control of her body and emotions because she is able to retain focus and attention longer. Your child's ability to control her emotions and refrain from acting on her first impulse also helps her cooperate and develop the ability to wait her turn and not grab toys from friends.

Self-
Awareness

Social
Development

Self-
Regulation

Emotional
Development

WHOLE CHILD: AGE TWO
Social-Emotional
Development Components

Social-emotional development is the foundation for all other areas of development, because in order for your child to be a confident and attentive learner, she must first feel safe and valued.

1. Social Development

Social development is your child's ability to connect with fellow friends and adults in a socially acceptable way. This connection forms the foundation for two year olds to have healthy relationships with others and fit into social environments both now and in the future.

2. Emotional Development

Emotional development is the start of a two year old's knowledge, understanding, expression, and management of her feelings. Emotional development does not happen without connection to other people or things; the nervous system, cognition, and regulating behaviors are involved in emotional development.

3. Self-Regulation

Self-regulation involves a two year old's capability to gain control of her body, control strong emotions, and retain focus and attention. The development of self-regulation is the foundation of early childhood development.

4. Self-Awareness

Self-awareness in two year olds is seen when they begin to recognize themselves in mirrors, react by giving a self-conscious grin, or display shyness when they are the center of others' attention. Two year olds build their understanding of themselves as individuals, which increases their confidence in interacting with people, objects, and experiences in the world around them.

Healthy social and emotional development begins with your child having an attachment to other human beings.

Social Development >
Can I Play?

Social skill development occurs when your child understands the feelings of others and can create positive relationships with peers and adults.

"I have pizza for you!"

When your child was an infant, he engaged in solitary play (playing alone). When your child was a toddler, he engaged in both solitary play and parallel play (playing beside other children rather than with them). During both forms of play, your child was only interested in what he was doing.

Now your child wants to experience what it is like to really have a relationship with a peer whom they may later call a best friend. Your child's social skills have developed so much that associative play is what he wants to do.

Associative play is when children play together.

Your child's cooperation with other children grows as he develops more empathy regarding others' feelings and wants.

Two year olds will borrow from peers and share toys, but this does not mean that they will necessarily play cooperatively. When children turn three, you will see more cooperative play experiences take place.

ACTIVITY

 Two-and-a-half-year-old Josie is playing with her peer, Thomas, during morning playgroup. Josie spots a bin with colored blocks near Thomas and picks it up. One by one she takes out the blocks and lays them on the table in the shape of a circle. Josie calls out to Thomas, "Thomas, want some pizza? I have pizza for you!"

Thomas replies, "Yes, I want pizza. I don't like pepperoni pizza. It's spicy."

Josie replies, "It's cheese." She then grabs a small toy shovel from the sand table across the room and comes back to scoop up a block "slice" of pizza for Thomas. "Here's your pizza, Thomas!"

Thomas scoots over to Josie and then says, "I don't want cheese pizza!"

Josie starts to cry and says, "I have your pizza."

Thomas looks up and says, "Okay, pizza please, thank you."

As your child grows older it is amazing to see how he learns to cooperate more with another person through the use of verbal interaction and understanding that relationship building involves give and take.

It is important for your child to be able to interact with others in a positive way because this skill will support him well into adulthood. Interacting well includes your child being able to cooperate, communicate, and work through problems that can and will happen during ordinary play with peers.

Every stride your child makes in social development brings him closer to forming healthy, positive relationships with you and others in his environment. Support opportunities for him to engage with others on a regular basis.

INSIGHT

Thomas is able to see that Josie is upset, shows empathy, and decides to have the pizza. Both children demonstrate cooperation and relationship building skills.

Emotional Development >
Feelings

Emotional development refers to how your child understands her own feelings, as well as how she can read the feelings of others.

Because your two year old has a better understanding of her feelings, she will be able to respond when you ask questions like "Are you happy or sad today?" or "Why are you happy?" or "Why are you sad?" When your child is able to communicate her feelings, it gives you the opportunity to respond appropriately to her wants and needs.

Your child's emotional security and confidence develop when parents give warm, consistent, responsive care to their children. Part of showing warm and caring behavior to your two year old is being attentive and in tune with her feelings. Demonstrating this behavior shows your child how to use kind, caring, appropriate behavior when dealing with others.

ACTIVITY

Stephanie is sitting with her mom and reading a book. Her brother Leo has a play date with his friend Erik. The boys are playing in the other room.

Suddenly Stephanie hears loud noises. She runs into the living room where she sees Erik and Leo face to face. They are talking loudly and gesturing. It looks to her as if they are fighting.

She runs back to her mom and cries out, "Mommy, look!" and points to the boys in the other room.

Mom smiles at Stephanie and says, "It's okay, honey. The boys are pretending to be like two superheroes on TV who were comparing powers."

Stephanie calms down.

"It's nice that you were worried about your brother and his friend," Mom adds.

As Stephanie sees the smile on her mom's face, she begins to smile, too.

INSIGHT

Stephanie looks to her mother for directions when trying to figure out how to react. Stephanie is able to read her mother's emotions, hear her words, and act appropriately.

Having the ability to read the emotions of others is an important social skill that two year olds are beginning to develop. As they learn how to read others' emotions and react appropriately, children often look to their parents for directions when trying to figure out how to behave in certain situations.

As your child grows older she will look less to you for understanding someone else's emotions and decide for herself how the other person is feeling. She will begin to understand when she is making her friends happy or sad, when to give space, and when her friends need a hug. In other words, she will start becoming more emotionally intelligent over time and with more experience with family and peers.

It is important to praise your two year old's successes and show your child that you see how she is growing and learning. This will help build her confidence so she can have more success making friends.

Self-Regulation >
Emotions

Self-regulation is the ability to control one's own behaviors and expression of emotions.

Parents can be overwhelmed by emotions, but over time we have learned some strategies to help us regain control. Strategies could include taking a moment to count to ten or calling a friend to talk about your frustrations. But when your child has such feelings, he is not yet able to use the same coping or self-regulating mechanisms.

Self-regulation is demonstrated by your child's ability not to act upon his first response. You will see your child use self-regulating strategies such as calming himself by sucking his thumb, tolerating waiting minutes for his turn, sitting and focusing on a book being read to him, or refraining from hitting another child who has moved into his space.

There will always be a time when your child does not like to hear the word *no*. It is important to take a moment and look at the situation from your child's perspective. Then ask yourself if you are expecting your child to understand or do something when he is tired or does not understand what is being asked of him. Are you giving your child time to calm himself down (waiting before you react)? And have you been teaching your child the skills he needs to calm down on his own (holding a beloved toy, sitting for a little bit)?

If the answer is no and you still require your child to accept your request then you are forcing obedience through control; this is not being supportive, and it will delay the development of his self-regulation skills.

In addition, **it is imperative that parents are also modeling self-regulating behaviors so that the child can imitate, practice, and internalize what is being modeled for him.** Self-regulation is the cornerstone of your child's social-emotional development and will be seen in all areas of development as your child matures.

ACTIVITY

 Mom needs to go to the grocery store because she has run out of formula for Tony's baby sister. Mom knows Tony has not had his nap today, but she still has to go.

Arriving at the grocery store Mom puts the baby in the cart and has Tony hold onto the side of the cart. Then off they go toward the infant aisle.

Walking through the aisles Tony sees the candy section and begins to grab a bag of candy off the bottom shelf. Mom says, "Tony, no candy. Put it back, please."

At the moment Mom says no, Tony throws himself and the bag of candy on the floor and begins kicking and screaming, "I want candy!"

Mom remembers that Tony has not had his full nap and says, "I know you're upset. I'll wait for you to calm down." Mom then hands Tony his little blanket out of the diaper bag.

INSIGHT

Tony's mom understands that Tony has not had a nap, so she gives him some time before she reacts to his tantrum. She also gives Tony his blanket, which serves as a comfort item he can use to help himself calm down. Tony's mom has realistic expectations and also provides support for her two-year-old son.

Self-regulation skills develop slowly over time; this is why it is important for parents to have realistic expectations of their children.

Self-Awareness >
My Identity

Self-awareness in two year olds means having a clear and positive sense of identity.

Your child is starting to identify herself as an individual who has her own body, thoughts, and feelings separate from those of others.

In your child's search for self-identity, she is eager to use her mind, have her say, and make decisions. Saying "I don't want to" or "Not those shoes. I want pink shoes, pink!" is normal behavior for two year olds. When you say, "Yes," they say, "No."

She wants to choose what she wears, so let her! Lay out three outfits and let her pick one from those choices. Then say, "You can choose from these or I can choose for you." This gives your child a sense of control over her own destiny. It can be tough to get a particularly stubborn child on board, but decisions need to be made, so why not enlist her help?

It really speaks to your child's self-esteem that she is developing

ACTIVITY

 Katy stands in front of a mirror, looking at her face. She points to her nose and then points to the nose in the mirror.

INSIGHT

 Katy realizes that the face in the mirror is hers. Katy is becoming aware of what she looks like. This is how a child first begins to see herself as an individual, separate from others.

into an individual who is separate from you. Your two year old is experiencing a very important stage in her development. **In order for your two year old to become a healthy, thriving adult, she must separate from you, and now is the time she will start doing this.** Don't panic. She's not going far!

Developing a sense of self as a unique being starts with recognizing superficial features and characteristics.

3. Language Development

> **Language development encompasses your child's emerging reading and writing skills as well as the development of her communication skills, such as listening and speaking.**

Two year olds typically have a vocabulary of between 70 and 225 different words. Your child will develop language more swiftly if you and other adults engage her in real conversations.

Language development improves social-emotional, cognitive, and physical skills. Your child understands and uses language to communicate successfully with others, build relationships, and express her needs in multiple ways.

Your two year old is learning language by making connections between the words she hears and the meanings of these words. She is now able to put together words to form short sentences and phrases.

And while it may be quicker for your child to express herself verbally, sign language can serve as a great outlet for your child to communicate not just her needs but also her feelings.

As you support your two year old's familiarity with storybooks, you will also increase her expressive vocabulary skills and early reading abilities.

WHOLE CHILD: AGE TWO
Language
Development Components

Besides having storybooks available, there are a number of ways you can create a home environment that promotes emerging literacy for your child, such as labeling objects around the house to expose your child to more print and promote future skills like letter recognition.

Your support is key when it comes to your child's love for written and spoken words, transforming your child into a critical thinker and effective communicator.

1. Listening and Understanding

Two year olds learn language by making connections between the words they hear and the meanings of these words. These connections between words enable your child to put together words to form phrases and make different words from a root word; for example, the root word *appear* helps your child make sense of the words *disappear* and *reappear*.

2. Communication and Speaking

Two year olds use sounds, gestures, and words to have their needs met. They are building their vocabulary and are able to use two- and three-word phrases to communicate with others.

3. Emerging Literacy

Two year olds are able to recognize and identify almost all common pictures and objects around them. They are developing story comprehension as well as engaging in more conversations with others. This is what is called emerging or emergent literacy.

"Reading" and being read to are some of the most powerful ways to develop cognitive and language skills.

Remember, the Whole Child Parenting Program offers appropriate developmental products and monthly activity books that walk you through supporting your child's skills. Using these in conjunction with the recommended age-appropriate room materials ensures faster development.

Listening and Understanding >
Bit by Bit

Receptive language is the aspect of communication that involves hearing, listening, and understanding. In other words, receptive language skills involve the ability to understand words and language by hearing and listening.

"Can you say bear?"

Your child saying the wrong word is a normal part of the language development process. Often your child is saying the word wrongly because he did not hear the correct way of saying the word or because he did not understand the meaning of the word. Demonstrate the correct way to say a word and repeat with him many times. Use the word in context if you can (e.g. "Bears have fur. Do you see the bear's fur? Can you touch the bear's fur?") By repetition and with your support your child will be able to speak words correctly.

Receptive language is important in order for your child to communicate. Think about a time when your child had difficulty understanding something you asked him to do; having difficulty following directions often occurs because the child does not understand one of the words you are using.

When your child is able to understand directions and what is happening around him, he will be better able to pay attention and listen. Thus, having a good understanding of language will also make it easier for your child to engage in learning activities.

It is important that when you hear your child use a word wrongly, gently pronounce the word the correct way and have him repeat it back to you. Refrain from saying, "No, you said it

ACTIVITY

Two-year-old Aaron is sitting with his mom at the table looking at a picture book about bears. He points to a picture of a bear and says, "That's a bar." (bear)

Mom responds, "Yes, that is a bear. Can you say bear?" (Here she is making sure she correctly says the word *bear* for her son and has him repeat the word.) "Good job! Now can you point to the bear?"

INSIGHT

By having Aaron repeat the word and find the pictures of the bear on the page, his mom is listening to hear how well her son hears the correct pronunciation and how well he understands what the word is. At this age your child mispronounces many words.

wrong" because that can discourage your child from trying again. Young children listen a lot! They listen to the sounds you make and the words and phrases you say. As your child develops more language and uses his receptive language skills, he will become more advanced in listening to and understanding information.

That is why it is important to give your child plenty of opportunities to develop his listening and understanding skills. After you have talked about a routine, follow up by asking your child if he can tell you what comes after breakfast or after hearing soft music or after a bath.

As your child listens and understands others, he is also learning that communication is important and useful in his everyday life.

Listening and understanding skills will play key roles in how your child communicates his feelings and how he interacts with others.

Opportunities can include:

1. talking during daily routines (e.g. "After breakfast we are going to brush our teeth.").

2. talking with your child about things that you are doing (e.g. "I am going to add eggs to the batter for our cookies.").

3. talking about things they can see in their environment (e.g. "I see a blue bird on the tree. He is building a nest.").

Communication and Speaking >
My Turn to Talk

Communication and speaking are how your child uses language to connect with others through avenues such as his voice to make sounds and his hands to sign words.

ACTIVITY

Mom makes a play telephone out of two empty cans and a piece of string for Tony and his neighbor to play with. Tony picks up the can on one side of the play telephone and says, "Nicole, can you hear me?"

Nicole says, "Tony, is that you?"

Both Tony and Nicole start laughing as they listen to the other speak through the can.

INSIGHT

This activity helps your child learn the organization of conversation and understand that people take turns communicating and speaking.

Be an interactive language partner with your child so that you are helping him learn to use language to communicate. When your child asks for something, respond appropriately, and he will begin to understand that exchanging information back and forth is an effective way of communication.

Describe how things taste, what they feel like, and how they smell. Speak with your child and ask him to reply—this will support the development of communication skills.

You should use two- or three-word phrases when speaking with your child. By the time your child reaches two, he should know and use 200 or more words when speaking.

It is important to stay in tune with your child's language communication and to talk often with him using a rich and varied vocabulary. The number of different words and phrases you use on a daily basis, as well as the number of conversations you have with your child, are both directly related to your child's language development. So keep up the talking!

Sign Language

Sign language is a form of communication used as your child combines hand and body movements to make words.

Mia is signing milk.

Your child is naturally drawn to speaking because it is the fastest and easiest way for her to communicate with others; however, during this age it is still difficult for your child to express exactly how she is feeling, especially during times of stress. That is because her vocabulary is still developing, and she is in the process of learning to pronounce words heard in his environment. Starting with simple signs, such as *happy* or *sad*, can give your child another way to express how she feels without using spoken language.

The other wonderful aspect of sign language is that your child will see it as fun. You use it as a way to support your child's language skills as you teach the signs for words and the alphabet. By teaching signs you are helping your child with letter recognition and vocabulary building.

In addition, teaching your child to use sign language as another outlet for communicating helps your child feel confident to "speak" her wants, needs, and feelings.

When you are able to understand her needs and be responsive, you are supporting your child's emotional development, which is crucial for developing self-esteem and the ability to learn.

Emergent Literacy >
The Written Word

*"Can we taste
with our nose?"*

Emerging or emergent
literacy relates to the
development of knowledge
and skills associated with
books and writing.

It is your child's experience with
reading and writing skills before she
learns how to read and write words.
Emergent literacy involves your child
in the process of becoming literate.

ACTIVITY

 Mother and daughter are reading a book titled *Silly Ways We Use Our Senses*.

Mom says, "It is so sweet to taste the lemon drop on the tree. We taste it with our nose. . . ." Mom pauses and repeats, "With our nose? Can we taste with our nose?"

Peyton says, laughing, "No! We taste with our mouth, not our nose."

Peyton then pretends to lick the lemon drops off the tree on the page, and her mom joins in.

INSIGHT

 We see that Peyton's mom does not give directions to show Peyton that we do not taste with our noses when reading the story to her, but rather she gives assistance. Peyton's mom also joins in when Peyton decides to expand the story by using pretend play and creative movement.

Picture book reading and story reading should be one of the most common forms of interaction that occur between you and your child. While reading to your child point out different words to help her make connections between the print and the pictures.

It is important to remember that emergent literacy begins at home. Two year olds who live in a home environment that includes lots of reading and writing will develop reading and writing skills before they start school.

As she understands her environment, your two year old will select and focus on important aspects of literacy, one of which is written language. Two year olds are immersed in written language. They see books, newspapers, magazines, and words on screen. Parents must show their children that reading, writing, and talking about words occurs in everyday life and serves different purposes. Immersion in reading and writing will help your child develop a love of learning that can last a lifetime.

Create a supportive environment for your two year old's emergent literacy development. You can do this by trying the following:

1. Read as much as possible to your child and have many books available for your child to look through and pretend to read as she flips the pages.

2. Allow your child to explore with tools for writing and drawing (such as pencils and crayons).

3. Make simple labels in your child's room. For example, label the drawer where your child puts her socks by writing the word SOCKS on white paper or on an index card in large, black, capital letters.

4. Talk with your child about writing. When you write something down, draw her attention to it. Say things such as "I am leaving a note so they know where we went."

4. Creative Development

> Creative arts engage two year olds' minds and senses.

Creative arts invite your child to listen, observe, move, solve problems, and imagine—all while using multiple modes of thought and self-expression. By actively involving your child in the creative arts, you are stimulating brain connections that support learning.

You may find your two year old now claps to a basic musical beat, experiments with mixing colors to make a new color, or moves like the animal characters in a story.

This year, your child is taking on a greater interest in music and is able to memorize words to her favorite songs. She will also start experimenting more with different dance movements. Her movements will start reflecting the beat, rhythm, and mood of the music. She can express herself while also strengthening her gross motor skills and exploring spatial relationships in her environment.

Your child will develop an interest in visual arts as she doesn't just explore art mediums and materials, but also starts to express herself by describing and discussing her art. Visual arts can include a limitless number of materials, which give your child infinite ways to express herself and explore her environment.

WHOLE CHILD: AGE TWO
Creative
Development Components

You will also see your child gravitate toward expressing herself through dramatic play. Through dramatic play your child is able to use her imagination to explore different roles, while also having an outlet to express her feelings by acting out familiar situations.

Each of these elements supports your child's imaginative thinking and self-expression, enhancing her progress in other areas of growth such as problem solving and emotional development.

1. Music

Music and words have a great connection for two year olds. Ask your child to sing her favorite song, and then sing it back to her. Repetition is key in early childhood learning. This is the age when children start to clearly use words to communicate needs and wants.

2. Dance

Two year olds move more freely than during the toddler stage. They are aware of their body parts and the reactions their movements make. They love to run and fall on the ground. Play games to encourage their understanding of moving slowly or quickly.

Remember,
the Whole Child
Parenting Program
offers appropriate developmental
products and monthly activity books
that walk you through supporting
your child's skills. Using these in
conjunction with the recommended
age-appropriate room
materials ensures faster
development.

3. Visual Arts

Two-year-old art is messy and hands-on. At this age, you might start to see the beginning stages of a story as your child draws. Ask your child what a line or form represents in her picture.

4. Dramatic Play

Two year olds get extremely excited by dress up and dramatic play. They combine their imagination and memory skills to express their thoughts and feelings. Objects have more meaning and are specifically chosen during dramatic play at this age.

Music >
I Got Rhythm

Music is sound that expresses ideas of emotions through rhythm, melody, and harmony.

"Let's play these drums."

Musical experiences for two year olds involve listening to, learning about, and making music.

Music calms your little one during rest time. It also promotes listening skills. Through music your child will learn about patterns, and through singing your child will learn about language and rhymes. **When your child is between the ages of one and three, he will look for opportunities to get rocking, rolling, clapping, and moving to a beat.**

It is important for you to have resources available whereby you can enhance your child's musical opportunities. Part of supporting your child in music is giving opportunities for him to not only listen to music, but also to become actively engaged in it by playing an instrument along with the music, making his own music, dancing with music, and play acting with music.

ACTIVITY

 Dad wants to give his son an opportunity to listen and play music with him. He goes to the garage and gets his small drums and two wooden drumsticks from when he was young.

Dad says, "Mark, come sit with me on the floor and let's play these drums I got from the garage." Dad hands the sticks to Mark and then turns on the piano concerto "Andante" by Mozart and begins to beat on the drums slowly with his hands.

Dad turns to Mark and says, "Mark, hit your drums like this, fast and then slowly like the music."

INSIGHT

Dad encourages Mark to bang out a rhythm and to imitate with his sticks what Dad is doing with his hands. As Mark continues to bang on the drums, he is also learning to keep a steady beat and coordinate his movements with the sticks in both hands.

Dance >
Moving

Dance is anytime your child moves to the rhythms of the sounds he hears.

Dance can be a sway, a twirl, or a jiggle. Dance can be fast or it can be slow, but most of all dance is movement.

Your child is learning about himself and the world around him through movement. Playing your child's favorite music and encouraging him to dance and play supports gross motor skill (large muscle) development and spatial exploration as your child moves in the space around him.

Movement includes exploration, experimentation, and discovery. Dancing helps your child explore all the new ways his body can move, such as using the large muscles of the body like his arms and legs to do a twist and a turn, a leap or a shimmy. Remember, dance is an art form, and when combined with the child dancing freely to the music (without following the moves of an adult) it will promote creativity and self-expression.

Visual Arts >

Little Artist

Visual arts can be experienced by your child using her sense of sight.

Art forms such as drawing, painting, crafts, pictures, and videos are all visual arts.

Your child can use materials such as crayons, paint, play dough, clay, glue, tape, paper, and everyday objects found around the house, along with tools such as child-safe scissors, brushes, rolling pins, and cookie cutters to express her ideas.

Visual arts benefit growth in all areas of your child's development. When your child describes what she has created she's using language. When your child uses cause and effect to see what happens when she combines two colors of paint she is developing her problem-solving skills.

It is important to enable your child to express her own ideas through the visual arts. Think of ways you can nurture her creativity and self ex-pression by letting her choose paint and crayon colors, asking questions about the colors she chooses, and discussing how she feels when she is painting or coloring a picture.

By playing an active role and praising your child's art, you are allowing her to feel confident to continue to express herself through further visual arts activities.

ACTIVITY

Molly's mom asks her if she wants to paint today. Very excitedly Molly says, "Yes!"

Mom gets a plain piece of white paper from the home office and tapes it to Molly's easel. Then Mom goes and gets a cup with blue paint and a paper towel roll and places them on the easel tray.

"Here you go, Molly," Mom says as she takes the paper towel roll and dips one end of it in the blue paint before handing it to Molly. Molly then begins to bang it on the paper, moving from left to right. "Mommy! Look! I made flowers!" Molly says.

"I love your flowers! They are so blue. Good job," Mom says.

INSIGHT

Mom gives Molly a chance to create any kind of picture she wants using paint. When she is done Mom does not ask Molly "What is it?" but instead waits for Molly to tell her and then praises her.

Dramatic Play >
Imitation Game

Dramatic play involves children taking on assigned roles and acting them out.

This is a time when your child will pretend to be a baker, doctor, or fire fighter with another peer or an adult.

The wonderful aspect of dramatic play is that it is spontaneous. You are able to see how your child perceives herself and the world when you watch her use her imagination to act out different roles and situations. Often your child will create a scene that is familiar or imitate family members. Let her have fun!

Dramatic play is a form of free play for your child to express herself. It is one of the most personal, individualistic, and intimate learning experiences your child can engage in because through dramatic play your child can explore the world by taking on the role of someone else or work through her feelings by recreating a familiar situation.

Overall, it is important to encourage your child to participate in dramatic play because it offers a wide range of opportunities for two year olds to use and expand their cognitive, language, literacy, memory, and social skills.

ACTIVITY

Clara goes for a walk with her mom in the morning after dropping off her older brother. During the walk, Mom and Clara see a crossing guard with a stop sign in her hand. The crossing guard holds up the stop sign, and together Mom and Clara cross the street safely.

When Clara gets home, Mom hears her yell "Stop!" She goes to Clara's room and notices that Clara has lined up all her dolls and is having them cross the road after she says "Stop!" to imaginary cars.

INSIGHT

 Clara creates a play experience that is familiar to her and acts it out using her dolls and an imaginary stop sign and vehicles. This is an example of an everyday activity blossoming into a dramatic play opportunity.

5. Physical Development

> **Physical development in two year olds includes gross motor, fine motor, and sensory motor experiences.**

A motor skill is defined as a physical capability.

You have probably already noticed your child has become more coordinated in his gross motor (large muscle) movements. Not only has he developed a much smoother, heel-to-toe form of walking, but he is also able to maneuver around corners, walk backward, and avoid running into things.

In addition, your child is combining his senses to engage in more complex sensory motor skills like kicking a ball and walking up and down steps; however, even though your child is displaying more coordinated movements, it is important to remember that his judgment and self-control are still lagging when it comes to testing his physical limits, both indoors and outside.

Fine motor skills usually take more time to develop than gross motor skills as they require more hand-eye coordination and concentration. Your two year old is still building the attention skills he needs to develop fine motor skills such as tracing and writing.

This year you will see your child engaging in fine motor movements such as grasping, reaching, releasing, and turning his wrist. He will become interested in building with blocks, turning doorknobs, and turning the pages of a book.

WHOLE CHILD: AGE TWO
Physical
Development Components

These fine motor movements will also play a part in your child building his independence through developing more self-help skills such as getting undressed and washing his hands.

Because fine motor skills take longer and are harder to develop, it is important to provide a wide variety of opportunities for two year olds to enhance their fine motor development.

So even though your child's physical growth has started to slow down this year compared to when he was an infant, you will see him continue to make tremendous strides in his physical development.

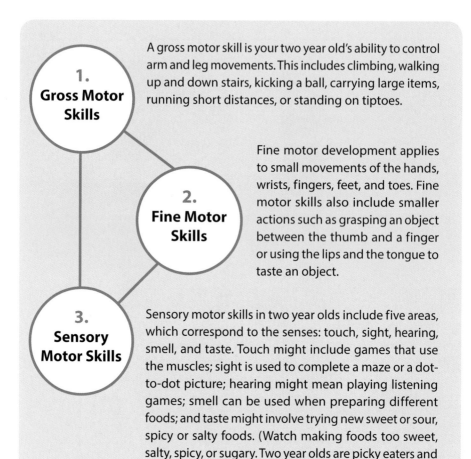

1. Gross Motor Skills

A gross motor skill is your two year old's ability to control arm and leg movements. This includes climbing, walking up and down stairs, kicking a ball, carrying large items, running short distances, or standing on tiptoes.

2. Fine Motor Skills

Fine motor development applies to small movements of the hands, wrists, fingers, feet, and toes. Fine motor skills also include smaller actions such as grasping an object between the thumb and a finger or using the lips and the tongue to taste an object.

3. Sensory Motor Skills

Sensory motor skills in two year olds include five areas, which correspond to the senses: touch, sight, hearing, smell, and taste. Touch might include games that use the muscles; sight is used to complete a maze or a dot-to-dot picture; hearing might mean playing listening games; smell can be used when preparing different foods; and taste might involve trying new sweet or sour, spicy or salty foods. (Watch making foods too sweet, salty, spicy, or sugary. Two year olds are picky eaters and will reject flavors that are too strong.)

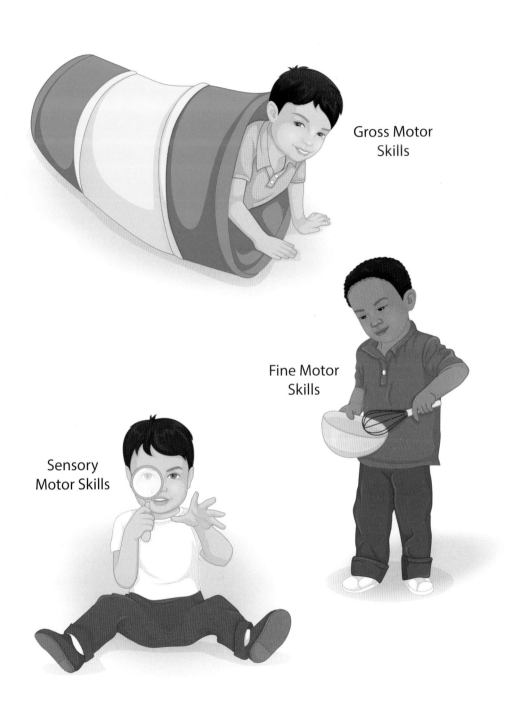

Gross Motor
Skills

Fine Motor
Skills

Sensory
Motor Skills

Gross Motor Skills >
Large Muscles

Gross motor skills are the larger movements your child makes with her arms, legs, feet, or her entire body.

ACTIVITY

 Mom and her daughter Morgan are getting ready to have lunch. Mom thinks it would be nice to play a game of Row, Row, Row Your Boat since they read the book earlier that day. Mom tells Morgan to sit so that they are facing each other, and they hold hands. They then begin to rock back and forth and sing the song "Row, Row, Row Your Boat." They start off slowly and then speed up, pretending that the boat has hit rocky seas.

INSIGHT

Using games to develop gross motor skills is probably the best way to engage your child in physical activities. Games are great for fun bonding, too.

Gross motor activities are movements of the entire body such as the ability to roll over, walk, hop, climb, crawl, and jump. These activities increase blood flow, which feeds the brain.

Movement experiences should be introduced early in life and built upon year after year with classes and team sports.

Guidelines for Everyday Gross Motor Activities

Your child should have at least 30 minutes of structured (adult-lead) physical activity each day. The following activities can be fun for the entire family: taking a walk in the neighborhood or playing T-ball. Activities such as T-ball also help to develop ball skills such as catching, throwing, kicking, and hitting.

Your child should engage in 60 minutes or more of unstructured (free play) physical activity each day and should not be inactive for more than 60 minutes at a time, except when sleeping. If your child is involved in active play at an early age she will stay active and be physically fit in the future.

A great example of unstructured play would be taking your child to the neighborhood park and using the playground equipment. Encourage your child to go on the slide; because she needs to climb up stairs and position her body to sit on the slide so that she does not tip over, she develops balance and strength.

As your child develops, her gross motor skills will go from mastery of simple skills like jumping and crawling to more complex skills like riding a tricycle and standing on one foot.

Fine Motor Skills >

Small Muscles

Fine motor skills refer to the small movements of the hands, wrists, fingers, feet, and toes.

Fine motor activities are built on four basic skills. These skills include releasing objects, grasping for objects, reaching for objects, and turning the wrist in various directions.

To support your child's fine motor skills you should make one of the following activities a part of your weekly activities at home:

* Mold and roll play dough into balls.
* Tear newspaper into strips.
* Squeeze water from a sponge.
* Roll small balls out of tissue paper.
* Sing songs with hand movements.
* Play clapping games.

Releasing

Releasing objects can be seen when your child is building with blocks. In order to build a tower, she has to pick up the block and then stack/release the block on top of another block. This is great for hand-eye coordination, as well as grasping and releasing movements.

Grasping scissors and then releasing them so she can cut paper is also a fine motor skill. Your child's mastery of grasping skills will not completely develop until she is three. Having your two year old pick up a bead (grasp) and place it on the string (release) helps strengthen fine motor muscles that your child will later need to build her writing skills.

Grasping

Grasping objects involves your two year old holding a writing instrument such as a pencil or crayon. Grasping objects can be seen in an activity such as scribbling.

ACTIVITY

 You are working in your home office. While you are writing something, your daughter is scribbling on a piece of paper with crayons. She is so excited to show you how she is "writing" just like you.

INSIGHT

Random scribbles come first, and then circular scribbles begin to emerge.

Reaching Objects

Your child's hand-eye coordination skills have improved as she has gotten older. This has lead to your child being able to have better small muscle control (grasping), which supports her ability to reach and grasp for objects because her hands and arms are working together to complete a task (picking up a ball and holding it or picking up a crayon from the table and grasping it).

Your child is now using her hand and arm together, and both arms are usually used together as well. You will see your two year old demonstrate a hand preference, if that one hand initiates the activity more often than the other. She moves her arm and hand together to get an object that she wants, and she usually starts by using the same arm and hand to reach for the object.

Hand preference is still emerging at this age, so it is not yet firmly established. As a result, your child may frequently reach for objects with alternating hands.

Turning the Wrist

This fine motor skill of turning the wrist involves your child moving his hand in circular motions. Working on this strengthens small muscles, which leads to further development of fine motor skills. Turning of the wrist movement is another fine motor skill that will lead to building strong writing skills as your child approaches age four.

ACTIVITY

 Peter is in the kitchen with his mom watching him. She is watching him make a cake. Peter says, "I want to make a cake!" Mom gives Peter a plastic bowl and a small whisk so that he can "whip" ingredients like she does. Mom says, "Peter, watch how I turn the whisk around and around. Now you try." Peter starts turning his wrist just like Mom. "I did it!" he says.

INSIGHT

Activities that involve your child whisking or scooping will support the strengthening of your child's wrist and support the development of further fine motor skills.

Sensory Motor Skills >
Touchy Feely

Sensory motor
experiences include
activities that combine
sight, touch,
and hearing with
fine and gross motor
movements.

ACTIVITY

 Charlie and his father are at the park playing a game of T-ball, which involves hitting a ball off a stationary tee.

This is a good activity for Charlie to develop his sensory motor skills, because he has to see the ball while swinging the bat in order to make contact between the ball and the bat.

INSIGHT

 In the activity, Dad can point to the ball to direct Charlie about what to hit. Charlie would then know what to look at when it comes to swinging the bat and making contact with the ball. Practicing movements like these leads to mastery over time.

For your two year old to jump up and down on a square, he must see the square and use balance to land on the square. In order for your child to Velcro close his shoes, he must have adequate fine motor skills and be able to use the sense of touch to grab the Velcro and fasten it.

Your child is now seeing obstacles that might cause him to stumble ahead of time, whereas before he might just have tripped. He can now balance, jump, and walk and hold things at the same time. This is because he is now using his vision and attention skills to see what is in front of him and can adjust his movements and balance. Sensory motor skills heighten your child's reflexes and responses because the child is using a combination of senses to be more aware of his environment.

Your child also uses his hearing to follow two- and three-step requests that may involve large muscle movements ("Walk to the trash can and throw away the paper."). He will incorporate his listening and understanding skills to direct his attention to items being named and directions such as "stop" and "go."

Sensory motor skills bring together your child's cognitive skills through attention and reasoning when he uses his visual sense to make contact with items and move more gracefully throughout his environment. Sensory motor skills are part of his growing language skills as he understands and responds to directions. It is important to remember that sight, touch, and hearing must all work together to support development of your child's gross motor skills.

As your child matures, so do his senses and ability to use his senses to improve his motor skills.

Remember, the Whole Child Parenting Program offers appropriate developmental products and monthly activity books that walk you through supporting your child's skills. Using these in conjunction with the recommended age-appropriate room materials ensures faster development.

6. Health and Care

> **Your two year old is more active than ever and is exploring everything around her.**

She is also running, jumping, and working up a sweat! There are a number of tips and care routines you do to help your two year old stay clean, healthy, and happy from head to toe! When it comes to feeling under the weather, your two year old will start letting you know how she feels and point to what hurts. She may point to her tummy if she is constipated or pull on her ear if she has an ear infection. Other times, changes in your child can be an indication that she has a fever or is in pain. Irritability can affect not just her mood but also her schedule. It can also affect her sleeping or eating habits.

Mind and Body

Hygiene

Health Visit

Diet

Potty Training

WHOLE CHILD: AGE TWO

Health and Care

Hygiene > Hair, Eyes, Ears, Skin, Nails, and Tooth Care

Working Together

* Let your child use the comb in her hair or on a doll before combing her hair yourself.

* When in the bath, let your child rub her fingers in the shampoo just like you do. You can let her wash her doll's hair in the tub as well.

* Let your child watch you wash her hair by placing a mirror next to the bathtub.

Hair Care

Your two year old's oil glands on her scalp and body don't become fully functional until puberty, so shampoo only as needed. Once a week is usually plenty.

Brushing

Brushing hair can help bring oils to the surface of the scalp. When trying to get out knots and tangles, try using a detangling spray and a wide-toothed comb or a brush with round-tipped bristles. Start combing or brushing out the ends and then work your way up to the scalp to avoid tugging and pulling.

Curly and Textured Hair

There are a number of products out there for curly and textured hair. **Try a variety of products to see which one fits your child best.** A good product for your child's hair is one that doesn't dry it out or weigh it down. With curly or textured hair, it is also a good idea to keep the hair short, let it air dry, and brush through it with just your hands or a wide-toothed comb only when wet to avoid frizz.

Eye Care

Your child's eyes can still change up to the age of two.

Check your child's eyes regularly to see if:

* your child's eyes are crossed,
* they are sensitive to light,
* one eye is wandering,
* both eyes cannot follow an object as it moves back and forth in front of her.

Conjunctivitis (Pink Eye)

Conjunctivitis has three forms: viral, bacterial, or allergic.

Symptoms usually include:
* watery discharge,
* veiny redness in the white area of an eye,
* itchy and swollen eyes,
* stringy discharge that causes eyelids to stick together, especially after sleeping.

Viral and bacterial conjunctivitis are contagious and usually occur from an upper respiratory tract infection, sore throat, or cold.

Conjunctivitis requires a doctor; you will need a prescription for antibiotic drops or ointments.

Allergic conjunctivitis is not contagious and is usually connected to seasonal allergies, irritation, or intolerance to medication or anything topical that is put on the face and comes in contact with your child's eyes. A cold compress can also relieve discomfort.

Ear Care

At bath time, clean the outside crevices of your child's ear with a damp, soft cloth.

DO NOT probe the inside of the ear. The middle ear is not fully developed, and you could end up puncturing the eardrum or pushing wax farther into your child's ear.

Ear Infections

Ear infections are most common in the middle ear. Until the age of three, the Eustachian tube that connects the outer and inner ear has not yet fully developed or grown. Because it is so small, the Eustachian tube gets clogged after a child has a cold.

Signs that your child has an ear infection may be pulling on her ear or seeing drainage come from her ear.

Skin Care

Dry skin can occur due to the weather as well as dehydration.

When caring for your child's skin:

* Try cutting back on bath time and sticking to 10-minute baths.
* Use a moisturizer on your two year old's body as soon as he gets out of the bath, before all the moisture in the skin evaporates.
* Have your two year old drink more fluids.
* Add more fatty foods to his diet such as avocados, flax seed, and olive oil.

When cleaning dry skin:

* Pat down skin and make sure not to wipe rough, chapped skin (especially face and cheeks).
* Use warm water (avoid hot water).
* Use an alcohol- and perfume-free moisturizer.
* Apply sunscreen when going outside because your child's sensitive skin can burn easily, causing his cheeks to be dry and predisposing him to skin cancer later in life.

Nail Care

Your two year old is constantly playing and exploring, so it is not uncommon for him to get play dough, food, or dirt in his fingernails. Try to keep your child's fingernails short so that they collect the least amount of dirt. **Wash your two year old's hands frequently, especially after activities or outside time.** You can use a nail brush or toothbrush to help clean under your two year old's fingernails.

Trimming

Trim your two year old's fingernails after getting out of the bath. The water softens the nails, making them easier to trim and cut. Sing a counting song or count the fingers to keep your child engaged and patient while you finish.

Tooth Care

Try to get your child in the habit of brushing her teeth as more teeth start to come in. Get a small-head toothbrush with soft, round bristles and brush your two year old's teeth gently in a circular motion along the sides and along the outer gum lines.

Brushing can help clean any food stuck in teeth and massage your two year old's gums while she is teething. Let her brush her own teeth for a little while before you take over.

Skip toothpaste until your child masters spitting out the toothpaste.

Teach your child to rinse by leaning over the sink and spitting. **Have your child say words like** *nuts* **or** *tooth* **to help her spit into the sink.**

Diet and your child's teeth:

Diet plays a key role in your child having healthy teeth. It is important to have her rinse her mouth out after eating or snacking. This is why brushing at night time is the most important!

Here are a few tips for snacking and mealtime:

* Snacks and meals should be served around the same time each day.

* Limit snacks in between meals. One reason is because you want your child to be hungry for mealtime. The other is because frequent snacking without brushing immediately afterward leads to plaque and tooth decay.

* When your child does snack include food that will help support healthy teeth. For example, raw broccoli, low-fat yogurt, or fruits like pear and melon cut into bite-size pieces.

* Remember to choose foods with low sugar content. Try to avoid processed foods whenever possible.

Diet >
Calories, Picky Eaters, Allergies, and Tummy Troubles

Two year olds need:

* 5 ounces of grains (one slice of bread or ½ cup of cooked rice or pasta),
* 1 ½ cups of fruits (¾ cups juice, ½ cup canned fruit, ¼ cup dried fruit, 1 piece of fruit or melon wedge),
* 1 ½ cups of vegetables (½ cup chopped raw or cooked vegetables, 1 cup raw leafy greens),
* 2 cups of milk or other dairy products,
* 2–4 ounces of high-protein foods (meat, poultry, eggs, and legumes)—1 ounce meat, 1 egg, ¼ cup legumes such as beans, 2 tablespoons of peanut butter,
* 3–4 teaspoons of healthy oils such as canola oil, olive oil, or tub margarine,
* Fats and sweets are empty calories and should be avoided.

Calories

Two-year old boys and girls need an average of 1,000 calories each day for healthy weight maintenance.

Based on the activity level of each child, two year olds may need more or less than the average. The more active the child, the more calories she will need.

* The food quantity averages to the left refer to two year olds who engage in 30–60 minutes of physical activity per day.

Calculate how many calories your two year old needs.

The average child needs 34–41 calories per pound of body weight each day.

Picky Eaters?

Offer your opinionated two year old two healthful options so she feels like she is more in control. Put small portions on her plate at first so she does not feel overwhelmed and then add more food after she finishes the first serving.

Adding dipping sauces or encouraging your two year old to be a part of making the meal can make her more excited about eating (let her assemble the sandwich or spread peanut butter and place raisins on celery for ants on a log).

Two year olds are becoming more social, so sit down for lunch or other mealtimes with your child. Moving from a highchair to a booster seat encourages more socializing. In addition, by sitting your child closer to you at the table, you can model how to use utensils and how to act at the table.

Utensils

Two year olds should be moving toward using utensils such as a spoon and cup. Nonskid plates and bowls help your two year old scoop food into her spoon. Cut up her foods into small, bite-size pieces so that she can easily go from spoon or fork to mouth.

Allergies

With the introduction of more varieties of food, some two year olds begin to develop allergies. Indications of allergies include sneezing, itching, swelling, and skin rashes.

Food allergies are usually quite rare and follow family genetics. If you have a food allergy that runs in your family, be careful when giving your child that food.

Food allergies in young children can go away with age.

Hay fever can occur with environmental or seasonal allergies when your child is allergic to pollen, grass, dust, or animal dander. Symptoms include watery eyes, sneezing, and a runny nose.

Because two year olds cannot yet blow their noses to clear their nasal passages, mucus drips down their throats, causing them to cough.

Tummy Troubles

Your two year old's digestive system is starting to change because your child is having more consistent bowel movements, and new textures of foods are being introduced. Your child may complain about stomach pain if he has to go to the bathroom and isn't yet in control of the feeling or is feeling emotionally stressed and can't put together the words to tell you. **Most complaints about stomachaches with two year olds are minor and can be helped by giving your child something to eat or having him try to go potty.** If his stomach pain is accompanied by a fever or vomiting, he may be sick.

Constipation

Constipation is not always a sign of illness but can make your child uncomfortable. Constipation is usually accompanied by hard or painful stools.

What to do:

* Increase fluid intake: Give your child more water to drink.
* Diet: Make sure you are giving your child correct portion sizes when it comes to food, and also change the variety of foods you serve. Provide more fruits and vegetables.
* Try prunes, dried fruits (raisins and apricots), oatmeal, or green vegetables.
* Stay away from cow's milk, yogurt, cheese, cooked carrots, and bananas when constipated.

Diarrhea

Diarrhea is the opposite of constipation and involves very loose or too many bowel movements. Diarrhea can cause your child pain as well as make him become dehydrated and lethargic. Diarrhea can be caused by a virus or contaminated food or can be a side effect of medication.

If diarrhea starts quickly but ends by the next meal your child eats and isn't accompanied by fever, you probably should not be concerned.

What to do:

* Try bananas, white toast, white rice, and electrolytes to drink (such as Pedialyte®).
* Avoid drinks with sugar like soda or ginger ale because the sugar in the drinks may upset your child's stomach.

If his stomach pain is accompanied by a fever or vomiting, he may be sick.

Vomiting

Vomiting is usually the result of a virus caused by bacteria or a parasite. It can sometimes be followed by diarrhea.

Vomiting can also cause dehydration. Signs of dehydration include:

* not urinating,
* dry lips and mouth,
* looking pale.

What to do:

If your child is having trouble holding down liquids or food, try to rehydrate him with an oral rehydration solution.

Examples of oral rehydration solutions include:

* water,
* Pedialyte®,
* watered-down juice,
* chicken broth.

When administering oral rehydration solutions:

1. Give your child only a teaspoon of fluid every five minutes to help him keep it down.

2. If your child is able to keep down the liquid, keep increasing the amount of fluid you give him.

3. Keep giving your child fluids until he stops vomiting.

4. If your child is ready to eat again, try to stick to these foods:

* dry toast,
* small amount of pasta (no sauce),
* hard-boiled egg,
* rice,
* bananas.

Potty Training >
Are We Ready?

Eighteen months to three years old is the average age to show interest in and start trying to potty train.
Your child may be ready to begin potty training if your child:

* begins to communicate having a dirty diaper—your child may verbally tell you or draw your attention to his diaper by patting it or pointing to it;

* begins to show discomfort when wet or soiled—walking in a wide stride or beginning to pull and take off his soiled diaper;

* shows interest in the potty— models potty training with toys, dolls, or even themselves;

* demonstrates independence— starting to pull his pants on and off, follows basic one- and two-step directions;

* is able to stay dry for up to two hours between diaper changes— shows that the bladder is maturing and is able to hold it in longer;

* starts to have regular bowel movements at the same time every day.

Ready to Start?

* Stay close to home.

* Try no underpants or underwear.

* Try to encourage the most tries as possible so your child can get used to the feeling of going.

* Use a timer to teach the feeling of going regularly.

* Give your child salty snacks to make him thirsty or let him have a special juice he likes.

* Have all materials present at the potty (toilet paper, underwear or pullup, clean clothing).

* Let him bring his favorite toy, doll, or stuffed animal to model potty training.

> **Verbal Praise:**
>
> Be excited about your child using the potty!
>
> * Sing a song, do a dance, clap your hands, and tell her with a smile you are proud of her.
>
> * Don't be upset or annoyed when she has an accident. Remind her that pee and poo go in the potty. Have her help you clean up, do laundry, or get clean clothes together.

Follow Through

Potty on the go

Invest in a travel potty to encourage consistency. It is important to keep up with your routine even when at Grandma's house, with your baby-sitter, or at school.

* The more days you get into potty training, the more consistent your child's potty times will become. Having a routine with nap and eating times adds to the consistency. **Routine allows you to be able to know times to encourage your child to try if she has not expressed to you herself that she has to go.**

* Have all your materials with you, such as wipes, clean underwear, and plastic bags for soiled clothes.

Potty time doesn't mean missing play time!

Don't make your child feel like going potty means she is missing out on an activity or other interesting or exciting things going on.

* Move the potty to the activity. If everyone is outside, let your child use the potty while she is outside so she doesn't put up a fight to leave because she feels like she is missing out.

* Encourage your child to try before you start an activity or before you go somewhere. Have your child try before lunch and after lunch, as well as before you start a game or put out different toys.

Potty training tips for help along the journey:

* Every 15 minutes, put your child on the potty, then put back on the diaper or pullups for three days. On the third day, have an all-day no diaper or pullup session.

* Have naked time; let your child wear nothing so that your child has to put the pee and poop somewhere.

* Give rewards such as stickers for the first full day in underwear.

* Make sure you read (see to the right) the differences in potty training boys and girls.

* Be proactive when you go out or drop your child at a neighbor's house. Bring a portable potty chair with you and encourage your child to ask to use it when she needs to.

Things That Come With Time . . .

Pooping on the potty usually takes children a little longer to master because it involves having to push out their poop, and that can take some getting used to and definitely requires a longer time sitting on the potty.

When you start to see a pattern as to what time of the day your child has a bowel movement, try to plan your schedule around that time so that she is more encouraged to try on a regular basis. For example, if your child usually poops about half an hour after lunch, plan a short activity or extend cleanup time and then have her sit down and try. That way, she won't get too busy with another activity and try to speed through potty time.

Encourage your child to keep trying. Charts with stickers are a great way for your child to be proud of all the times she sat on the potty.

Boys vs. Girls

Have girls sit farther back on the potty with their knees apart. This will relax their muscles as well as make them more comfortable if they end up sitting and trying for a few extra minutes. Adding a stepstool for her when she gets older and is sitting on the toilet can help her relax, too.

Boys will start using the potty while sitting down so that they can focus more on the feeling of having to urinate and take the pressure off learning to aim. When they are ready to urinate standing up, it may be a good idea to get a stepstool for your toilet to make it easier on him.

Finding something flushable for boys to aim at will help. Gummy bears or mints work great and can be an incentive as well. If he aims at the gummy bear in the toilet, then he can have a fresh one to eat when he is done.

Remember: Every child is different. Do not force your child into potty training. If your child doesn't show an interest right away or puts up a fight, try again in a couple of months.

Health Visit >
What to Expect During a Wellness Visit

The well-child visits during your child's second year are similar to those you had when she was younger, though now you can expect to have deeper discussions with your doctor about behavior and habits.

Fevers

Once your child is two, you can take your child's temperature via the axillary method (underarm) or orally (mouth). To help your child keep a thermometer in long enough to get an accurate temperature, try holding a timer your child can watch or hold a thermometer under your armpit or in your mouth at the same time.

Underarm:
96° F to 99° F is a normal temperature; 99.6° F and up means a fever is present.

Mouth:
96° F to 99° F is a normal temperature; 99.4° F and up means a fever is present.

Eighty to ninety percent of all fevers in young children are related to self-limiting infections (these infections get better without treatment).

Unless a fever rises above 102° F, try these methods of treatment:

* Increase fluids: Fevers can occur if your child is dehydrated.

* Cool down: You don't want to overheat your child, so cool her down by having her wear fewer layers and bring in a fan. Make sure your child is comfortable and not too cold.

* Slow down: Discourage running around or heavy activity that can increase temperature.

Common Cold

Colds are also known as upper respiratory disorders and are usually caused by rhinoviruses, which spread from hand to hand. The duration of a cold is usually seven to ten days, although some symptoms, such as a cough or runny nose, can linger longer.

The average child gets six to eight colds per year.

Symptoms of a cold:

* runny nose
* nasal congestion
* sneezing
* dry cough
* fatigue
* crankiness
* loss of appetite
* a mild fever
* sore, scratchy throat

Treatments for a cold:

* plenty of warm fluids and vitamin C-enriched foods,

* humidifiers to help clear nasal passages,

* saline solutions to soften dry mucus that clogs your child's nostrils.

To help prevent a cold: wash hands, disinfect toys, and clean surfaces on a regular basis to get rid of germs.

Your child's checkup will include:

* a complete physical examination;

* measurement of your child's length, weight, and head circumference; growth will be plotted on a growth chart;

* a review of your two year old's development through simple observation. How is she walking: on tiptoes or flat feet? Is she combining two words? The doctor may ask you these questions and others like them;

* safety questions such as asking if your child is in an age-appropriate car seat;

* a discussion of your child's eating habits. Is she eating a variety of foods? Using a spoon? Using a cup? Weaned from the pacifier?;

* advice on what to expect in the coming year;

* immunizations;

* discussion between you and the doctor. Talk about any questions or concerns you have, and write down any specific instructions the doctor gives you regarding special care. Keep updating your child's permanent medical record, listing information on growth and any problems or illnesses.

Immunizations

Most doctors schedule your child's two-year-old visit on your child's actual two-year-old birthday. Your doctor will weigh and measure your child as well as ask you questions about your child's development and overall health.

Your doctor will discuss your child's eating habits as well as examine your child's teeth for tooth decay, abnormal tooth development, or other problems and recommend visiting a dentist no later than your child's third birthday.

The two-year-old checkup includes a number of screenings and required immunizations.

You child will be screened for anemia, lead poisoning, tuberculosis, and high cholesterol.

Lastly, your doctor will talk to you about other safety issues such as wearing helmets when riding bikes or scooters or skating and how to stay germ free.

The immunization chart on the next page can give you an idea of the ones required early in life.

Well-child visits with a pediatrician are yearly routines that will continue through the adolescent years.

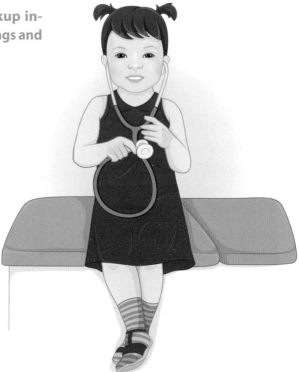

Recommended immunizations by age two:

Age	Birth	2 months	4 months	6 months	12–18 months	19–24 months
HepB Hepatitis B	✓	✓	✓	✓		
DTap Diphtheria, Tetanus, Pertussiss		✓	✓	✓	✓	✓
HiB Haemophilius Influenzae Type B		✓	✓	✓	✓	
Polio		✓	✓	✓		
PCV Pneumo- coccal Conjugate		✓	✓	✓	✓	
RV Rotavirus		✓	✓	✓		
MMR Measles, Mumps, Rubella					✓	✓
VAR Varicella					✓	✓
HepA Hepatitus A					✓	
HPV Human Pappiloma- virus						
MCV4 Meningo- coccal Conjugate						
In Influenza				✓		✓

Mind and Body >
Yoga

Having two year olds participate in yoga gives them the ability to exercise both their bodies and minds.

Yoga encompasses the whole child by strengthening bodies and calming minds to encourage better focus and build self-confidence. Through yoga, children are able to develop and foster more than just physical skills.

Yoga helps your two year old develop social-emotional skills such as self-awareness.

Physically, your two year old is developing more body awareness through yoga by testing and pushing her balancing and physical capabilities. She is able to become more confident and have higher self-esteem when it comes to movement and mobility.

Yoga is a great tool to build creativity and imagination. Your child can express herself through different movements. As a parent, you can incorporate different music, relatable animal or nature poses, and dance. Because your child is young, you will have to show her how to do each movement.

1. Three-Legged Dog Pose

Step both feet together so your big toes are touching. Bend over and put your hands flat on the floor in front of you. Shift your weight onto your hands and your left foot, then raise your right leg into the air. Then lower your right leg and switch sides.

2. Frog Pose

Bend your knees and sit down. Place your palms on the ground, but make sure your knees don't touch. Move your heels upward and put a little pressure on your toes. Slowly, put your heels on the floor and stand up.

3. Reverse Warrior Pose

With the right knee bent, drop left hand down to rest on left leg. Then reach right arm up toward the ceiling on an inhale. Keep right knee bent and press firmly into feet, keeping legs strong. When you feel solid, begin sinking hips down. Check to make sure shoulders are soft. Hold the pose for up to five breaths, and repeat it on the other side.

1. Three-Legged Dog Pose

2. Frog Pose

3. Reverse Warrior Pose

**Remember,
the Whole Child
Parenting Program**
offers appropriate developmental
products and monthly activity books
that walk you through supporting
your child's skills. Using these in
conjunction with the recommended
age-appropriate room
materials ensures faster
development.

Reaching Milestones >

Your child is two years old, now ranging in age from 24–36 months. At this age your child will develop very quickly and will develop most of these skills as he approaches the age of three. Now, as a two year old, his learning process has become more thoughtful. He's beginning to form mental images for objects, actions, and concepts. He also can solve some problems in his head, performing mental trial and error.

Now is a great time to get in the habit of checking your child's progress on a more frequent basis. You can do this twice a year or every three months. Time passes quickly and you can miss progress in the blink of an eye.

The information below is a guide to explain some of the developmental milestones an average two year old will achieve. Theses skills may not all occur in order; skills can occur within a six-month to a year range. Consider what you read in the context of your child's unique development.

COGNITIVE

- Places large puzzle pieces in appropriate empty spaces.
- Can sort shapes, complete puzzles with eight pieces or less, and stack a set of rings on a peg by size.
- Will begin to recognize the purpose of numbers in counting objects—especially the number two.
- Can solve simple problems with the "trial and error" method and will practice an activity many times to master it. Becomes much more interested in winding up toys and turning lights and appliances on and off.
- Recognizes patterns with daily activities and understands concepts like "tomorrow" and "yesterday."
- Spends about two minutes on a single activity. The usual preference is for almost constant attention from an adult. With or near a small group of children, can play peacefully for 10 minutes.

SOCIAL-EMOTIONAL

- Enjoys playing alongside other children, usually will keep to himself.
- He is more independent and can do things for himself (e.g. pour milk, dress himself in simple clothes).
- Begins to label feelings that he recognizes in himself and others. Controlling emotion is difficult, so frustrations may trigger emotional meltdowns.
- New fears—the dark, monsters, and people in costumes—will emerge. He does not really know the difference between fantasy and reality. Comfort objects like blankets or a teddy bear will be desired.
- Conflicts will require adults to step in to prevent aggression.

LANGUAGE

- Enjoys having books read to him and will pretend to "read" as he independently looks through familiar books.

- New language discoveries will lead to him picking up most parts of speech to form more complete sentences. Can understand and say hundreds of words.

- Makes a variety of scribble marks anywhere and everywhere and may attempt to write the first letter in his name in this scribble pattern.

- Sings A-B-C song.

- Understands simple directions and many common phrases used in routine situations.

CREATIVE

- Can make sounds by banging and shaking instruments and household items.

- Might substitute one object for another in play, like using Legos® to represent food in a mealtime scene. Acts out chants and simple songs.

- Draws a face (no arms and legs). Enjoys sensory pleasures of the art materials you provide and focuses on the process of creating art.

- Gains more control over his voice and joins in singing the refrains of favorite songs.

PHYSICAL

- May be able to ride a tricycle forward using the pedals and steer it around corners.

- Can kick a small ball forward, catch a rolled ball, and throw a ball overhand (with little accuracy).

- Can stand on one foot for a few seconds. Has learned to go up and down the stairs with only one foot on each step. Stands on tiptoes.

- Carries large toys or several toys while walking.

- Turns doorknobs, unscrews lids, and has improved his skills in using utensils.

HEALTH AND CARE

- Points to body parts.

- Helps with undressing and dressing, puts feet in shoes and arms in sleeves.

- Learns to use toilet.

- Feeds self with spoon.

Environment >
Two Year Old's Room

"Help me do it by myself" is probably the most important concept to keep in mind for your two year old.

It is important to intentionally create an environment that will help her learn and gain as much independence as possible. There's no better place to do this than in your home.

Your home is already a rich environment full of learning opportunities. We will help you set up practical activities that will tap into her natural curiosity and support her ability to test the world around her.

This can best be achieved by designing a space with materials and toys that stimulate thinking, creativity, and support all **six areas of development: cognitive, language, social emotional, creative, physical, and health.**

The goal is for your child to have an area in her room that is well organized using your **Six Drawer Whole Child Color-Coded Organizer.**

You are creating a space that's free from clutter, multi-functional, and efficient. At right is a sample of a two year old's room with must-have items for optimal learning.

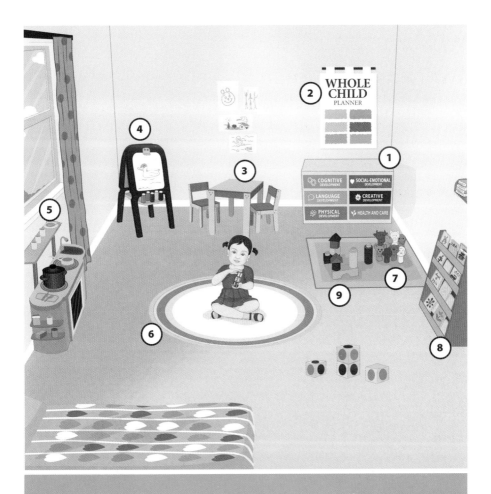

Whole Child: Two Year Old's Room

The following list contains must-have items for your two year old's room. These items will be used interchangeably with your other Whole Child Parenting materials.

1. Six Drawer Whole Child Color-Coded Organizer
2. Whole Child Wall Planner
3. Table and Chairs
4. Easel
5. Kitchen Set
6. Carpet
7. Puppet/Pretend Play Materials
8. Bookshelf
9. Blocks and Manipulatives

three >

Milestones for a Three Year Old

 **COGNITIVE** 1

- Names some colors
- Understands the concept of counting
- Recognizes some numbers and letters
- Develops a sense of time

 **SOCIAL-EMOTIONAL** 2

- Acts more independent
- Plays with other children
- Develops empathy for others

 LANGUAGE 3

- Speaks in five- to six-word sentences
- Tells stories
- Asks questions

 **CREATIVE** 4

- Draws a person with two to four body parts
- Engages in pretend play with peers

 PHYSICAL 5

- Moves forward and backward
- Stands on one foot for five seconds
- Kicks ball forward
- Copies and traces shapes

 HEALTH AND CARE 6

- Gains independence with brushing teeth
- Develops daily routines
- Exhibits preschool readiness

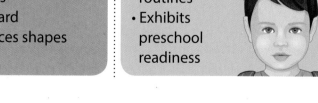

three

At three years old, children have better control of their emotions and begin problem solving and thinking of solutions to their problems instead of acting out by hitting or screaming. They are developing a better sense of time and a clearer understanding of their daily routine. Because of this, three year olds are able to become more independent with personal care routines such as dressing and undressing themselves and washing their own hands. Three is a big year.

1. Cognitive Development

> **Cognitive development skills enable your child to process information, reason through problems, and develop language and memory.**

Cognitive development is the building of thinking methods, which includes how your child will remember, problem solve, and make decisions from now and into adulthood.

Three year olds are able to sit and focus for longer periods of time, which enables them to take in more information. They also ask a lot of questions and are very inquisitive.

During cognitive development, children will grasp language, persevere through problems (like puzzles), ask a lot of questions (about things they see or hear), and remember past and upcoming events.

Remember, your child will develop at his own pace; however, there are still typical cognitive goals he must achieve during this age in order to be developing on track.

The following chart provides you with an image that walks you through the stages of your child's intellectual development.

Understanding these areas of cognitive development will help you learn how your child thinks, how to support learning, and how to teach new skills.

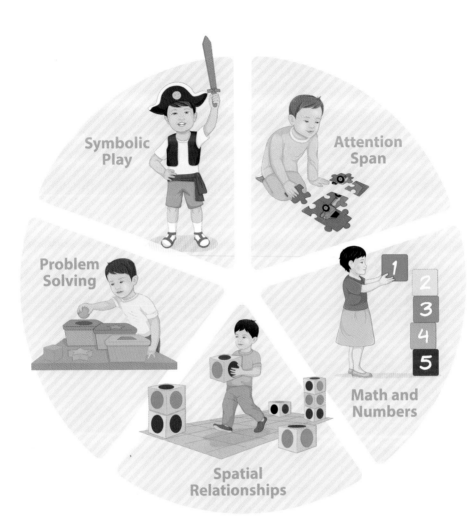

WHOLE CHILD: AGE THREE
Cognitive
Development Components

Attention Span >
Stimulate My Brain

Attention span refers to the amount of time your child is able to concentrate on or focus on a single activity.

Supporting the development of your child's attention skills, along with his self-regulation skills, will form his foundation for learning. Strong attention skills will set the stage for your child to have success in everything from learning math to his social relationships. In addition, strong attention skills can help your child learn to read before age five, have improved memory, and achieve a host of other amazing milestones.

ACTIVITY

 Gabe wants to have a friend over for a play date. Mom agrees to have one friend come over. Mom says to Gabe, "Your friend is coming over. What should we do?" Gabe says, "A dance party! We love to dance. Look at me move." Mom thinks for a moment and says, "Okay! Dance party it is. You have to help me get things ready." Gabe says, "I'll get the music!" Gabe goes to his parents' room and grabs Mom's guitar for her. "Here you go, Mom!"

Gabe's friend arrives with her mom, and they go downstairs to have fun. In the beginning the children are talking and playing. Gabe's mom says, "It's time for a dance party!" Gabe and his friend scream "Yeah!" and jump up and down.

Mom tells the children, "For the first part of our dance party you can dance until the music stops. When the music stops you should stop dancing." Mom begins to play her guitar. After a few short minutes she stops and starts it again. After doing this several times, Gabe's mom says, "Now I want you to listen for me to strum the guitar fast. When you hear me stop you should stop dancing and listen." Gabe and his friend dance and stop for 30 seconds then dance again until they are all danced out. Gabe's friend says, "That was so fun, Gabe! Can I come to your house again?"

INSIGHT

Through this activity Mom gives the children an opportunity to practice attention skills, especially when she asks them to listen for the guitar playing. Mom also helps the children develop attention skills because this activity allows both children to actively participate as opposed to passively listen during the entire activity.

Help build attention span

1. Speak a language of attention—Attention is a set of three skills: focus, awareness, and a set of mental skills that helps your child get things done, e.g. planning and decision making. Play Spot the Letter on a car ride. As you drive, call out a letter for your child to spot along the way, choosing easy to see objects like a stop sign for the letter S.

2. Focus on one another—A meeting of the minds comes from focusing on something together. Set the table for dinner together with your child.

3. White space, also known as uninterrupted time—Put an end to distractions to support developing attention skills in your child and provide a space for him to focus. Limit TV time, video games, and other electronics.

4. Eat mindfully—You may have noticed we are a society that eats on the run. Take time to stop and eat as a family, talking together about the food you are eating, how it smells, looks, and tastes.

Typically, your child will have the most difficulty with paying attention during activities that involve sitting and listening. This is normal behavior, and it occurs because at this age your child will become bored very easily and needs a variety of activities to stimulate his whole brain.

Your child's left side of the brain, which deals directly with logic, language, critical thinking, numbers, and reasoning can be referred to as the "seat of learning;" it is eager to take on new information. Provide lots of simple brain-stimulating activities so that your child can learn and develop his attention span.

Your three year old has a limited attention span. Build up attention skills over time. Do an activity for a minute, and then later do the same activity for a few minutes longer.

Over the next week, do at least two of the listed activities in the box to the left with your child. Start doing the activity every three days and then build up to every day. Building your child's attention span takes time and encouragement, and development must continue well into adolescence.

The quantity, quality, and consistency of stimulation you provide through experiences with your child will play a part in the developing structure of his brain and its capacity. By strengthening your child's brain, you will improve his ability to focus and pay attention to any task that he becomes involved in.

Remember, the Whole Child Parenting Program offers appropriate developmental products and monthly activity books that walk you through supporting your child's skills. Using these in conjunction with the recommended age-appropriate room materials ensures faster development.

Math and Numbers >
I Spy with My Eyes

Math and number awareness involves your child counting, recognizing numbers and patterns, learning one-to-one correspondence, sorting, and classifying.

ACTIVITY

Adam is on the floor of his bedroom playing with a variety of toys he has taken out of his toy box. He discovers a few rocks of different sizes, a plastic frog, and a plastic tree branch.

Mom comes in his bedroom and says, "Adam, you're so quiet. What do you have?" He replies, "Look at all this stuff I found in my toy chest!" Mom replies, "Oh, wow! Look at this rock. It has all of these light colored lines on it." "Let me see," says Adam.

Mom asks, "Why don't we see how many other rocks we can find that look just like this rock here and count them?"

INSIGHT

Adam's experience playing with a collection of rocks is a powerful math experience. As he learns to match the rocks he is learning concepts of math through play and hands-on experience. Mom supports her son by asking him to pay attention, notice how the rocks are the same, and group them in like categories. Mom also extends the learning experience by the two of them counting out how many rocks they have that look the same. Using simple materials and bonding together creates a meaningful math experience.

Mathematical thinking involves seeing how your child uses his brain to play with the concepts of parts and wholes and his ability to see math in everyday life.

Mathematical thinking is important for three reasons: it is a necessary skill to master in your child's schooling experience; it is a way of learning mathematics itself; and it helps your child in solving problems later in life.

One of the best ways to build early mathematical thinking skills in your child is to make numbers and math concepts fun and relatable to the everyday experiences he has. This will increase his desire to learn more and have an appreciation for math in the future.

Early math concepts appropriate for your child include shape sorting, matching games (putting one part with another part), color sorting, and simply playing with collections of things (seeing math in everyday life).

In this next example, you get a glimpse of how Maria is on her way to becoming a mathematician by interacting with ants. Learning about numbers is one of the first steps to your child becoming a mathematical thinker. She will become a mathematician through counting, number recognition, and one-to-one correspondence activities.

ACTIVITY

Maria is in her backyard kicking around a new ball Mom just bought her, when she accidentally kicks the ball in the area of the garbage cans. Maria runs over to get the ball and stops in her tracks, staring down at the ground. There are a bunch of ants in a line.

Maria runs inside to tell her dad. "Dad, come see the ants!" Maria grabs Dad's hand and heads toward the backyard. While she is walking with her dad, she begins to sing. "The ants go marching one by one, hurrah, hurrah. The ants go marching two by two, hurrah, hurrah."

Maria bends down to look at the ants on the ground and pulls Dad down with her. She tries to count the ants but they are just too small and numerous to count.

INSIGHT

Even though Maria cannot point to and count each ant on the ground, she is singing about numbers and uses simple counting while she sings the song and marches. This is counting using a **math rhyme**. It is simple and fun and happens through an everyday experience. You see how fun math can be for your child, and you have the distinct pleasure of being a part of the process!

Spatial Relationships >
The Genius of Seeing

Spatial relationships are related to how your child can maintain her body in connection to the surrounding environment when she is at rest and during movement.

ACTIVITY

Aubrey and her parents have just come back from the theater. Aubrey is so excited to get into the house because Grandpa is back from his fishing trip. She jumps out of the car and runs into the house and into the kitchen. Aubrey does not notice that the kitchen chair by the wall is going to be in her way and runs right into it, stubbing her toe.

INSIGHT

Aubrey is unable to navigate and avoid the contact with the chair either because she doesn't see it, or because she doesn't realize just how big she is and that she cannot fit in between the chair and the wall without moving the movable object. Aubrey's spatial relationships skills are still developing.

Understanding spatial relationships is a required skill for your child to have as she learns to navigate through life.

When your child has the ability to understand her position (where the body is) in relation to things around her, then she can avoid obstacles. Your child's brain has to consistently think about where everything is, especially her own body.

Spatial relationship skills will continue to develop naturally over time as you support your child's skill building. Your child will also increase this skill through making more observations of where things are in her environment. Help her out by making obstacle courses at home with sheets and chairs. Also play Hide and Seek with your child; you'll both have a good time.

Problem Solving >
Independent Thinking

Problem solving refers to your child's ability to use the knowledge and information she has already acquired to find answers to difficult or complicated issues that are occurring now.

ACTIVITY

Three-year-old Elizabeth is trying to stack all of the blocks she got from her birthday, but they keep falling over. She wants to make a tower that is taller than she is. She remembers watching her older brother make a really tall tower yesterday. Fascinated with the idea of doing the same things her brother does, Elizabeth decides to solve her problem by imitating what she saw her brother do.

Elizabeth begins by putting the larger block on the bottom, and then she continues by stacking the blocks one on top of the other. She makes sure that the blocks are a bit staggered as opposed to lined up the same exact way. She smiles and says, "It's working, they are not falling over!"

INSIGHT

 Through this simple experience Elizabeth finds a solution to her problem by remembering back to something she has seen her brother do, and then applying her problem-solving skills to come up with a solution to keep the blocks from falling over. When parents or siblings see a child engage in problem solving skills, it is very important to provide encouragement and praise for the efforts they are making to think independently and make decisions for themselves when and where appropriate.

Every day your child takes in new information and then tests that new information. Your child's ability to acquire this information and store it for later problem solving is dependent on the support and nurturing you provide through these experiences. The information she already knows enables her to use a variety of approaches to solve problems. Even if she fails the first time, she will try one or even two different strategies before she begins

---

Many problem-solving skills are important for brain development. Here's how you can nurture the development of problem-solving skills:

1. Open the window for learning opportunities by creating hands-on problem-solving experiences with learning toys and materials or even everyday household items.

2. Be responsive to your child's signals for support or attention; this builds trust.

3. Create a safe environment, allow mistakes to be made, and reduce stress.

4. Give time each day to practicing songs and stories and looking at books with words.

5. Always remember to give opportunities for your child to work above her current abilities with help from you (toss a ball and expand how far you toss over time).

to get overwhelmed and frustrated.

You will notice that your child is learning from her mistakes and using the feedback given to her when you see how she changes her techniques to solve the next problem. Your child's ability to use trial and error thinking skills—by touching and doing—is one of the most important cognitive developments during this age.

Encouraging independence promotes problem-solving abilities. When your child has a "problem," such as a toy that won't make that special noise, she becomes motivated to figure out why. Motivation drives children's problem-solving skills.

Remember you must be present and provide support to your child when needed. If she becomes too overwhelmed with trying to find a solution to a problem, she will give up and the learning opportunity will be lost. Problem-solving skills are tools that your child will use for the rest of her life.

Learning continues throughout your child's life. But there are "prime times" or "windows of opportunity" when the brain is a super sponge, absorbing new information each day. Now is one of those prime times!

ACTIVITY

Justin is playing with his new puzzle on the basement floor of his house. He is having a hard time trying to fit one of the puzzle pieces into the puzzle board. After turning the piece in several directions (up then down, right then left), Justin starts huffing loudly and says, "I can't." Dad hears Justin and comes over onto the floor next to him. Dad asks, "What's wrong? Can I help you?" When Justin says yes, Dad gives him some clues that will help him find where to place the puzzle piece.

INSIGHT

Here we see that Dad supports Justin before he becomes too frustrated. Dad also asks if he wants support instead of jumping right in. This shows that he acknowledges his son's own efforts, which in turn builds Justin's self-esteem.

Teach problem solving to your child slowly, patiently, and consistently! Learning is a process that happens over time.

Symbolic Play >
Thinking

Symbolic play is a type of thinking in which symbols or internal images (images in your child's mind) are used to represent objects, persons, and events that are not present.

"I got you!"

ACTIVITY

 Kieran's next-door neighbor comes over for a play date with his pirate hat and sword. The two boys go outside in the backyard; Kieran finds a medium length stick on the ground and together the boys begin to play swords. Going back and forth they trade shouts, "I got you!" "No, I got you!" Kieran and his friend transform themselves into pirates fighting for treasure.

INSIGHT

Kieran finds an object to represent a sword and thus uses symbolic thinking to play with his neighbor. A parent can provide support by extending the play experience. Give the child unusual materials to play with, perhaps items that are not usually used for playing, like a frying pan for a shield or a bandana for an eye patch.

You can see symbolic thought occurring in your child's play, especially during times when he is engaged in social interactions.

Symbolic thinking involves symbols or internal images used to represent objects. When we provide three year olds with socio-dramatic play opportunities, we must also include materials (e.g. a box, broom, empty cans) to play with. By doing so you encourage your child to use his symbolic thinking skills. These materials allow your child to use objects to stand for things that are completely different, thus supporting symbolic thought.

Your child puts a lot of thought into a symbolic play event. He has to think about what he wants to be, think about what objects he wants to use to transform himself, and think about how to be or do something new. It requires a lot of imagination and memory.

Memory goes hand in hand with symbolic play because in order for your child to imitate the behavior of what he sees in his mind, he must store and later retrieve information about the behavior from his memory. As your child grows, his ability to store more information over a period of time (weeks and months) and pull from his memory for later use will increase. This will then make his symbolic play more complex and longer in duration. In a few years you can sign him up for a play at school or a theater class.

Symbolic play provides a great example of your child integrating experiences from her past into her present to plan for her future.

2. Social-Emotional Development

> **During the preschool years, social-emotional development is about socialization, which is the process by which your child learns values and behaviors accepted by society.**

Social-emotional development is also about becoming a confident person who has a sense of self and can take responsibility for himself. Children who develop the skills to make and keep a friend, to cooperate with others, and to participate in groups are more likely to adjust to and be successful in school.

WHOLE CHILD: AGE THREE
Social-Emotional
Development Components

Your child's social-emotional development provides him with a sense of who he is in the world, how he deals with stress, and also helps him form relationships with others. The development of these skills is what stimulates him to communicate with others, resolve conflicts, gain confidence, and reach personal goals. Social skills serve people well throughout their lives as does emotional intelligence.

1. Social Development

Your child likes to be around other children his age. He will play alongside other children, using toys and playing games. Children learn to understand how to take turns and can now use words to express themselves in social settings.

2. Emotional Development

Emotional development at this age is observed as your child becomes strong-willed and disagreeable. He may at times become emotionally insecure and anxious. He may also be picky and hard to please. This emotional instability is due to his gaining more independence.

3. Self-Regulation

Self-regulation refers to your child's ability to regulate his thinking, emotions, and behavior. Self-regulation is critical for school and relationship success.

4. Self-Awareness

Children this age are excited about what they would like to become; they engage in many different imaginative activities, which enables them to discover themselves. They discover what type of athlete, musician, peer, and friend they really are.

At age three your child can express empathy as part of her toolbox of social-emotional skills.

Remember, the Whole Child Parenting Program offers appropriate developmental products and monthly activity books that walk you through supporting your child's skills. Using these in conjunction with the recommended age-appropriate room materials ensures faster development.

Social Development >
Let's Talk About You and Me

Empathy involves your child's ability to put herself into another person's shoes and to experience something as that other person would.

ACTIVITY

 Mina is sitting on the ground waiting for her friends Tegan and Gia at the park, while the moms watch nearby. The two girls began to whisper in each other's ear about who has the best dress on. Tegan turns to Gia and whispers, "My dress is better than Mina's!" Mina drops her head and folds her hands. Mina starts to cry. Gia walks over to Mina and begins to comfort her by patting her on the back. Gia asks, "Mina, are you okay? I'm sad you're crying. I'll get my mom."

INSIGHT

Gia is showing empathy toward Mina by asking if she is okay and even offering to get support so that her friend can feel better. When Gia says she is sad that Mina is crying it is her way of putting herself in Mina's shoes. This is a newer skill for a three year old. Gia's social skills have developed over time.

At age three, your child takes a huge leap into the world of socialization. When children this age are exposed to social opportunities, they will most naturally gravitate toward social play. **It is the role of the parent and caregivers to help "coach" their child through social interactions when needed.** Parents and adults need to give their child the words to join into play and give her options about how to resolve conflicts.

Starting to learn these skills now will help promote self-confidence in your child and make her feel positive about playing with other children. During this time, your child will also start developing a sense of humor and the ability to show empathy for others.

When your child was younger she would look to you for guidance about how to deal with social situations with friends. **As children get older, they become more confident and independent and less dependent on others to work through social events.**

Help your child understand empathy for others by modeling empathy and pointing out situations that call for empathy. If you and your child see someone getting hurt on TV, talk with your child about how that person must feel. Read books about characters showing empathy and helping to find solutions for another character's problem.

And encourage your child to interact with family members, peers, caregivers, and teachers.

Emotional Development >
Calm, Cool, Collected

Social-emotional wellness involves developing the ability to experience and control emotions, form secure and positive relationships, and explore and learn in all areas of your child's environment (family, community, and culture).

Reading your child's emotional cues will help her identify her emotions. Also model for her the behavior for dealing with the emotion so she can store that information and use it the next time a similar situation arises or the feeling is experienced again.

Your child mirrors your own expressions and gestures. It is important to always model and provide emotional support for your child. Social-emotional maturity is a necessary skill to have in social settings, and each age has its milestones in this category.

ACTIVITY

Aunt Lisa comes over to see Helen's new baby brother. Helen is upset that she has not come to see only her. Mom sees Helen with her arms crossed and sitting on the couch. Mom asks, "Helen, are you sad?" Helen nods. Mom says, "Helen, it's okay. I will sit with you, and we can ask Aunt Lisa to bring your baby brother over while we all sit together." Mom comforts Helen with a hug and a kiss. As they wait for Aunt Lisa they sit together on the couch having some special together-ness time.

INSIGHT

In this situation Mom takes the time to identify to Helen how she is feeling, then she provides comfort to her and brings her into the experience so she does not feel replaced in everyone's affections by her baby brother. This is also very important to do since Helen is feeling excluded from the situation, and feeling left out brings feelings of sadness and isolation.

Three year olds form relationships and learn to express their feelings during play experiences with others as the children work toward a common goal and communicate how they feel.

Relationships play a key role in cultivating your child's social-emotional well-being, providing a sense of stability and belonging, and allowing the child to make the most of learning opportunities. Social relationships between children also allow the child to learn appropriate ways to express herself when interacting with others.

Your child's emotional development requires your support by helping her have a positive self-image. When your child accomplishes a physical feat or deals with an emotion in a positive manner, praise her. **A "good job!" goes a long way in reinforcing appropriate social-emotional reactions.** You will keep coaching and encouraging your child's emotional development into her adolescent years.

Self-Regulation >
Control

Self-regulation involves your child's ability to take what she experiences and turn it into information she can use to control thoughts, emotions, and behaviors.

ACTIVITY

Theresa is sitting at the table with her parents, and they are all ready to eat. In their family they pass the food to one another, and the person waits to receive the dish in order to serve him- or herself. Mom serves herself some mashed potatoes and then passes the bowl to Theresa's brother, Hoyt. He then serves himself some mashed potatoes. Now the bowl reaches Theresa, and she takes her spoonful of food. Theresa says, "Thank you, Hoyt!"

INSIGHT

Theresa watches her mother and brother wait for the food to be handed to them so they can serve themselves. Theresa then takes these cues and uses her self-regulation skills to wait for her turn. She also spontaneously says thank you. This takes intentional effort on her part.

For instance, when your child stops playing and begins cleaning up when asked or impulsively shares a toy with a friend these are demonstrations that she has regulation of her emotions, thoughts, and behavior. **Much practice is required for your child to learn how to regulate herself in the first five years of her life.**

You play a key role in helping your child regulate her thinking and behavior. The best way to help her is through modeling during ordinary activities. Your child is getting cues from you, for instance, in situations that require turn taking, such as waiting to be served food.

Self-regulation is not a skill that stands alone; it also affects other areas such as cognitive development. **Thinking affects emotions, and emotions affect cognitive development.** When your child cannot self-regulate effectively, she will move from one activity to another as opposed to engaging in each one.

For instance, you have probably observed your child become frustrated during an activity and say, "I'm not good at this!" showing she cannot regulate her anxiety. She then walks away from the task, unable to persist in a challenging activity.

If your child uses self-regulation skills, she will say, "This is hard, but I can do it" (the emotion leads to positive self-esteem behavior). She will then try to figure out how to accomplish the task (the cognitive skill is persisting in problem solving).

Self-regulation requires your child to intentionally make a decision to do something other than what her impulsivity directs her to do. Think about a time when you witnessed your child take a friend's toy; you had to step in and help her return the toy. This resulted in her getting upset and crying. Your child was unable to use self-regulation skills and acted on the impulse of wanting the toy and taking it. As a parent, you know this behavior is not acceptable and involves thinking and emotions that do not support appropriate or effective social development.

Therefore, you must help your child develop self-regulation skills by using different strategies, such as modeling (playing a sharing game), using hints and cues ("Remember, whose crayon is that?"), and gradually withdrawing your support to let her practice these skills.

Modeling is how your child sees you react to situations. Cues are the directions and gestures you give to help her move in the right direction.

It is very similar to a mother bird and its baby: Mother bird shows her child how to fly and then she just has to let the baby do it herself. You show your child how to self-regulate, and then you have to let her try. You will have to demonstrate appropriate behavior more than once, and that is normal.

Helping your child learn to persist in difficult learning experiences is one of the most important results of developing her self-regulation skills. Also helping your child control her stress-based or anxious or angry emotions by modeling appropriate responses helps her develop into an emotionally well-balanced adult.

Self-Awareness >
Mirror, Mirror, on the Wall

Self-awareness refers to your child's ability to see himself as having a sense of belonging, being able to do things well, being independent, and being accepted.

As your child gains self-awareness he is beginning to answer the question, "Who am I?"

Your child sees his ability to successfully complete a given task. This develops as your child completes tasks and receives feedback about how he did. Self-awareness plays a role in the communication your child will have with others, and it is de-veloped by the experiences he has and the observations he makes.

An important part of under-standing your child's emotional development is the establishment of self-awareness, or your child's overall perception of self, including his own traits, habits, abilities, motives, and social roles.

Self-awareness supports self-

Self-awareness can best be explained by discussing the three steps it takes for your child to reach this state.

1. When your child was two years old he displayed **self-consciousness**, which is embarrassment or pride in situations such as looking at himself in a mirror.

2. Now at the age of three your child displays **self-awareness**. He knows that what he sees in the mirror is "I," not anyone else, staring back at him. He knows he has an identity.

3. The third step will occur between the ages of five and seven, when your child is able to see himself beyond the mirror experience. He can identify himself in a movie taken a few years back, or in a picture that shows him significantly younger and in different clothes. With your child understanding he has an identity, another aspect of self-awareness comes into the picture: **self-efficacy**, which is the belief that he can succeed in accomplishing what he puts his mind to.

identity. Self-identity supports your child in discovering "I." The discovery of "I" supports self-efficacy or "I can do it!" This all leads to confidence!

Self-efficacy creates positive emotions that your child needs to be successful in facing challenging tasks as he enters school.

Be sensitive and responsive as well as physically and emotionally available to your child. Promote trust, security, and exploration through nurturing relationships. Be consistent and create stimulating environments—all of these will support your child's development of self-awareness and positive self-esteem.

3. Language Development

> **Language encompasses all of the language arts: listening, speaking, reading, and writing. Language development is the way in which your child learns to communicate and understand spoken or written words.**

Three year olds use these skills now, creating a foundation for their use of language throughout their lives. A rich language environment is essential for the rapid development of a child's brain. Language and literacy are the links between learning to talk and learning to read.

When parents and caregivers speak with a child in a timely, responsive manner, the child learns new words and is soon able to hold a conversation. This can be a hard task to achieve sometimes, especially when you are doing several things at one time. For instance, let's say that your child has asked you, "Why do birds fly?" The question comes out of the blue, and it is not a topic you know much about. But it is a hot topic for your child! Take a moment, stop what you are doing, and say something like this, "Birds fly so that they can get from one place to another, like when we drive the car from the house to the store. It is their form of transportation." From this simple answer you have responded, introduced words like *transportation* and *drive*. You have also created a conversation opportunity for the two of you to talk back and forth.

Listening and
Understanding

Emerging
Literacy

Communication
and Speaking

WHOLE CHILD: AGE THREE
Language
Development Components

Learning language and practicing communication skills help your child obtain information and express herself in a variety of ways and settings. These skills will help your child develop an expressive vocabulary, as well as learn to read and to communicate through writing. Your child is learning language by listening to others in her environment and by listening to a variety of books and simple stories. Through this process, your child will notice the sounds of language and may play with rhyming or finding other similar sounds.

Think about a simple rhyme like, "Rabbits." *"Rabbits-rabbits one, two, three, will you come and play with me? Camels-camels four, five, six, why do you have a hump like this?"* In just two lines your child has heard sounds of a rhyme, used counting skills, been pulled into a story about different animals, and been given an opportunity to interact by continuing the rhyming.

1.
Listening and Understanding

Your child's communication involves much more than speech, and certainly more than writing, because her writing skills are still developing. She will communicate in many different ways by using nonverbal gestures, glances, and changes in tone of voice when speaking. How your child observes people in her environment helps develops her communication and speaking skills.

2.
Communication and Speaking

Listening is an active process that has three steps:

1. *Hearing*—Your three year old listens just enough to catch what is being said.

2. *Understanding*—Your child takes what is heard and comprehends it.

3. *Judging*—After your child understands, she decides if it makes sense to her.

3.
Emerging Literacy

Emerging literacy explains how your child uses knowledge of reading and writing skills before she actually learns how to read and write words. Three year olds are in the process of becoming literate. The process will continue through college and beyond.

Listening and Understanding >

New World, New Words

Listening and understanding involves your child paying attention to what someone says and making sense of what was heard.

Listening is a very important communication skill to teach your child; it is not a skill that develops naturally. Children this age especially have a great way of using selective listening skills, tuning out the things they do not want to hear.

ACTIVITY

 Peter is playing a game of Simon Says with his parents. Peter loves this game. In a very slow voice his mom says, "Siiimon saaays touuuch your toessss." Peter listens then touches his toes. In a really fast voice Dad says, "Okay, touch your nose!" Peter touches his nose. "I didn't say Simon says, Peter. Listen for Simon says before you move." As his parents continue to take turns giving directions they each go faster and faster until no one can keep up.

INSIGHT

Peter has to listen and understand the question in order to produce the correct action. The instructions are simple yet fun enough to keep Peter entertained. Peter is also hearing vocabulary words *toes*, *nose*, and *touch*.

Your child's vocabulary expands as he understands what he hears and uses words he hears in his communication with others such as:

* **nouns**: *flower, banana, towel, bath*;

* **verbs**: action verbs (*walk, jump*), being verbs (I *am*, you *are*), helping verbs (Do you *need* a tissue?), and irregular verbs (The dog *bit* me, not, The dog *bited* me.);

* **adjectives**: *pretty, colorful, mad*;

* **adverbs**: *quickly, happily*.

These types of words are used more in your child's sentences because they signify a simplified manner of speech in which only the most important words are used to express ideas.

However, some children this age have cognitive limitations on the length of words they can produce. Given these limitations, they sensibly leave out the least important parts but still get their point across.

You might hear a your child say, "Adam make tower." As your child continues to expand his words, he will begin to use prepositions (*up, down, below*) and pronouns (*he, she, you*) along with the other words. He will now say, "*I* (pronoun) will *make* (verb) *my* (adjective) *tower* (noun) *on* (preposition) *grass* (noun)."

As you teach your child new words make them concrete by helping him visualize them. If it's an adjective like *scratchy*, point out the scratchiness on Dad's chin.

Your three year old's use of nouns, action verbs, and adjectives allows him to better understand the language he is using. Therefore, communicating with your three year old is one of the most important, pleasurable, and rewarding parts of your parenting experience. The more interactive conversations you have with your child, the more your child will learn to listen; the more you encourage the use of words, the more your child will understand.

Communication and Speaking >
Making More Sense

Your child will use a greater variety of closed-class words (e.g. prepositions) between now and four years of age.

Closed-class words or **function words** are limited in number and act as guides for sentence structure. The use of closed-class words makes your child's sentences easier to understand.

For example, as your child's language skills develop he will use the prepositions *in* and *on*. He will understand the preposition *under*. He will also use gestures to tell the meaning of locational prepositions (such as pointing).

Prepositions like *on, in, under* are easier for your child to understand than *behind, beside,* and *between.* Have you ever asked your child to bring you a ball? You give clues such as "It is in front of the door." Even with this clue, he still has difficulty locating the ball. This is because your child has to identify the relationship between the front and the back of an object (a ball has no identifiable parts). Therefore, for your child to use a preposition correctly, he must first understand its meaning. This skill develops beyond the age of three.

ACTIVITY

 Three-and-a-half year old Max points to some other children at the park and says to his dad, "They are eating ice cream on the grass and not making a big mess." If Max just said, "Eat ice cream no messy," it would have been more difficult for his dad to understand what he meant.

INSIGHT

In order for Max to use the preposition (*on*) correctly and the adjective (*messy*) he has to expand his speech and word knowledge to communicate the meaning of what he is seeing. This comes with time and practice.

Phonology

Phonology is how speech/word sounds are used and organized in your child's language as he learns to talk. This area of development is a cognitive skill, and it is a strong predictor of future academic success. Your child was not born being able to make all the word choices and patterns of language.

He goes through this developmental process because he is learning to coordinate his tongue, lips, teeth, etc. Think back to the time when you heard your child say something such as "baba" for bottle. Even now, if your child just turned three, you may hear him say "nail" for "snail." As your child continues to develop, he will stop using incorrect speech sounds and articulate and enunciate increasingly complex sentences.

"They are eating ice cream on the grass and not making a big mess."

Emergent Literacy >
The Printed Word

Emergent or emerging literacy refers to how your child interacts with books; it also includes when she reads and writes, even if she cannot actually read or write in the traditional way.

The ways that your child will learn to read and write are similar to how she develops language.

Your child must learn about written language before she can read and write in the traditional way. Very early on your child becomes immersed in written language even if you do not do this intentionally by reading to her. This occurs as she sees environmental print—books, magazines, and advertisements on TV. Words are already a part of her world way before she can read or write them.

Did you know you instinctively engage in reading, writing, and talking experiences with your child on a daily basis? For example, every time you leave a note for your child in her lunch box for the teacher to read, share a story, label objects, communicate, or sign you are engaging in literacy. Interactions between you and your child cannot occur all the time; it is for this reason your child has already started thinking about written language.

Just as your child wants to learn written language, she also becomes excited about using pictures and letters to communicate. She will use symbols invented by herself as printed words; this may include poorly copied words, gestures, or marks on paper.

Reading starts for your child when she gives meaning to the symbols around her, such as stop signs, labels on food, symbols on an electronic device or a restaurant billboard. Take a moment to look at your child's "writing." She will write lots of wavy lines; interspersed between the wavy lines you will see a symbol that looks like a circle or another kind of shape.

If you were to ask her what she "wrote," she may say, "I wrote your name and mine." This is how your child is showing emerging literacy skills with her attempt at writing, using symbols to represent print.

Through natural exposure to books and print and through conversations with people, your child will discover that written words are another way to communicate. Three year olds continue to grow in understanding and in their use of language.

As her vocabulary continues to grow, your child will be able to produce longer and more complex sentences. During the preschool period, children's speech becomes clearer as they master new sounds and new syllable structures.

Learning to read and write must be a gradual process that is nurtured over time. Parents should be intentional in providing activities to support development of these skills. Activities include parents having purposeful conversations with their children and children having purposeful conversations with other children; this will support language development.

Provide your child with access to many different books and other reading and writing materials. It is important to also offer opportunities for exploring and engaging in literacy activities, which include reading, writing, and learning letters and sounds.

Your child's learning in literacy cannot be separated from her learning in other areas (e.g. fine motor skills). Her interest in various subjects and activities can fuel her verbal language and create opportunities for learning to read and write.

For instance, you might have recently taken a family vacation; on the trip, your child sees dolphins and whales. This experience can result in looking at pictures of different types of whales, naming those pictures, seeing the names in print, and making up stories about the whales. This is teaching and supporting literacy in a natural way based on your child's current interests and environment. The more you read and speak and engage with your child, the more her emerging literacy will lead to actual literacy—reading and writing on her own.

Storytelling

Storytelling is developed from social interactions and play scenarios that children have with each other and adults.

It is amazing to see how three year olds have learned the art of story-telling: how to sequence events, how to set actions in place and time, and how to organize a story around characters. It is hard to imagine that this is possible when they are still in the midst of developing elementary language skills.

Another way in which children acquire storytelling skills is through talking about the past with their parents. A child might say, "Mommy, do you remember when we went to the ice cream store?" This starts the story, and the adult and child will then build on the story together.

Children tend to talk about experiences they have with others; this builds intimacy between parents and children. Storytelling is a three-phase process in your child's development; it begins even before she turns three. In the beginning of storytelling, your child will listen to stories that you tell. She will watch your face, listen to your voice, and take cues from you on how the story should end.

ACTIVITY

Wini is playing with a doll. She holds the doll in her arms as she gives it a drink. Wini says, "Let's have milk! There you go, dolly, are you happy? You drank your milk. Do you want more? You burped! Mommy can get you more milk. Here you go. Drink it slow."

INSIGHT

Wini has just told a story through her play. It has a beginning (having milk), middle (drank all of the milk), and an end (more milk). She even includes characters (dolly) and emotions (happy).

Next, when your child has learned all she can from you about telling stories, you will hear your child add elements to the story you started that you never imagined. By the time your child has turned three, you have a certified storyteller who captivates the attention of all who will listen.

Organizing Stories

Your child can organize stories when she is able to give descriptions of the setting (faraway place), give detailed information about the characters (he was so big), and provide a sequence of action to communicate a story verbally.

Young children follow different strategies when organizing their stories. One of these is called **centering**.

With centering, your child will create a story around a central topic. Each object, action, or event included in the story relates to the topic, but the listener may have difficulty recognizing the relationship between them. Your child will give you as much lively detail as she can about the story. You may hear your child say, "A Mars bar bush growing out of the earth." Remember: You will have difficulty understanding; that is normal.

ACTIVITY

The following story told by three-year-old Eve to her friend Nathan about her day at the park with a pink burger (topic) provides an example of centering. "I ate a pink burger like this," mimes eating, "with the swings" (detail), "I was high" (detail). "Mommy threw the ball" (detail), "burger" (topic), "like this. I didn't get the burger ball. My burger is pink. I liked my pink burger. I had chips with my burger, chips pink just like my burger."

INSIGHT

This is a perfect example of Eve having a topic and using detail in her story. It is very difficult for the adult listener to put all the pieces together. For two three year olds the story makes sense. Eve demonstrates her early ability to organize her story for the listener. Remember, organizing has a setting (park), characters (pink burger and Mommy), and a sequence of actions (swinging, throwing a ball, and eating chips).

"I had chips with my burger, chips pink just like my burger."

4. Creative Development

> **Creative development activities invite your child to listen, observe, move, solve problems, and imagine while using several operating systems.**

Creative development consists of your child's participation in art, music, movement and dance, and dramatic play. Active involvement in creative arts promotes learning and brain development. Three years of age is a good time for parents to continue to support their children's imaginative thinking and self-expression and enhance their growth in these areas.

Children can count musical beats, experiment with colors to make a new one, create a dialogue for a story, or move like animal characters in a book. Activities like these will support development in the social, cognitive, and creative processes. Creative play activates the mind and senses, allowing children to expand or contract their universe and shape it any way they please with whichever characters, objects, words, or music they choose.

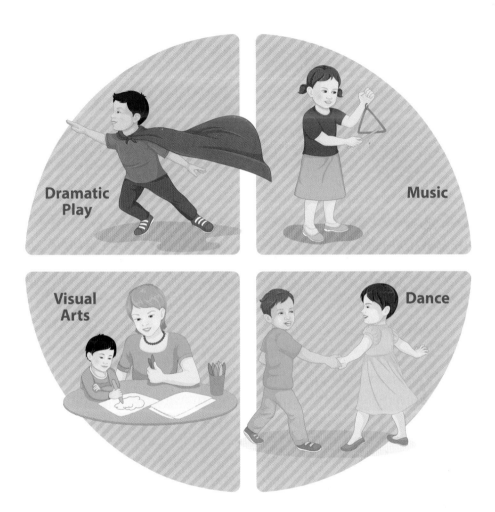

WHOLE CHILD: AGE THREE
Creative
Development Components

1. Music

Music involves listening to, learning about, and making melody or harmony. Your child will listen and respond to different kinds of music by moving her body, dancing, painting, or talking about how the music is making her feel. Music can include all types of instruments, songs, singing, and live or recorded music.

2. Dance

Dance includes movement and moving the body in different ways, which enables her to learn what her body can do and how to express herself. Your child will imitate how animals move or how to move when happy or sad.

3. Visual Arts

Visual art involves giving three year olds the opportunity to explore materials through painting, drawing, mixing colors, making 3-D sculptures, and creating mosaic patterns. Participating in visual art enables children to explore their environment and discover connections and meanings using art materials to express and communicate their discoveries.

4. Dramatic Play

Dramatic play is when your child pretends to be a "teacher," for example, and gives a lesson to a younger child. It includes your child pretending and mimicking what she sees, as well as her having the opportunity to take an object and use it for anything she can imagine.

Have various instruments available to your child to encourage her to experiment with melody, rhythm, and sound to create music on her own.

Remember, the Whole Child Parenting Program offers appropriate developmental products and monthly activity books that walk you through supporting your child's skills. Using these in conjunction with the recommended age-appropriate room materials ensures faster development.

Music >
Rhythm in My Bones

Music is a vocal or instrumental sound that is combined or done separately to create a melody, harmony, or rhythm.

ACTIVITY

Michael is in his bedroom looking outside through the window. It's raining. He puts on his headphones, closes his eyes, and starts singing "Itsy Bitsy Spider." He sings it again, this time doing the actions with his hands.

The itsy bitsy spider
climbed up the waterspout.
Down came the rain
and washed the spider out.
Out came the sun
and dried up all the rain.
And the itsy bitsy spider
climbed up the spout again.

INSIGHT

This is a song Michael has sung in music class with his friends. By doing the actions and singing the song he demonstrates his ability to listen and understand. Singing reinforces the rhyme staying in his memory. This is how literacy and music come together. His ability to sing and chant will help develop language skills and auditory discrimination.

Your child enjoys listening to all musical styles.

Just hearing a specific type of music over and over does not seem to affect your child's listening preferences, but your approval and support do have a positive influence on your child's musical preferences. By nature, music is a social experience because it is shared with others as your child shows you how he sings, dances, or plays instruments.

Music is also an area of creative development that provides your child opportunities to enhance his cognitive thinking skills by providing practice in patterns, math concepts, and symbolic thinking skills.

As your child learns to distinguish different sounds in music, his thinking and memory skills will grow. Repeating songs he has heard before helps your child remember sounds and words in order for a certain amount of time.

These skills are learned through the enjoyment of music. For instance, many children's songs have counting in them, such as "One, Two, Buckle My Shoe" or "Five Little Monkeys." The rhythms of these songs make it easier for your child to absorb math concepts.

Singing is natural for your child. Parents frequently hear their child break into a song or chanting; these chants are not true songs but consist of repeated tones. Physical, rhythmic movement, such as walking, hopping, pounding, or rocking, may accompany singing and chanting (e.g. "Ants Go Marching").

Don't get too ahead of your child's development at age three. Even though he breaks into spontaneous chants, he is still having difficulty carrying a tune.

Dance >
Moving and Grooving

Dance is defined as creativity through movement; this involves your child's problem solving, self-expression, and imagination skills.

The random movements of the infant and the spontaneous swaying and bouncing to music of the toddler develop into the more dance-like movements of your three year old.

He is motivated to dance to music, but his movements are not always coordinated to the music he hears. Thus a steady beat, rhythm, or overall musical effect may still not be accurately connected to his body movements, though he is moving closer to coordinating himself to the music. Simple exercises in movement are best to encourage skill development for this age child.

Your child loves having a dance partner. Set a time during the day to dance with your child to different genres of music.

As you encourage dancing in your child, you also encourage him to express himself and be creative. This will help him later in life as he learns to improve his coordination, build his spatial awareness skills, and think through ways of how to move his body.

ACTIVITY

Tito and his friend are in music class. The teacher says, "How about if we sing my favorite song about dancing trees?" She stands up. "How tall are trees? Children, stand up and grab a friend's hand as you dance and sway like me."

She begins to sing, "He swings and he sways and he shakes all his limbs. The little ole tree loves to dance with the wind. He rustles and bustles when the wind comes to call. He dances so hard I'm afraid he will fall." Tito and his friend love the song so much because they are swaying and dancing to the beat. They also get to tumble to the floor at the end. The boys want the teacher to sing the song again.

INSIGHT

This class is a great example of helping children use problem-solving skills as each one thinks about which direction to sway, shake, swing, and dance. This simple activity fosters development of both imagination—each child has to first imagine dancing like a tree—and self-expression.

Your child can move fast or slowly and stop and turn with some smoothness and control, but he still has difficulty understanding that a relationship exists between the sounds he hears and what his muscles can do. Thus, your child will limit his movements, repeating a few patterns consistently during his musical experience. To unlock creativity, think along the lines of facilitating music and movement with him. Present a challenge or question to which there are many possible ways your child can move his body in response (e.g. Can you move your legs?).

A dance session will require mental concentration and active participation from your child. **Dance will help your child become aware of his own body and learn gross motor coordination skills. These are critical to other developmental skills.**

Dance gives your child a sense of accomplishment in his abilities as he learns new steps and ways to move his body and work together with his dance partner—that's you! Dancing together provides a fun and physically beneficial bonding experience.

Visual Arts >
Artist

Visual art is anything your child produces that can be seen. This can be a drawing, a painting, a photo she takes of an object, or a sculpture she makes from clay.

ACTIVITY

Mom is sitting in the kitchen with Dad while Taylor is taking her afternoon nap. Mom says, "I saw Taylor drawing today. I wanted to draw with her." Dad asks, "Why didn't you?" Mom replies, "I can't draw very well, and I really didn't want Taylor to see what I was doing so I just sat and watched her."

INSIGHT

In this situation Mom's lack of drawing skills and lack of creative confidence causes her to worry about transferring her deficits to Taylor. Rather than doing this, Mom should show her confidence in herself and sit down to draw beside her daughter. It is important to engage in art with your child and enjoy the process, not worry about the end product.

Art builds self-confidence in your child because your child believes that she can draw, and she enjoys drawing. **The amazing thing with children is that they have no fear of engaging in artistic activities especially when you build their confidence.**

Engage in the following to support your child's art experiences at home:

* Do you help your child feel good about her art? By saying something like this, "I love how you used the color blue in your picture. It reminds me of the ocean." Don't name objects in the painting for your child because your meaning could differ from your child's; let her tell you what something is.

* Do you engage in art with your child? Sit at the kitchen table and do a coloring page with her.

* Do you give your child different ways to use art materials? Give your child crayons and let her make crayon shavings using an automatic pencil sharpener. Then glue those shavings to a piece of construction paper. Then cut it into stars or other shapes. Add string and you have a mobile!

* Do you have a special place to display your child's artwork? Make space on the kitchen refrigerator or kitchen walls and use letter magnets to hold up the art.

> * **Art promotes creativity.**
> * **Creativity brings out your child's personality and builds her self-esteem.**

Encourage your child to experiment with art products in the following ways:

* Have faith in your child's artwork and tell her you like her art.
* Refrain from offering too much help.
* Accept your child's creative products without placing a value judgment on them.
* State the confidence you have in your child to make the project her own.

When you view your child's artwork and ask questions, she realizes the creative process involved is of great value to you. In other words, the process is more important than the product you want to hang on your wall or refrigerator. To allow for true creativity there must be no boundaries to what she is allowed to make or draw.

Dramatic Play >
Playing House!

Dramatic play is when your child transforms into something he is not; it fuels imagination and is driven by the materials available to him as well as the experiences he has had.

If you just went for a checkup you might see your child take on the role of doctor. He may become an astronaut and turn the house into a spaceship after watching a movie about aliens.

During dramatic play, you will see your child take on a new role—and he would love for you to join in. Your child will use many different areas of the house as settings for dramatic play.

You should offer many opportunities for your child to engage in role-playing and make-believe activities by having a play area in your home with seating and storage for a wide variety of props, such as boards, scrap lumber, dress-up clothes, cooking utensils, banners, signs, and other items that support dramatic play. You don't have to go out and buy these things; simply look for unused items around your house or ask a neighbor.

Dramatic play offers opportunities for your child to use and expand his creative life skills and mimic what he sees you do. These activities will help him make meaning of his environment.

Even without any props, your child will engage in dramatic play by telling stories and acting them out. Imagine how much fun you could have participating in this important developmental skill together. Take a chance. Play a part. You're missing out if you don't give it a shot!

Here are some steps you can take to support dramatic play:

1. Focus on the process of dramatic play by asking questions that help to extend the experience. Your son is making honking noises as he pushes a race car on the carpet. Mom: "Where is that race car going?" or "That is a fast car. What is it honking at?"

2. Model your own creative thinking and expression by making up voices and sound effects. Using recycled items for a microphone (e.g. a can of soda).

3. When your little one says he wants to role play a character, encourage the problem-solving process by asking open-ended questions such as "What will you need to be the character?" Questions like these help your three year old recognize the creative process in himself.

5. Physical Development

> By the beginning of her third year, your child is becoming very active and agile.

You see your child spend a lot of time getting to know her body and how to control it. In accordance with how three year olds develop, parents will see that their children will gain about four to five pounds, grow at a rate of two to three inches, and reach about half of their adult height during the third year. Because of these advancements, your child will discover just how much her fine motor and gross motor skills have improved.

Your child's balancing abilities increase in the way that she walks, runs, and jumps. Your child jumps on two feet, and she can catch a smaller ball than she could at age two. Your three year old is super excited because now she can pedal a tricycle, which will prepare her for a bicycle. Your child can hop on one foot, copy a circle, and place small objects in a small opening. Because she loves to move and be active, it is a perfect time to support further growth in physical development. As we learn more about gross motor (large muscle) and fine motor (small muscle) development, you will be given support and solutions to help your child advance her physical skills.

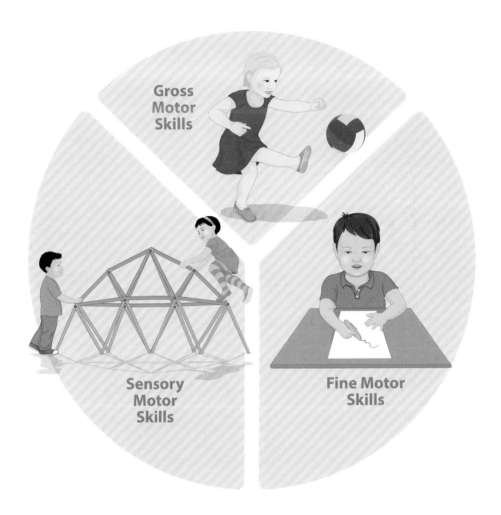

WHOLE CHILD: AGE THREE
Physical
Development Components

1. Gross Motor Skills

A gross motor skill is your child's ability to control arm and leg movements. This includes climbing, walking up and down stairs, kicking a ball, carrying large items, running short distances, or standing on tiptoes.

2. Fine Motor Skills

Fine motor development applies to small movements of the hands, wrists, fingers, feet, and toes. Fine motor skills also include smaller actions, such as grasping an object between the thumb and a finger or using the lips and the tongue to taste an object.

3. Sensory Motor Skills

Sensory motor skills in three year olds include five areas, which correspond to the senses: touch, sight, hearing, smell, and taste. Touch can involve games that use the muscles; sight can be used to complete a maze or dot-to-dot puzzle; hearing might include playing listening games; smell can be experimenting with plants and flowers in the garden; and taste might involve trying different kinds of foods.

The ability to kick a ball indicates a big jump in gross motor skill development.

Remember, the Whole Child Parenting Program offers appropriate developmental products and monthly activity books that walk you through supporting your child's skills. Using these in conjunction with the recommended age-appropriate room materials ensures faster development.

Gross Motor Skills >
Developing
the Large Muscles

Gross motor skills are skills that involve moving different body parts such as feet, legs, head, and arms.

Gross motor skills are important because they are the foundation for your child having the ability to do more complex skills, like karate or little kid soccer.

Gross motor skills can be broken down into three areas: loco-motor skills, balance skills, and ball skills. All of these gross motor skills are necessary for your child to move through life with confidence as he learns to play games and sports and engage in other, more complex activities like swimming.

Your child needs a lot of opportunities for physical development in these specific areas; therefore, active play is important for getting those large muscles moving. Gross motor skills develop through activities in which your child has the opportunity to move his legs, arms, and lower body.

1. Loco-motor skills—Running, jumping, hopping, and leaping forward are examples. Mickey stands with his knees bent and his arms stretched in back of him; he then propels himself forward and leaps, landing on his feet.

2. Balance skills—are movements in which your child's body remains in place, but moves in a horizontal or vertical direction. With his arms bent and lifted to waist level during take off, Nicholas steps forward with his lead foot followed by a step from the foot behind as he gallops forward.

3. Ball skills—are throwing, kicking, and catching. Mark prepares to catch the ball by holding both hands in front of his body with his elbows slightly bent. He stretches his arms in front of himself to reach the ball as it comes to him.

ACTIVITY

Mom decides that her son needs something to do since it is raining outside. She finds masking tape in the drawer and tapes down a straight line on the floor. Mom asks her son to walk on the tape with his arms stretched out and try not to fall to the right or left of the tape.

INSIGHT

Mom supports her son's physical development when she encourages him to use his legs and arms to balance.

Help your child develop new skills:

1. **Observe the behavior in others**, e.g. Tommy watches Dad shoot a basketball through the hoop.

2. **Form a mental image of the behavior**, e.g. Tommy then visualizes how his dad bends his knees and propels the ball up with his arms.

3. **Imitate the behavior**, e.g. Tommy then stands next to Dad, bends his knees, and propels the ball up with his arms.

4. **Practice the behavior**, e.g. Tommy does not get the ball through the hoop the first time, so he tries again.

5. **Be motivated to repeat the behavior**, e.g. Tommy's dad says, "You can do it," which motivates Tommy to keep trying.

Three year olds need a lot of opportunities for physical development; active play is important for getting those large muscles moving.

When your child is having difficulty kicking a ball, first give him a moment to try to solve the problem on his own. Then you can help your child problem solve using a different strategy that you illustrate for him so he can learn to kick the ball better. Then help your child think about how he could practice this new skill.

Fine Motor Skills >
Developing the Small Muscles

Fine motor skills refer to the movements we make with the small muscles of the hands, wrist, and fingers.

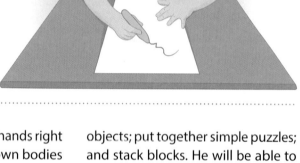

Children start to use their hands right at birth to explore their own bodies and the world around them. Their fine motor skills develop as their bodies start to move more in different ways and become more stable in their movements.

During his third year child will be able to hold a crayon or pencil in his fingers instead of his fist, draw or color a picture, and copy simple lines. He will be able to cut paper with scissors, although not in a straight line; manipulate small objects; put together simple puzzles; and stack blocks. He will be able to turn the page of a book and begin to lace—but not tie—his shoes.

The two popular terms that come up when learning about fine motor skills in three year olds are **fist grip** and **pincer grip**. An example of a fist grip is when your child uses his whole hand and wraps it around a pencil to write his name. A pincer grip refers to the pinching muscles that use the thumb and pointer finger.

ACTIVITY

 Andy is at home with his dad playing in his dad's office. He asks his dad for a pencil and some paper so that he can "write" his mommy a letter. He takes the pencil and looks at his dad, and then he tries to hold the pencil like his dad, but ends up making a fist. Dad stops what he is doing and shows Andy how to hold the pencil with his thumb and pointer finger.

INSIGHT

As Andy learns to fine-tune his pincer grip he still has a tendency to hold his pencil with a fist. Even though many children do the same thing until they are five, it is really okay only for a toddler to do this. Andy should have mastered this skill already, so his father should keep practicing with him to help him nail it down.

Even if your child has not mastered a fine motor skill it is never too late to teach him. Take the time to stop what you're doing and show your child how to develop his skills.

Your child can get lots of practice with fine motor skills by engaging in simple activities such as zipping and unzipping zippers, picking up connecting blocks or finger foods, and stringing beads. Strengthening the pincer grasp is an important skill because it will prepare your child for holding pencils, markers, crayons, and paintbrushes, which support the development of prewriting skills.

Wrist control and finger strength are also important parts of ultimately mastering writing and drawing. Fitting pieces into a puzzle will develop dexterity of the hand and wrist.

All types of fine motor skills are important to practice. Practicing and mastering one fine motor skill can lead to the development or refinement of another. Practice is key.

Sensory Motor Skills >
The Five Senses

Sensory motor skills involve the ability to use fine motor skills or gross motor skills through the senses of touch, smell, taste, sight, and hearing.

As your three year old spends more time moving, listening, touching, and smelling, he will learn more through the opportunities you provide to interact with his surroundings while using his senses. Try some of the activities on the next page.

ACTIVITY

 Hollis and Anne are restless. They've been inside doing art and playing with blocks for hours and need to get moving. The children ask permission to go out and play. Their mom is more than happy to encourage outdoor play, and she opens the door with enthusiasm. The kids run outside, straight for the climbing structure happy to be free of the four walls of their home.

INSIGHT

Your child must use fine motor skills to coordinate eye and hand movements and to adjust his grip on playground equipment. He must coordinate the action of climbing and using many large muscle groups to maintain his balance.

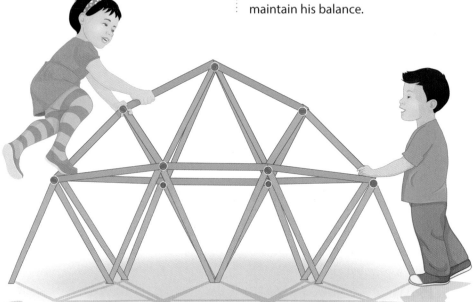

Do the following activities with your child to encourage sensory development:

* Squirt a small amount of shaving cream onto the kitchen table. Ask your child how it smells, then ask if he has ever seen someone in the house use shaving cream (getting him to think and pull from his memory to develop his cognitive skills). Encourage your child to draw shapes or animals in the shaving cream, making a game out of the experience.

* Mimic Me is the name of this step in the game. Write the first letter of your child's name on a piece of white paper. Use a black marker and write in very large print. Ask your child to mimic you and draw the letter they see on the paper.

This type of activity helps your child in the following ways: Your child must pay attention to the letter you wrote on the paper; he must focus to draw the same letter in the shaving cream; he must use his fine motor skills to hold out only his pointer finger to draw the letter; and he must use his hand-eye coordination skills to get it all on target. Sight, touch, and smell are involved in the activity above.

Even though larger muscles usually develop before smaller muscles, more advanced motor abilities require your child to coordinate large motor (large muscle) skills with small motor (small muscle) skills.

6. Health and Care

> **All children grow at different rates. Your child's growth rate will include genetic and environmental factors.**

Environment plays a role in your child's growth because the conditions of your child's environment are important in how she progresses both physically and emotionally. It is crucial for parents to understand the different aspects of environment to ensure that their children are getting what they need to grow and develop. One aspect in their environment is **nurture**: the loving, responsive care you give that has an effect on how your child grows. When your child feels loved and supported, she can focus on learning and growing instead of worrying. **Nutrition** is another environmental factor. Good nutrition leads to growth; offering a variety of foods to your child will give her the nutrients and vitamins needed for her brain and body to grow.

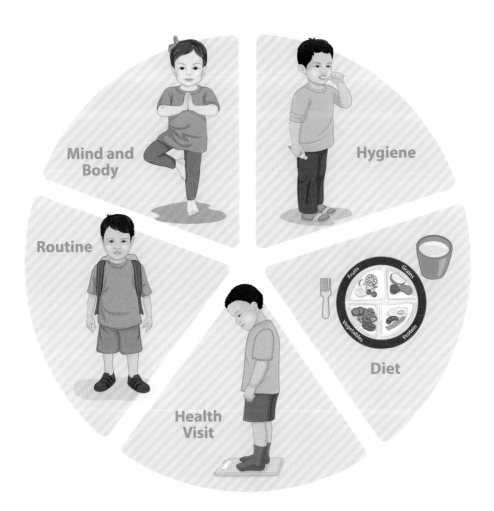

WHOLE CHILD: AGE THREE

Health and Care

Hygiene >
Keeping Clean, Oral Care, First Aid

Because your three year old has better listening and understanding skills, she can understand why she needs to:

* bathe regularly,
* brush her teeth twice a day,
* use tissues to blow her nose,
* cough into the crook of her arm,
* comb and brush her hair,
* and change her clothes daily.

Your child is capable of understanding not only the reasons for good hygiene, but also what happens when you don't practice good hygiene.

I'm Clean!

Good health is connected to grooming and hygiene. It is important for your child to learn the importance of personal hygiene to avoid the spread of illness. **At three years of age, it is necessary for parents to guide and tell their children about personal hygiene and set the example.** Good hygiene skills will help your child the rest of her life.

Teaching hygiene may seem difficult and frustrating at times as your child may boycott taking a bath, brushing her teeth for two minutes, or even washing and combing her hair. You can read books to your child as a means of keeping hygiene practices in her mind. Elizabeth Verdick has an entire series of books for children ranging from *Germs Are Not for Sharing* to *Noses Are Not for Picking*.

Don't forget washing clothes; now that your child is three, she can help you sort the laundry by color and even drop clothes into the machine. Remember, you are the role model; what she sees you do will set your child on the path to healthy hygiene practices in the future.

Oral Care

The American Academy of Pediatrics and the American Academy of Pediatric Dentistry recommend that you take your child to the dentist within six months after her first tooth erupts, or by her first birthday, whichever comes first.

After your child's first visit, the dentist will tell you when your child needs to return. Most children see a dentist every six months.

Just as you took the time to prepare your child for his well-child visit you need to do the same for a dental visit.

When your child was a toddler, you may have noticed that she had an inclination to want to brush her teeth herself; however, your child still needs your assistance when brushing. **Young children do not have the ability to brush their teeth effectively.**

To help your child still have a sense of independence, you can let her brush her teeth using a pea size amount of toothpaste, but then you must brush her teeth again to make sure no spots are missed.

The general rule is when your child is able to tie her own shoes, she can brush her own teeth because you will know her fine motor skills are developed enough to do this; however, you still need to monitor your child and make sure she is brushing for a full two minutes.

Correct brushing techniques

You can have your child lie down on a bed with her head in your lap, or you can have your child sit with her body between your legs and her head tilted back into your arms. You can also do this standing in front of the sink with your child's head tilted back.

Brush the teeth gently using small, circular motions, being sure to include the area where the teeth meet the gums. Start by brushing the outside surface and then move into the inside, brushing the bottom of the teeth last. Remember to use a circular motion. As you assist your child, use a timer so that she can help you track the two minutes.

First Aid

Your child will get bumps and bruises, cuts and sores. It is difficult for a parent to see a child get hurt. It is our natural instinct to protect our children from all injuries, and when we can't we feel we have somehow failed in our responsibilities.

It is very important to attend to your child's emotional needs while doing a quick assessment of the injury, moving close to her body and listening for a regular heart beat and breathing to insure these functions have not been compromised. When you have determined no other medical attention is needed outside of ice, a bandage, and/or washing, give your little one a hug, a kiss, and some cuddle time, letting your child know you care and are there to help.

Every parent needs a well-stocked first-aid kit at home and in the car for on the go. Kits for the house and car should be big enough to hold a wide range of supplies.

It is important to have the necessary first-aid materials for patching up a wound and calming your little one so you can make the boo-boo better.

Burns

1. Place under cold water.
2. If there is no broken skin, apply a burn cream, not petroleum jelly.
3. If there is broken skin, apply antibiotic ointment and a bandage.

Call a doctor as soon as possible if burns are on the face, hands, or if they are larger than ¼ inch anywhere on the body.

Splinters

1. Clean the area of the splinter with soap and water.
2. If the splinter is small and does not hurt, it will make its way out in a few days.
3. If the splinter is big, clean a pair of tweezers with alcohol and pull the splinter out. If the tip of the splinter breaks, you can sometimes nudge out a splinter with the edge of a credit card.
4. Wash the skin again.
5. If the splinter isn't out after a few days or is causing your child pain, turning red, or has pus, see your doctor to have it safely removed.

Bumps and Bruises

1. Place ice on the bumps.
2. Apply over-the-counter ointments for bruising or muscle aches.
3. Have your child rest.

Cuts and Scrapes

1. Wash your own hands.
2. Wash the cut with soap and water.
3. Pat dry.
4. Bandage the cut or scrape to keep out dirt and germs.

If the skin is broken, apply a thin layer of an over-the-counter antibiotic ointment, then cover with a bandage or gauze and surgical tape.

Apply pressure to the wound if it is still bleeding. If bleeding does not stop after 10 minutes, head to the emergency room because your child may need stitches. Head to the doctor also if your child's cut is longer than half an inch, there is something stuck inside the cut, or the cut is on your child's face because it may leave a noticeable scar if untreated.

* Antibacterial lotion (not petroleum jelly) can help clean the cut and should be applied with each bandage change; however, avoid rubbing alcohol and hydrogen peroxide because they can cause discomfort for your child and slow the healing process.

* Make sure to clean the cut, use an antibiotic cream or ointment, and keep it under a protective bandage. Change the bandage daily. After a few days, remove the bandage and allow the cut to air dry. This will lead to the formation of a scab, which shows the wound is healing. Encourage your child to leave the scab in place as it will fall off naturally and lessen the chance of scarring.

Diet >

Three year olds need:

* grains: 4–5 ounces (half from whole sources),
* vegetables: 1 ½ cups,
* fruits: 1–1 ½ cups,
* milk: 2 cups,
* meat and beans: 3–4 ounces.

When it comes to your child's diet it is your responsibility to set an example by making sure your child has healthful food options at every meal.

Active three year olds need between 1,200 and 1,600 calories each day. Compared to a toddler, a three year old has a smaller stomach and energy needs relative to her size, so she tends to stay full on a smaller amount of food.

It is important at this age to be cautious of portion sizes and how much your child eats. It is especially important to make sure you give small portions of any treats or high-fat foods because these can cause her to want to overeat.

We want to give our three year olds the best nutrition, but knowing how to do that without giving in to quick fixes of empty calories can be challenging.

Foods to Introduce at Three

Around the age of three, it's time to switch to skim or 1% milk and find more healthy fats and oils for your child in sources such as nuts and full-fat cheeses. Limit the amount of milk and juice your child drinks, especially between meals, because it can make your child not hungry for solids.

It is important to keep up with a routine of regularly planned snacks and meals so that your child can eat throughout the day. This helps her not overeat and be able to recognize her own hunger cues.

High-Fiber Foods

As your child grows older, the recommended portion will increase to roughly 14 grams of fiber per 1,000-calorie intake.

Fruits and vegetables are excellent sources of fiber, so you should encourage your child to eat as many as possible. Other high-fiber foods include beans, whole grain breads, and cereals.

To figure out how much fiber your child (age 3–18) needs, take the child's age and add 5. The sum is the number of grams of fiber your child should have each day.
For example, for a 3-year-old child:
3 + 5 = 8 grams of fiber.

Other high-fiber foods that are over 5 grams of fiber include barley, navy beans, baked beans, split peas, lentils, wheat flour, refried beans, prunes, and spinach, just to name a few. Many of these foods may be new to your three year old, so show them to your child before you cook them and let her learn a little about them. We want to help that picky eater consume more high-fiber foods.

A high fiber diet should be used to:

* relieve and/or prevent constipation,
* increase stool volume,
* help manage the symptoms of irritable bowel syndrome.

Family Style Eating

Your three year old's diet should now reflect your family's diet in the types of foods she is eating. Now is a good time to start introducing manners at the dinner table.

Try to have all meals at a table. This will help your child establish more routine meal times.

It is also a great time to socialize and have family time with your child. Practice those language skills with your child and model the back and forth of conversation.

Lastly, you can model manners and safe eating habits. Put food in bowls and encourage your child to serve herself with a spoon. Have your child say *please* and *thank you* when she wants more of something, use a napkin, and help her clean up any spills.

Finding time to eat with your family may actually leave you feeling less stressed. Plan ahead by preparing the protein part of your meals for the week on a Sunday. Leave salad, vegetables, and fruit for right before. Planning cuts down on prep time.

Health Visit >
Healthy and On Track

Height and Weight

One of the most important ways your pediatrician will determine your child's physical growth is by measuring height and weight to make sure she is growing at a steady rate. Most three year olds fall between these two numbers (but don't worry, all children grow at different rates): Three-year-old girls range from 35 to 40 inches in height, and boys are roughly a half inch taller. Girls typically weigh 25 to 38 pounds, and boys weigh 27 to 38 pounds. In order to determine how your child compares to other children your doctor will use the pediatric growth chart.

As long as your child is growing at a regular rate, the position she holds on the chart is not terribly important.

Keep a monthly log of your child's height and weight to see how your three year old is growing.

Another measurement your doctor will take is the circumference of your child's head. This is important for determining healthy brain development.

Head Circumference:

Girls: 18.25 to 20 inches
Boys: 18.5 to 20.5 inches

Questions doctors may ask:

* Is your child still taking an afternoon nap? (Most still need one.)

* How much and how often does your child eat? Is he eating a variety of foods?

* How is potty training going? If your child hasn't shown any signs of being ready to toilet train, be sure to let your doctor know.

* Is he left- or right-handed? By age three, most children have a dominant hand.

* Does your child play well with others? Three year olds normally have a hard time sharing their toys.

* Can your child recognize his name when called out or in print?

* Does your child jump, kick a ball, or ride a tricycle or other three-wheeled bicycle?

* Does your child always wear a safety helmet while riding a bike or a scooter and while roller skating or inline skating?

Other important areas your doctor will discuss with you is how your child is progressing in his self-help skills, language skills, social skills, and behavioral development by asking the following questions:

* Does your child dress and undress himself (with a little help)?

* Does your child brush his teeth, wash hands, and brush his hair?

* Is your child able to form sentences using three or more words?

* Does your child walk up stairs with alternating feet?

Having routine yearly well-child visits with your little one's pediatrician enables you to address concerns (if any) early on, and give you peace of mind in knowing that your child is healthy and that his development is on track and age appropriate.

Routine >
Every Day the Same, Sleeping, Starting Preschool, and Safety

Every Day the Same

Routines and consistency are very important when it comes to your child's development and overall happiness. Your child will also begin to have expectations and pick up on cues when it comes to discipline, sleeping, and eating habits.

Your child has a hard time understanding why one day you read her a story before bed and another day you are too busy. Being consistent and reading a short bedtime story every night can help your child know that after the story she will be left in her room to sleep. That can be more comforting than just putting her in bed at a different time with a different routine every day.

Tattling occurs a lot at age three. In most cases, it is not because your child is trying to get another child in trouble. **Children at this age tattle when they see another child doing something they were told not to do; they are testing you to see if the rule set earlier still stands.**

In addition to handling tattling, try not to overreact when your child starts to tell stories or lies. Your child's imagination is growing, so she may just be testing out a story to see your reaction. She may lie about something she did, such as denying she broke a toy. Your response can be "We can fix this together" or "I understand that you don't feel good about breaking the toy."

It is also important to be consistent with discipline.

Your discipline must be clear, consistent, and immediate so that your child makes the connection between her act and the disciplinary action you take. Disciplinary actions should also make sense whenever possible. If she took something without asking, limit her time with that thing. If she broke something on purpose, have her make amends to the owner. Also note if your child is hungry or tired as these two states often lead to misbehavior.

Sleeping

Three year olds should start becoming pretty consistent with their sleeping. Most three year olds still take a nap during the day and generally sleep a total of 11 to 12 hours a day overall.

Try not to overschedule your child with activities, and respect her naptime. Do not sign up your child for a soccer class that starts at the same time your child naps. She will be cranky and won't enjoy being there because she is tired. Also, it is important to be active, but having too many activities going on every day can be exhausting. Make sure your child has some time every day to choose what she wants to do.

Talk to your doctor if your child is having trouble sleeping or wakes up constantly in the middle of the night. Nightmares are common at three years old because your preschooler's imagination is very active.

Nightmares can be inescapable, but having a daily routine and consistent naptime can alleviate any extra stress or irritability when going to sleep, which can trigger nightmares.

If your child has a nightmare, it is important to comfort her and help your child fall back asleep, especially between the ages of two and six.

Your three year old is maturing more and more each day, and now is the time to help her get a good night's sleep by doing the following:

1. Move your child to a big bed and out of the toddler bed. Give a lot of praise when she sleeps in it.

2. If your child gets up because she is not used to the bed, simply take her back to bed and firmly tell her that it's time to go to sleep and leave the room.

3. Read a story, sing a song, and give a small glass of water. If you want to help her feel independent, allow one request of her choosing, but only one, and be firm.

Starting Preschool

When your child turns three it is important for you to start looking into preschool programs.

Whether a half-day or full-day program, three times a week or five, preschool helps your child get ready for kindergarten. **Attending a high-quality program prepares your child for future academic success.**

When you are choosing a preschool—an organization that promotes quality in early education—it is important to visit the school without your child the first time. Take the time to ask questions (see below). The next time take your child with you, see how he responds to the environment, and watch how the caregivers and teachers interact with him.

Children at this age learn by observing each other. Your child will catch on to the classroom routine by watching other children take directions from the teacher and follow along.

Going to preschool helps your child socialize with other children his own age, learn to share, take turns, and build relationships.

Things to look for in a preschool:

* How is the staff interacting with the children? Is the staff engaged and excited to be working with the children? Are the expectations for the children appropriate?

* What is the teacher's experience with young children? What is the teacher's background and how does the school train their teachers?

* What does the schedule look like? Is the whole day structured and planned out? How much free play is incorporated?

Structured activities with the teacher are important. Your child's teacher should spend time with each child during structured activities to help make connections and encourage the students to socialize with other children in the class. Free time should be incorporated into the schedule as well so that your child has the opportunity to explore her own interests.

* What is the school's guidance and discipline policy? How do the caregivers handle stressful situations without losing their patience?

It is important that you follow a similar guidance and discipline policy at home so that expectations are consistent for your child. It is also crucial to see if the teacher is consistent and fair with all the children in the class.

Getting ready for preschool:

* Allow him to get his outfit for preschool ready the night before so there are no anxious last-minute battles over clothing. If your child chooses a hideous outfit, rest assured that her teacher will know that it was not your choice but your child's. Allow plenty of time to get ready each day.

* Schedule: Ask your preschool for the daily schedule ahead of time so you know what time you want to arrive and transition your child into the classroom.

* Adjust your child's sleeping schedule gradually to accommodate when he will have to wake up for school.

* Talk to your child about what he will be doing at school. Drive or walk by the preschool and point it out to your child. Ask the school if you can come for a shadow day or orientation so that your child can meet his teacher and see the classroom.

* The chances are your child won't be ready for you to just drop him off and leave on the first day, so be prepared to hang around until he's settled.

* You'll probably be feeling just as anxious and emotional as he is, but try to stay cheery and confident; children pick up on your feelings of apprehension.

* Explain to your child when you'll be back. Don't use fibs such as "Mommy's just going to move the car" when you make your exit. Tell him you'll be back after lunch time/ drink time or snack time/storytime. Leave your contact number with staff in case they need to call you.

* If your child cries and won't let you leave, ask the staff for advice. In most cases in the first few days they'll ask you to stay for a while with your child.

* When you've said your goodbyes, try not to worry. If there is a problem, you'll be contacted, but in most cases your child will be enjoying his exciting new experience.

* Remember that every child is different. Some children transition into preschool quickly, and others take more time.

Going to preschool is a time of great transition for your child. Preparing together as a family will make him more confident when the time comes.

Remember, the Whole Child Parenting Program offers appropriate developmental products and monthly activity books that walk you through supporting your child's skills. Using these in conjunction with the recommended age-appropriate room materials ensures faster development.

Safety

Your child is getting bigger and moving easily on her own. She is riding a tricycle, running, jumping, and climbing with ease.

Most injuries are preventable; they happen because parents are unaware of what their children can do. Because your child is learning so much, she is at risk for injuries from falls, burns, and even water. Your child does not remember "no" when she is exploring or playing. Stay aware of where she is and what she is doing.

Some simple guidelines for keeping your fast-moving child safe are listed here.

Electrical outlets:

Cover all electrical outlets in your home. Your three year old has a good grasp on spatial orientation and will start experimenting by sticking different objects in holes and openings to see if they fit.

Chemicals:

Keep chemicals and cleaning solutions out of reach.

Gates:

If you are letting your child explore your backyard on her own, make sure you lock any gates, especially those around pools or other unsafe areas.

Helmet:

When your child is ready to learn to ride a bike or scooter or try skates, buy her a helmet. Make sure you have one with a proper fit and one that is not too loose or too snug on the head.

Traffic and street safety:

Do not have your child play near streets, and talk to your child about not chasing any balls or toys that go into the street. **Teach your child his or her name, address, and telephone number (with area code).**

Car seats:

At this age your child still needs a car seat. Between two and three years old is a good time to change to a forward-facing car seat with a harness and tether. It is important to follow the recommended weight and height requirements for each car seat.

Playground equipment:

Before letting your child explore the playground, take a walk around the park and check the equipment to make sure it is sturdy. Keep her in sight so you can monitor how high she climbs.

Strangers:

This age is an important time to start talking about strangers. Talk to your child about what to do if someone she doesn't know approaches her. Let her know that if a stranger approaches her, she should run away yelling, immediately tell you or her caregiver, and not take anything that a stranger gives her.

Mind and Body >
Yoga

Having three year olds participate in yoga gives them the ability to exercise both their bodies and minds.

Yoga encompasses the whole child by both strengthening the body and calming the mind to shape focus and build self-confidence. Through yoga, children are able to develop and foster more than just physical skills.

Yoga helps three year olds build problem-solving skills when testing their balance. They try to move their bodies and muscles in different ways until they find the best way to achieve the position.

Yoga also helps three year olds' imagination and creativity skills. You can turn yoga into a story with your child and build language skills by having her name and sequence positions that go along with the storyline.

1. Happy Baby

Have your child lie on her back, pull her knees toward her belly, and then grab on to the outsides of her feet. Then tell her to open her knees as wide as her chest and press her feet into her hands. This pose is great for the spine, so it is important to instruct your child to keep her tailbone on the ground during this pose.

2. Butterfly Pose

This pose is great for opening the hips and a good stretch for the ankles. Remind your child to sit up straight. Pushing down on the knees or thighs with elbows as your child keeps her feet pressed together allows the hips to open up more.

3. Crescent Moon

This pose benefits the flexibility of the sides of the body. Help your child extend arms into the air and stretch fingertips off to both sides, which will cause him to balance the weight of his chest while at the same time strengthening oblique muscles and stimulating flexibility.

1. Happy
   Baby

2. Butterfly Pose

3. Crescent
   Moon

Reaching Milestones >

A three year old goes through many changes from now until she reaches the age of five. These developmental changes take place over time; no two three year olds will develop at the same pace. One three year old may reach a milestone early and another at a later time. Also, all children have a difficult week or day. Take time to observe your child a few times a week to see how she is progressing.

Use these milestones as a general guide. They are not all-inclusive. What matters most is your child's progression at a fairly steady pace. Reaching a milestone later does not mean there is a problem. It simply means she needs more time and practice to master the skills.

COGNITIVE

- Can put together simple puzzles and understand that a whole object can be separated into parts.

- Names eight colors in a crayon box (red, yellow, blue, orange, green, purple, black, brown). Can count up to five and begin to recognize written numerals 0–9.

- Can label each object with just one number word to determine the total, also known as one-to-one correspondence.

- Begins to understand time in terms of morning, night, and days of the week. Working on grasping sequence of events.

- Better able to ignore distractions and focus on task at hand. Persists in completing something that is a bit more difficult and can think more creatively when solving problems.

SOCIAL-EMOTIONAL

- Starts to play with children (as opposed to playing side by side).

- Takes turns while playing (may still need prompting by adults).

- Begins to find simple ways to solve arguments and disagreements with peers.

- Begins to be able to give comfort and show concern for a peer who is unhappy without adult prompts.

- Shows a variety of emotions beyond happy, sad, and mad (though may not name these feelings). Can better manage emotions, but may still fall apart under stress.

LANGUAGE

- Listens and understands conversations, stories, songs, and poems. Understands spatial words like *in, on, behind*, and *next*. Asks "wh" questions such as "why" to get more information.

- Turns the pages of a book one at a time. Realizes that print in books tells a reader what to say.

- Communicates in simple sentences and is refining her use of grammar. Uses five or six words in a sentence and has a two- to three-sentence conversation with others.

- Learning letters and will sometimes refer to numbers as "letters." Notices print in the environment and will ask what it means. Scribbles begin to appear more like letters and may string these "letters" along to form mock words.

- Aware of the uses for writing and may dictate to an adult to write something down.

CREATIVE

- Developing greater control over her voice and can recognize, name, and sing favorite songs.

- Plays a simple rhythm instrument with a developing ability to control beat, tempo, and pitch.

- Art begins to include recognizable subjects.

- Loves dramatic play and will get involved in her imagined scenario. Prefers real objects and costumes in her pretend play.

PHYSICAL

- Runs and walks without tripping over own feet.

- Jumps and hops on one foot.

- Kicks and throws a smaller ball; catches a smaller ball using two hands and her body.

- Starts peddling a bike and pumping a swing.

- Walks backward and climbs playground equipment.

HEALTH AND CARE

- Helps with brushing teeth.

- Puts dirty clothes in hamper independently.

- Puts on shoes without ties.

- Washes body with help.

- Puts trash in the trashcan.

- Washes and dries hands, though may need some help reaching.

Environment >
Three Year Old's Room

For three year olds the world is filled with wonder. Everywhere she looks there is something new to discover, and each discovery gives rise to learning new skills.

An environment that enhances learning excites her wonder and invites her to explore. Your home environment is full of opportunities for imagining and skill-building in the **six areas of development: cognitive, social emotional, language, creative, physical, and health.**

All children appreciate an environment that is organized, uncluttered, interesting, and attractive.

Here is a basic checklist of recommended features for your home learning environment:

1. The environment is safe for your child to explore and free from clutter.

2. The environment includes your **Six Drawer Whole Child Color-Coded Organizer** with all the materials that are appropriate for independent exploration and making choices.

3. A wall calendar/organizer is available so your child can get into a routine while using the space.

Routines include regular times for learning activities to occur. Making time for daily learning in a well-organized space will set the expectation that your child have regular learning times at home.

The following picture shows what a recommended space for a three year old's room looks like with furniture.

Whole Child: Three Year Old's Room

The following list contains must-have items for your three year old's room. These items will be used interchangeably with your other Whole Child Parenting materials.

1. Six Drawer Whole Child Color-Coded Organizer
2. Whole Child Wall Planner
3. Table and Chairs
4. Easel
5. Carpet
6. Kitchen Set
7. Bookshelf
8. Puppet/Pretend Play Materials
9. Blocks and Manipulatives

four >

Milestones for a Four Year Old

 **COGNITIVE** 1

- Focuses attention more
- Uses five senses to learn math concepts
- Uses spatial language
- Uses problem-solving skills
- Memory and recall improve

 SOCIAL-EMOTIONAL 2

- Builds strong peer ties
- Uses language to express feelings and thoughts
- Controls emotions better
- Develops positive self-esteem and self-identity

 LANGUAGE 3

- Attention span increases
- Understands and comprehends meanings
- Uses around 1,500 words
- Gains phonetic knowledge and writing skills

 CREATIVE 4

- Creates music and responds to music patterns
- Creates and invents new forms of art
- Dances and performs other body movements

 PHYSICAL 5

- Hand-eye coordination skills develop
- Uses senses to guide locomotion
- Balance and endurance increase

 HEALTH AND CARE 6

- Better understands healthful lifestyles
- Is independent with self-help skills
- Understands some other cultures

four

Welcome to age four! This is a year with great changes in your child's growing independence as well as in your relationship with your child. This year will bring more than just problem solving but also reasoning skills and curiosity. Age four is a great time to start communicating openly and comfortably with your child about all the questions and concerns he can articulate about himself and his environment and those in it.

1. Cognitive Development

> **Cognitive development refers to the building of thinking methods, which includes how your child will remember, problem solve, and make decisions from now and into adulthood.**

At age four your child is now able to focus his attention more accurately and is less influenced by distractions, which is important because it will enable him to complete and engage in more challenging tasks. The eagerness to ask questions increases as your child develops a strong curiosity about the world around him.

By this age, your child will have increased memory, which accounts for a big part of his learning capability. This increase in memory supports your child in retaining more and different information at the same time.

Cognitive development at this age includes your child learning more about cause and effect as well as similarities and differences through everyday activities. Cognitive skills are at the forefront of your child's ability to process information, pay attention, memorize, and perform many other learning tasks.

The following chart provides you with an image that walks you through your child's stages of intellectual development.

Understanding these areas of cognitive development will help you learn how your child thinks, how to support learning, and how to teach new skills.

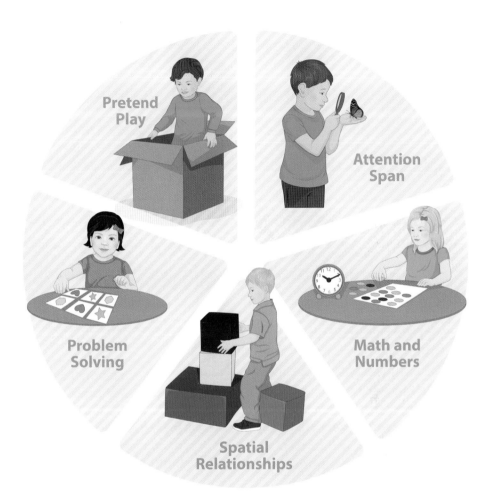

WHOLE CHILD: AGE FOUR
Cognitive
Development Components

Attention Span >

Concentration and Focus

Attention span involves the amount of time your child is able to concentrate and focus on a single activity.

If your child fails to develop strong attention skills, she will have problems with everything from math to social relationships.

Your child now has the ability to focus her attention more accurately and will be less influenced by distractions going on around her, which is important because this will enable her to engage in and complete more challenging tasks later on.

ACTIVITY

Sam and Mom are sitting at the table. Mom pulls out one of Sam's favorite memory games. "Are you ready to play Animal Memory?" says Mom. "Yes, I am!" Sam takes out the 12 game tiles, flips them all over face down, scrambles them up, and arranges them into a grid. Sam goes first, by flipping over two tiles at a time. "Aw, I got a zebra and an elephant," Sam says. "It's your turn, Mom!" Her eyes wander to her electronic tablet. Mom takes her turn and gets a zebra and a goat. "Sam, over here, it's your turn!" says Mom. Sam proceeds to turn over a tile; the first one she gets is a lion. She pauses for a moment, then turns over another tile, getting a giraffe. "Sam, did you notice what my tiles were?" says Mom. Sam says, "Zebra and . . . elephant?"

Left brain activities to do with your child to develop attention skills:

1. This is the first and most important activity to do. Change your child's diet by reducing sugar, increasing raw vegetables and fruit, using fewer processed foods, and increasing the amount of water your child drinks. A simple change of the diet makes a tremendous difference in your child's attention span.

2. Take five to 10 minutes each day to listen to music such as Mozart and Putumayo's *World Sing Along*. Talk about one instrument in the music (for example, piano or drums); this will require your child to pay attention and listen for the instrument. You may ask, "Did you hear the drums play fast or slowly?"

3. Play a game once a week of stacking blocks, then build in another day the following week, and continue till you are doing building projects a bunch of times a week. You would start this game by gathering six blocks, stack them any way you like, and then have your child copy you. This will require focus and attention to stack the blocks like yours.

INSIGHT

During this game Sam is not paying close attention to what tiles are being revealed and placed back down by Mom. Mom even has to remind Sam that it is now her turn to play. It is actually not unusual for Sam to lose attention at her age. She is still learning to focus her attention on a task for longer periods of time. Memory games are a great way for Sam to exercise her brain by improving her concentration, focus, and visual memory skills while increasing her attention span. As Sam grows older and the two of them play more memory games, she will become better and better at using her new skills in other areas of his development, such as in math.

Attention is a very sophisticated skill; the average attention span for your child is five to 15 minutes. This seems like a short time by adult standards; however, it is a perfect amount of time for your child to focus on one concept or activity without distraction or loss of concentration. Five minutes is long enough to listen to a story, and 15 minutes is long enough to do an art activity, such as cooking something together. Typically the more hands-on an activity is the longer your child will pay attention.

Take a moment and reflect on an activity you have observed your child engaging in, something simple like coloring in a coloring book. Was he able to stay focused and color the entire picture without stopping for a period of time? Or did he constantly stop after each stroke of a color placed on the paper? When your child has to use too much energy to stay focused on his work, then this is a learning block for him.

You may say to yourself, "It is just a coloring page, he can sit without moving around when he watches TV." TV and videos require little energy for your child because he finds these to be interesting but largely undemanding. A coloring page requires effort as your child has to think and focus on staying near the lines, using different colors, and trying to color in one direction. A short attention span will cause task avoidance, meaning that your child will not want to do it no matter how interesting you think it is.

We discussed earlier that your child has about a five to 15 minute attention span; however, one must understand that this does not hold true for all four year olds, because every child develops differently. When this is the case, parents play a key role in helping their children develop their attention skills.

Instead of getting frustrated or labeling your child as having an "attention problem," there are strategies parents should do to increase attention span.

Avoid flooding your child with a lot of options, as this will create distractions and disrupt your child from paying attention.

Following strategies like those on the next page gives a child brain balance and thus supports the development of his attention span, which will serve him throughout his life in all areas of development and interaction.

Strategies to increase your child's attention skills:

1. Help your child pay longer attention to an activity using toys he likes. If he likes his figurines or stuffed animals, line them up in a row, and ask him to point out certain details in the stuffed animal or figurine (e.g. size, shape, and color).

2. Use daily routines to build attention span. When going to the grocery store talk about the process as you are driving. "We will drive to the store, get a shopping cart, go over to the fresh fruit area, and pick out strawberries. After we have our fruit, we will go to check out, pay, load the car, and then drive back home." Have your child repeat the process back to you to see how well he was paying attention.

3. Help your child slow down. At this age he wants to move around quickly from one activity to another and sometimes without completing what he was working on in the first place. Do a game of Slow Motion. Ask your child to slowly walk to an object on the floor, pick it up, and bring it to you. Ask your child to count the steps as he goes along; this will increase the complexity of the task.

Math and Numbers >
Mathematical Thinking

Math and number awareness involves your child recognizing numbers, counting, learning one-to-one correspondence, recognizing patterns, sorting and classifying.

ACTIVITY

Matthew is at the table with his blocks and a new scale that was given to him by his dad. He decides to try it out by putting several blocks in one of the scale baskets. As he continues to add blocks, Matthew begins to see that the basket is tipping to one side and is full. Matthew then decides to pick up more blocks and add those to the other side of the scale.

INSIGHT

In this scenario Matthew is demonstrating his ability to measure and weigh blocks as he figures out how he can get balance on both sides of the scale. Measuring and weighing are math activities; they allow him to think mathematically and strengthen his math skills. Parents can support their child by asking questions during the activity (e.g. "Why do you think the scale is tipping?").

Math and number awareness comprise the foundation for learning more advanced math concepts.

Even before your child starts school, he is developing an understanding of math concepts through everyday interactions (as your child walks up the stairs he counts each step). Mathematical thinking involves your child using his brain to play with the concepts of parts and wholes. Mathematical thinking also occurs when your child becomes fascinated by the insides of things and how different parts make the whole thing work (e.g. puzzles).

Early in your child's life, he was learning about math by using his senses and body to make sense of the environment. When your child held your hand and saw that yours was big while his was small, this demonstrated an early math skill. This experience was preparing him for understanding and naming *small*, *big*, and *bigger*—all mathematical concepts—when he got older. Everything you will see your child do from this point forward will be more complicated.

Engaging in mathematical talk using quantity words *more* and *less* supports math thinking skills.

It is hard to imagine that your child can develop such comprehensive early math skills, but he can. Using mathematical thinking skills includes his working not only on counting numbers, but also learning about geometry, measurement, algebra, data analysis, and probability.

Encourage your child's mathematical thinking and understanding during play. Ask your child questions such as "What can you do to make your tower taller?" or "How many dolls did you put in the crib?"

Math is part of everyday life for your child, meaning you can provide a lot of opportunities for your child to think about math and to physically engage in math through regular routines.

Remember, the Whole Child Parenting Program offers appropriate developmental products and monthly activity books that walk you through supporting your child's skills. Using these in conjunction with the recommended age-appropriate room materials ensures faster development.

ACTIVITY

Dad and Marcus are in the kitchen; together they are cutting the pizza for the family dinner. Dad asks, "Marcus, would you like to help me cut the pizza?" Marcus replies, "Yes." Dad gives Marcus the pizza cutter. "Marcus, can you tell me what shape the pizza is?" "It is a circle," replies Marcus." Dad then asks, "How do you think we should cut it so all four of us get one piece of pizza?" Marcus replies, "Let's cut it here." He proceeds to cut on the corner of the pizza.

INSIGHT

In this example Dad engages in simple math talk with Marcus. He uses the math words *shape* and *four* and *one*. By Dad giving time for Marcus to respond to the questions, he is giving Marcus an opportunity to look at the pizza and think about how he will cut it into pieces for everyone. Marcus may not be able to correctly cut the pizza into four equal parts, but Dad can help him figure that out.

"Marcus, would you like to help me cut the pizza?"

Over the course of the next week focus on intentionally doing at least three of the following math routines with your child.

1. Lay out your child's outfit for the day on his bed. Ask your child to first put on his undergarments, and then have him count how many pieces of clothing are left on the bed. Next ask your child to put on his pants, and count how many pieces of clothing are left on the bed. Keep going till he is all dressed. This is providing an opportunity for your child to work with subtraction in a simple, age-appropriate way.

2. Before dinner ask your child to set out the napkins on the table. As he sets out each napkin have him count by saying, "One napkin, two napkins, three napkins, four napkins . . ." This is giving your child an opportunity to learn addition.

3. Give your child a banana or apple for afternoon snack. Cut the piece of fruit in half while he watches you, then ask him to put the fruit back together. Let him demonstrate his ability first by watching, then give verbal cues (perhaps by saying "two halves") and contextual cues such as indicating where the pieces might fit together. This is giving your child an opportunity to play with the concepts of *parts* and *whole*.

4. After dinner, have a frozen treat for dessert. Ask your child to count how many people are at the table, and then have him count how many treats he needs so everybody gets one. This will give your child an opportunity to listen to math language (*how many*).

Spatial Relationships >
Spatial Concepts

Spatial concepts
define the relationship
between your child and
objects, as well as the
relationship of objects
to each other.

ACTIVITY

 Genevieve sits at her table drawing a picture of her family. She starts by drawing a circle the size of a quarter at the top right hand corner of the paper; she puts one larger circle (the size of her palm) under the smaller circle, and then adds straight lines to represent arms, legs, and a body. Genevieve uses smaller circles to draw eyes and a mouth inside the larger circle.

Genevieve repeats this same process to draw four additional forms. Each form is larger than the next, each form is placed on different parts of the paper, and one of the forms is on top of another that is missing legs. The beautiful part about this picture is Genevieve's ability to draw shapes (circles) for objects/forms, show her understanding of spatial relationships in how the forms are placed on the

paper (by making use of the entire piece of paper), and making sure everything is inside the paper (nothing drawn off the side).

INSIGHT

As Genevieve grows older and continues to develop her spatial skills she will begin to draw pictures with distinct heads, arms, and torsos. Each shape will start at the bottom of the page (as opposed to the middle of the page); additional objects will be added to the paper to create a complete picture (sun, clouds). As your child develops strong spatial intelligence, she will draw amazing figures, drawings, and paintings. Four year olds are truly dynamic and will always enjoy tools for sketching (e.g. pens, pencils, paint boxes, and drawing paper) as gifts. Take the time to pay attention to your child's drawings. See what you can learn about her spatial development. Make comments to her about where her objects are on the page.

Spatial thinking is very important because as your child becomes aware of the world around her, and the objects that make up her environment, she will show this in her drawings. The objects your child draws will rarely be drawn in connection to one another (where they are drawn on the page). Nor will the drawing be organized on the paper. An example of this is when you look at your child's drawing and see everything "floating" on the paper.

When you see this, your immediate thought is that the picture is wrong, people and objects/forms don't float in space. Don't focus on the product, rather focus on the process your child went through to show you her ability to arrange the objects/forms on the page.

Specific kinds of play are associated with development of certain cognitive skills. Spatial play will support your child's ability to discern where she is in relation to an object and where objects are in relation to other objects.

Parents should support their children's development of spatial skills as early as the age of two, but let's say for a moment you were not thinking about this when your child was two. It is not too late to start teaching the concept because now that your child is four she will be able to grasp the concept of spatial skills more quickly.

And there are fun ways to practice!

> **Turn an everyday routine into a spatial activity for your child:**
>
> 1. Talk about things your child can see in a modified version of I Spy, as in "I spy a pink cup in the kitchen on the counter next to the stove" and then have her go find the pink cup.
>
> 2. Hide an object that is of interest to your child and then give instruction for her to find it, e.g. "The doll is in the toy chest in the playroom."
>
> 3. Ask your child to tell you which things are closer or farther away, e.g. "Which is closer to you: the couch or the TV?"
>
> 4. Sit together and complete a 3-D jigsaw puzzle.
>
> 5. Build a model together that has detailed instructions and pictures showing how to complete it.

Problem Solving >
Life's Challenges

Problem solving refers to your child's ability to use the knowledge and information she has already acquired to find answers to difficult or complicated issues.

ACTIVITY

Melissa and her brother Robert are thinking about how they will both use the electronic tablet as they sit on the floor, each one wanting a turn at the same time. On this particular day the bickering is louder than usual, and Mom can hear each of them in her room.

Mom comes out of the room and asks, "What are you two so upset about?" Each one explains that the other was not sharing the tablet. Mom asks, "Who used the tablet last? Melissa, I see the tablet in your hand. Did you just have a turn?" Melissa says, "No, I just got the tablet." Mom turns to Robert and says, "Tell your sister you'd like a turn when she is finished. She has ten minutes. I will set the timer." Mom then asks Robert what he would like to do while he is waiting for a turn on the tablet.

INSIGHT

Challenges and frustrations are inevitable, but you have the ability to support your child by giving him problem-solving skills. Mom helps her children solve the problem with the tablet by first identifying the problem (both want a turn using it), giving them an option for a solution (wait ten minutes for the timer to go off), and asking what activity they might engage in to make waiting less difficult. The strategy Mom uses will help the children think about different ways to solve problems of sharing and waiting. Mom is also teaching her children cooperation skills, which are necessary in life for engaging in social interactions.

Your child's ability to learn problem-solving skills is a significant contributor to his social-emotional wellness or self-esteem. Problem-solving skills will empower your child to think about himself and others and what roles he plays. In order to problem solve, your child needs support from you in learning to apply the five-step process of problem solving in every difficult situation that occurs. Remember, the more you practice this process with your child the easier he will learn it until it happens naturally (between ages nine and ten.)

The five steps of effective problem solving:

1. Calm down.
2. Identify the problem.
3. Brainstorm an alternative.
4. Choose a solution.
5. Determine if the solution is successful.

First, your child needs support in calming down. This can be done by encouraging your child to walk away from the situation or listen to soft music. Sometimes children need time to calm down by themselves before they are ready to talk and use language to express their emotions.

Follow by helping to identify the problem. Parents can do this by asking questions such as, "How are you feeling right now?" "Do you know why you are so upset?" or "What happened to make you so upset?" Once you have been able to identify the problem together, you can brainstorm alternative ways to solve the problem.

Once your child identifies the problem, he then acts upon the solution and discovers if it was successful. If it is not successful, try one of the other solutions you brainstormed.

By working through this process with your child, you are modeling how he can do it himself. He will likely feel supported. Your attention is always appreciated and beneficial.

Symbolic Play >
Thinking

Symbolic play is a type of thinking in which symbols or internal images (images in your child's mind) are used to represent objects, persons, and events that are not present.

Most symbolizing (using an object to stand for something else) can be observed through your child's ability to use her imagination in make-believe roles (e.g. playing doctor). **Your child's ability to symbolize occurs in gradual steps and is dependent on interaction with other people and objects in her environment.** One example of symbolic play could be your child using a large, empty box as a car after visiting a transportation museum.

It is important for your child to have a variety of opportunities to express herself symbolically; this would include encouraging your child to engage in art, drawing, and writing experiences to enhance symbolic thinking. Dramatic play or pretending also supports symbolic thinking. When your child uses symbolic thought, she accesses her memories to recall what she may have seen an object used for before,

or how she could take what is seen and use it in a different way.

ACTIVITY

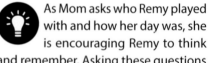

Remy gets home from half-day preschool. Mom asks Remy, "What did you do today at school?" Remy replies, "Nothing!" Mom then asks, "Well, who did you play with? Did you see your friend Tegan?" Remy replies, "We played princess today."

INSIGHT

As Mom asks who Remy played with and how her day was, she is encouraging Remy to think and remember. Asking these questions is very easy to do; however, remembering is on the lowest level of thinking skills. At the same time, remembering is necessary because it builds the foundation for higher cognitive thinking.

Your child can take in, remember, and recall information at this age fairly easily. You want your child to do more than just spit out information she has heard before; you want her to use her thinking skills.

Remembering is one of the areas parents support the most by asking the five W questions (*who, what,*

"Can I pour some tea for you, bear?"

when, *where*, and *why*). By this time you are probably wondering why remembering is discussed with symbolic play. The answer is very simple: **Play improves memory and stimulates your child's brain.** Your child will pay more attention to a task when she can have periods of play without direction from you. When you give this period of time to your child it supports her capacity to think about play; to plan what will happen; what actions, language, emotional expressions will be given to a specific character your child will play; and what real, symbolic, or invented objects she will use during play. Symbolic play supports this entire process.

ACTIVITY

 While sitting at her little table, Lea says to herself out loud, "We have to find something to do until the food is ready. Let's pretend we are going to a tea party." Lea gathers her teacups and places a stuffed bear in the chair. "Can I pour some tea for you, bear?" she asks. "Okay, here you go," she informs the bear. "I just poured your tea. It is hot so blow like this." As Lea pretends to do this with one of the bears, Mom watches from the bedroom door in silence.

INSIGHT

In this example Lea is planning what she is going to do, carrying out her plan, and then recalling what she did. Lea is developing key cognitive skills such as working memory, self-regulation (e.g. being aware of and controlling her feelings and actions), internal language or "self-talk," and the ability to organize, focus, plan, strategize, prioritize, initiate, and perform other skills that will determine her success in school later on. Pretend play helps your child develop these abilities.

2. Social-Emotional Development

> **Social-emotional development is vital because it creates a foundation for lifelong learning; it is related to later academic success and prevents future social and behavioral problems.**

During the preschool years, social-emotional development is about socialization, which is the process by which your child learns values and behaviors accepted by society. It is important to support social skills and your child's ability to control emotions with others. Development in this area leads to school readiness by teaching your child self-regulation, cooperation, and how to develop relationships with others. This skill also allows your child to develop a positive sense of self and sense of his place within the family and community.

Self-
Awareness

Social
Development

Self-
Regulation

Emotional
Development

WHOLE CHILD: AGE FOUR
Social-Emotional
Development Components

1. Social Development

Social development at this age reflects how your child develops the skills needed to make and keep a friend, cooperate with others, and participate in group activities, which in turn supports school success.

2. Emotional Development

At four, your child has better control of her emotions and has a better understanding of her feelings and what causes those feelings. Having a better understanding of why and how certain feelings come about gives your child the opportunity to problem solve and handle emotions such as anger and sadness. You will also see your four year old picking up on emotional cues when it comes to activities that make her happy and excited. Adults play an important role in helping a child discover her interests and pursue activities that make her happy, thus building her self-esteem.

3. Self-Regulation

Self-regulation is the ability of a child to recognize her own emotions and behaviors. By age four, she has enough language to begin using speaking and listening skills to solve social problems; however, this is also the age when her behavior tends to become more aggressive and more issues with aggression tend to manifest.

4. Self-Awareness

Your child is developing a sense of self through attributes she considers important such as her appearance or the ability to perform certain skills like throwing a ball. Four year olds become aware of their peers' abilities and appearances, too, and will begin to see differences between themselves and others. Your child will continue to build her independence as she sees herself as a person separate from others.

Learning how to appropriately express emotion in social settings is one of the most important social-emotional skills.

Remember, the Whole Child Parenting Program offers appropriate developmental products and monthly activity books that walk you through supporting your child's skills. Using these in conjunction with the recommended age-appropriate room materials ensures faster development.

Social Development >
Friendships

Social development
involves your child's
ability to learn how to
communicate better
with others, make
connections with peers,
resolve conflicts,
and gain confidence
in her abilities and
herself.

Building a strong social foundation is key to your child's happiness because it enables her to better handle stress ("Don't give up!") and keeps her pushing through difficult situations to a satisfactory conclusion ("I did it!").

Characteristics your child will display when she is on the path to satisfying social development:

* mastering basic interaction skills (e.g. smiling, making eye contact, and listening),

* independently approaching other adults and children,

* sharing her feelings with others (can be as simple as mentioning likes and dislikes),

* communicating needs and ideas.

Social development is also defined by culture. What is considered acceptable social behavior in your family, community, or culture may not apply to others. Given the amount of cultural diversity in our world, determining a set social behavioral practice is impossible. Therefore, parents should work toward helping their children learn behaviors that will help them become successful in their school and their environments. By doing so, parents teach their children to respect and value other cultures.

It is important for you to take time to teach your child to be pro-social by doing the following: Teach your child social skills in settings where the skill will be used. For example, when your child arrives at a neighbor's house for a play date make sure she lifts her head, looks into the other parent's eyes, and says hello in a loud, clear voice. If teaching is not possible in a natural setting then engage in a dramatic play experience and role-playing.

Teach social skills that are valued in a natural setting. For example, peers and parents value when your child is polite, uses phrases like "excuse me" when interrupting a conversation, or thanks someone appropriately.

Teach social skills consistently. Teaching must be done several times a day, using simple language, and reinforcing skills in different situations. Since you have your child use manners with others in their environment, make sure she is using manners at home with you. Often children can be more relaxed in their behavior at home and not be so polite. When you teach your child social skills in a proactive way, you will have better success in the skill being used on a continuous basis.

Be highly motivated to improve your child's social skills because social skills problems lead to peer rejection and this can be devastating to your child.

Being a four year old is tough, and being a parent is equally as hard. When children are expected to have good social skills, it will improve behavior and attachments to others. Social skills build trust in others, which supports taking risks to do activities with friends and know that she will be accepted and can accept others.

Emotional Development >
Feelings

It is important for you to look for emotional cues from your child so that you can support her in understanding her emotions.

ACTIVITY

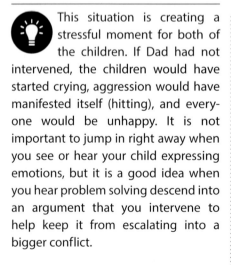 Lucy and Krish begin to argue about which one of them should have the next turn with the Dr. Seuss book. Lucy begins to cry. Dad comes over and says, "Lucy and Krish, let's take a deep breath together and talk this out. I am here to help you."

INSIGHT

This situation is creating a stressful moment for both of the children. If Dad had not intervened, the children would have started crying, aggression would have manifested itself (hitting), and everyone would be unhappy. It is not important to jump in right away when you see or hear your child expressing emotions, but it is a good idea when you hear problem solving descend into an argument that you intervene to help keep it from escalating into a bigger conflict.

Emotional development involves your child's ability to control emotions, express verbally how she feels, have positive self-esteem, and feel that she can accomplish any task she sets her mind to.

Emotional well-being involves a child's ability to understand the value of her emotions and what causes them. Having emotional well-being will enable your child to build happiness and self-esteem as well as coping abilities for emotions such as anger and sadness. Without strong emotional well-being your child will experience rejection, depression, mood swings, anxiety, and lack of appetite, and poor relationships will be formed.

Encourage your child to use more complex language to express her understanding of feelings and their causes (e.g. your child should say, "I want to try riding on that, but I'm scared.")

Stress plays a big role in your child's emotional development. When your child is always worried, anxious, scared, or unhappy, it affects her health and interactions with others.

Interact with your child affectionately, show consideration for her feelings, and express pride in her accomplishments. Give support in times of stress!

Relationships play a central role in fostering your child's emotions of joy, fear, and anger. When your child has good emotional health, she feels good about herself and is better able to handle stress and engage in relationships. You play an important role in the emotional wellness of your child by providing support as she learns to control her emotions and form good relationships with family, friends, and community. Do one of the following activities with your child at home to build your relationship:

1. Get into her space.
Your child spends a lot of time on the floor. You should be down there, too—playing games, pretending with dolls, building block forts. Work through your feelings of embarrassment and meet with your kids at their level. You might be surprised how fun it can be.

2. Enjoy family time.
Connect with your child by eating together as a family. This is a daily routine and is easy to do, even if it is just for 15 minutes. Talk about the day and how she felt about her day.

3. Do projects together.
Do a family project like cleaning up the garage or collecting recycling materials around the home. At this age you have a child who can and wants to be involved; you don't have to do it all alone.

When you do things as a family and build a strong relationship with your child, this enables you to take time to really learn to read your child's emotional cues so that you can help her identify her emotions. This can only occur when you stop what you're doing, *listen*, and participate!

Self-Regulation >
Self-Control

Self-regulation means children taking what they experience and turning it into information they can use to control thoughts, emotions, desires, and behaviors.

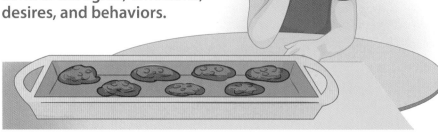

ACTIVITY

 Lizzie loves sweets! Mom has just made a batch of chocolate chip cookies; she can smell them all through the house. Lizzie runs to the kitchen and says, "Yum, cookies! I want a cookie, please. Cookies!" Mom replies, "Honey, you will have to wait for them to cool. They are right out of the oven." Lizzie sighs and decides to sit down at the kitchen table while waiting.

Mom hears the baby cry and has to leave the kitchen. Lizzie sits a few minutes more then gets up and walks over to the counter where the cookies are. She looks at them again, stretches out her arm, and opens her hand ... Mom comes back in with the baby.

INSIGHT

Many children love sweets. Try this activity with your child. Leave your child's favorite sweet treat on the kitchen counter. Tell her not to eat it until you return (she has no idea when you will return). See how long it takes before she devours it. This will give you a baseline to see how much self-control your child has.

Self-regulation starts in infancy; some children regulate arousals and sensory motor responses by sucking their thumb when they hear a loud noise. When your child was a toddler, she started complying with your requests.

Now at age four, your child is showing more complex self-regulation skills. For instance, your child will clap after she sees you put on a silly show, but she will not clap while you are giving directions. Self-regulation skills develop gradually over time.

Parents of four year olds can see firsthand how difficult exhibiting self-control can be by witnessing how four year olds push limits. This can be frustrating for you, especially when you are told by pediatricians to make sure you repeatedly and consistently set clear limits.

However, when you state limits repeatedly and then hover over your child to follow through, this will not support her ability to learn self-control. It just creates a situation in which you and your child go back and forth, ultimately ending with her crying and you raising your voice.

Try walking away when your child loses control and see what happens. When your child loses the audience, she tends to calm down. Return later and ask your child if she would like to talk about what just happened.

You play a critical role in shaping your child's self-control. You want your child to learn through you and not through lecturing and attempts to persuade or bribe. Remember, parents must model self-control and not expect it to come naturally for children. It is a skill that can take well into adulthood to master.

Modeling can take place in the following ways:

1. Include your child in decision making (e.g. food choices and what clothing to wear).

2. Offer your child periods of uninterrupted play.

3. Engage in conversations with your child about situations that happened with friends (e.g. sharing toys).

4. Help your child name her emotions and give her suggestions of ways she can calm down independently (e.g. listen to music, look through a book, engage in art).

Self-Awareness >
Self-Identity

Self-awareness refers to your child's sense of self that is retained over time and is based on various attributes he considers important.

For example, "I am the strongest, fastest boy in school." This is a statement by your child that demonstrates his sense of self based on attributes that he considers important (strength and speed). Parents help their child form healthy or unhealthy self-identity concepts of self. Identities in four year olds are encouraged by the parents and environment. For example, you could say to your child, "You are really smart," letting him know what you think about him (self-identity also comes from how he thinks others perceive him). Or you could give a negative image to your child, e.g. giving him the idea that he does not say anything that matters to you. You either increase his intelligence or increase his so-called incompetence. The road you take will help form his self-identity.

Four years old is a critical time for helping your child develop positive self-awareness and a sense of self-esteem. Achieving these goes well beyond making books about themselves, labeling body parts, and stating reasons why he is special or what makes him different.

Self-awareness is a cognitive capacity that initiates a specific step in self-development. Your child's capacity for self-awareness sets the stage for self-conscious social emo-tions such as embarrassment, pride, and shame that come from your child comparing himself to others.

ACTIVITY

Allie stands in the mirror looking at her face; she notices she has some hair on the side of her face near her ear. Allie calls for her mom and asks why she has hair on her face. Mom replies, "Some children have facial hair and others do not, and those differences are what make you who you are."

Allie is beginning to see different features about herself that she has never noticed before. Mom supports Allie by building her self-esteem and letting her know everyone looks different and has unique and special features.

INSIGHT

Encouraging self-awareness and self-identification means giving your child's positive self-esteem a boost by showing her how her differences support what it means to have an identity. The self is now recognized not only from a first-person perspective, but also from another person's viewpoint.

Self-awareness starts before your child has strong language development, as seen when she is a toddler and points to her body parts as she looks in the mirror. Your child is evaluating herself against what is perceived by those around her when she shows embarrassment and other painful emotions in a social setting.

Even at this age, your child does not have a full grasp of self-awareness because this is a gradually developed skill and develops continuously. Until your child has a definite conception of self as an independent person, she cannot understand the relationship she has to the surrounding world and thus cannot fully develop self-awareness. As your child matures, however, she will learn more and more about who she is. This learning process continues well into adult-hood.

3. Language Development

> **Language development is the process by which four year olds produce sounds, put words together to convey meaning, and communicate.**

It is suggested that language development occurs before children are born, that as fetuses they were able to identify the speech and sound patterns of their mothers. This is why doctors suggest that mothers talk to their babies while in utero. At four months, your child was able to discriminate sound and even read lips; now she is able to make full sentences and invent her own language. There is nothing more remarkable than the emergence of language because it occurs so quickly and is so obvious in a child's interactions with others.

WHOLE CHILD: AGE FOUR
Language
Development Components

Parents facilitate language development in their children through imitation and reinforcement. How parents interact with their children through language develops their children's language skills. Therefore, it is critical to always have language interactions and support children in developing their language skills as proficiency will lead to lifelong academic success.

1. Listening and Understanding

Listening occurs when your child tunes in to what he can hear and pays attention carefully. By listening, your child learns to hear the differences between sounds, which is a precursor to reading and writing. **Understanding** is how your child makes sense of spoken language, beginning with simple, short sentences and building up to more complex sentences.

2. Communication and Speaking

Speaking is how your child uses words to express his needs, ideas, and feelings and share what he is thinking with those around him. Four year olds need lots of opportunities to talk and **communicate** before they can start writing.

3. Emerging Literacy

Emergent or **emerging literacy** is how four year olds interact with books and develop the foundations necessary for learning to read and write. This is an area that uses sensory motor skills because your child will use his vision skills and fine motor skills to form letters and interact with print.

Soon your four year old will begin to start reading and writing if he has not already begun.

Remember, the Whole Child Parenting Program offers appropriate developmental products and monthly activity books that walk you through supporting your child's skills. Using these in conjunction with the recommended age-appropriate room materials ensures faster development.

Listening and Understanding >

I Understand

With listening and understanding come attention skills. Four year olds' ability to focus their attention is a developmental stage vital to the entire process of acquiring language.

ACTIVITY

 Camille goes to the public library with her older brother. As she goes off to look at books she sits and listens to the story *The Princess and the Pea*. As the librarian reads the story to the children, she speaks in an animated voice, using high-pitched and low-pitched tones. She also uses props to catch the children's attention. When the story is over, Camille goes over to her brother and excitedly tells him about the story she just heard.

INSIGHT

Camille demonstrates her listening skills by sitting while the librarian is reading. The librarian's use of props enables Camille to focus and gain a better understanding of what the story is about as well as entertaining her. Developing language skills using play and entertainment makes learning fun.

Parents can provide a variety of opportunities for their children to focus their attention and listen carefully. This skill will support all aspects of learning and development, including emerging literacy skills such as phonetic and phonemic awareness, which lead to reading and writing.

When your child was two, she listened with interest when you read stories to her and encouraged her to respond to familiar sounds. At ages three and four, you encourage your child to listen one-on-one or in a small group, such as going to a reading at the bookstore, because she can focus her attention and listen, which leads to understanding.

As your child continues to develop listening skills, you will see improvement in her speaking skills. Your child will say all speech sounds in words. Mistakes will be made with the more difficult sounds, such as "l," "s," "r," and "v," but this is not a cause for alarm.

She will talk without repeating words; name letters and numbers; use sentences that have more than one action word, such as *play* and *jump*; tell a short story; and—best of all—keep the conversation going. It is critical to build your child's vocabulary.

Model listening skills by making sure you are truly listening. Playing games such as Stop, Look, and Listen will encourage your child to pause and pay attention to what she hears.

Give definitions for new words, and use them in sentences: "A taxi is a type of transportation. It is a car. A double decker bus is another type of transportation. So are motorcycles and bicycles."

Understanding involves the way your child comprehends meaning and her interpretation of instructions and problems given to her. Parents will often ask their four year olds, "What did I ask you to do?" When parents do this, they are asking their children to explain what they heard in order to make sure the children understood the directions given to them so the task can be performed.

ACTIVITY

Tanni's neighbor comes over to play. Mom comes in the bedroom and says to Tanni, "When your friend leaves, you need to clean your room and put the dirty clothes in the laundry." At the time, Tanni is so busy playing that Mom is not sure if Tanni has been listening or even has a clear understanding of what she is supposed to do. When Tanni's friend leaves, Mom asks Tanni to come to the room. "Tanni, did you hear what I asked you to do? Please tell me what you are supposed to be doing now that your friend has left." Tanni begins to tell Mom she is supposed to clean her room.

"Please tell me what you are supposed to be doing now."

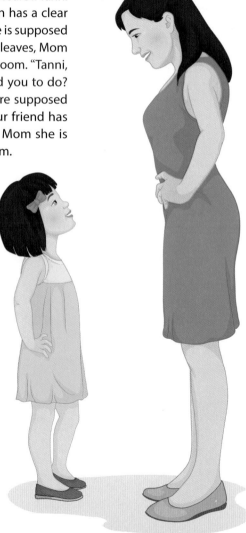

INSIGHT

It is very important for Mom to take the extra step to see if Tanni has listened to her and understands what she is supposed to do. When you do this type of follow up with your child, it encourages her to stop, think, and make meaning out of what she hears. Children need practice more than simply following directions; they need help practicing attending to oral language and interpreting what they hear. So give your child many opportunities to listen carefully to specific requests you have each day.

Your child has the ability to retell a story she has heard or create a story using a wordless picture book.

In a storytelling event, your child has not memorized the words; rather, she is interpreting and paraphrasing the words as she understands them through a spontaneous performance, assisted by audience interaction. For children to retell stories, they must understand what they heard.

They are able to understand the main idea of the story, recognize the characters, and organize the facts.

Understanding is important to your child's ability to build her language and literacy skills because it is also a necessary cognitive skill used in storytelling.

Stories provide a four year old with the mental framework for thinking so she can shape experiences into a whole that she understands. Storytelling allows your child to mentally map experiences and see pictures in her head; it gives her a model of language and thought she can imitate. Remembering and understanding occurs when your child answers questions that require her to organize previously gleaned information.

It is important for parents to create an environment that is rich in language opportunities for their children.

Communication and Speaking >
I Said That?

Language development incorporates an ever-growing vocabulary. Four year olds will understand how sounds and words can be married to create sentences and communicate with others.

ACTIVITY

Robert goes to the park with his older sister. At the park he gets really excited because in the distance he sees something really big. He cannot figure it out at first. Robert says to his sister, "A bear! I see a bear on the grass, by the tree!" His sister looks up and says, "Oh Robert, it's a deer not a bear. We don't have bears here!"

When Robert arrives back home, he runs into the living room where his mom and dad are sitting. Robert says, "Guess what? I saw a bear at the park! Oh, no, not a bear. What did we see?" His sister replies, "A deer." Robert says, "Yes, I saw a deer, and it was huge like the size of a bear!"

INSIGHT

Robert comes home and tells a short story about his experience during the day. He demonstrates his ability to communicate using descriptive words (*huge*) and complete sentences; he even uses connecting words (*by* the tree).

A rich language environment has an essential impact on the rapid development of your child's cognitive abilities (brain development). Communication and language support personal, social, and emotional development because your four year old can communicate feelings, needs, and ideas, as well as develop a strong sense of self-awareness.

At four, your child uses more than 1,500 different words, knows about 4,000 words, and understands even more. Words four year olds speak and understand fall into four categories:

1. **Connecting words, such as *when* and *but***—"When I grow up, I am going to play soccer."

2. **Words that explain emotions, such as *upset* and *angry***—"I am angry at you."

3. **Words that explain something that is on his mind, such as *remember***—"Remember, Mom took us to the park? We played on the rocket slide."

4. **Words that explain where things are, such as *on top of* and *below***— "The cat is on top of the car."

Connecting words come from your child's increased language development. He now has the ability to connect words and make a sentence or statement using those words.

Emotion words come from your four year old's social-emotional development. Your four year old is showing you how he uses words to express feelings as opposed to acting out those feelings.

Words about things on his mind come from having a better understanding of what he recalls and how well he can remember events from the past.

Using words about where objects or people are shows your four year old's growth in spatial development and his ability to see the location of objects around him.

Retell Stories

For your child to retell stories, he must tap into his creative and imaginative skillssets to recreate the story.

Children are taking everything that they have learned in the past and applying it to present skills they are developing, which prepares them for learning new skills in the future.

Remember to give yourself praise and encouragement for supporting your child's language growth.

A child's growth in language is one of the most obvious manifestations of cognitive development, and it provides great joy to parents as they watch it progress.

Emergent Literacy >

Learning to Read and Write

Emerging or emergent literacy development describes how children acquire reading and writing skills.

Language, reading, and writing are linked together, and they develop together continuously through the use of literacy materials. Literacy materials are things such as magazines, books, newspapers, crayons, and markers.

Everything your child has done at previous ages, from gumming a book to singing nursery rhymes, has paved the way for literacy development. Language and literacy skills are learned best when four year olds can enjoy books independently and interact with other children and adults, as well as through literacy rich experiences provided by you.

Printed words, in storybooks or in the environment, allow children to connect themselves to faraway places. Exposure to books and print, as well as having conversations that prompt children to discuss the people and important events in their lives, encourages children to discover that written words are another way to share ideas. It is important to practice literacy skills every day with your four year old by making literacy a part of your routine. Have your four year old repeat a simple story after you read it.

ACTIVITY

Patty is reading a book with her niece. Patty reads, "It was a dark and stormy—" and then stops reading. Patty asks her niece, "What comes next?"

INSIGHT

By asking this question, Patty is helping her niece make simple predictions about the story being read to her. This helps her develop literacy skills.

Some children are starting to recognize different letters, especially ones in their name; they can connect a letter with the sound it makes and understand that these sounds make up words. Some can already "read" common words they see, like the word *stop* on the sign at the corner.

ACTIVITY

Amelia picks up a book about cookies from the floor and begins to "read" the book. Some of the words she is making up, but when it comes to the word *cookie*, she is able to sound it out and read the word. Mom helps her by pointing at the picture and breaking the word into two parts.

INSIGHT

Amelia is demonstrating emerging literacy skills. She can recognize certain words that are important to her. By giving her contextual cues and breaking the word into parts, Mom is supporting her child's largely independent efforts.

Once your child understands and recognizes more words in print, you will find that she loves to play games with words. She wants to have fun with literacy. So join in with her. Read a book and then play act the characters. Using only the pictures in a book make up the story yourselves. Dress up like the characters in a book and write down a new story about them. Literacy skill building can be lots of fun.

ACTIVITY

Mona's mom wants to play a reading game called What Can You Read? Mom writes names of objects around the house (e.g. *window*, *sink*, *mirror*, *rail*, etc.) on paper and tapes the words next to the object. Mom says, "Mona, let's play What Can You Read? Go around and find all the words and read them out loud. The ones you can't read we will do together."

INSIGHT

Because Mom puts the labels next to the objects, she supports her daughter's early literacy skills. Offering to help keeps the activity from becoming overwhelming or boring.

Earlier we discussed how reading, writing, and language develop together. In Mona's game What Can You Read? Mom can extend the learning further to include writing skills. Since your four year old is developing more control over her hands and fingers, she can use literacy materials like pencils. Remember that she is still learning to write letters, so let your child practice with pencils and paper as often as possible.

In this example, after all the words are collected from Mona's What Can You Read? game, Mom asks Mona to pick two of the words she wants to learn to write. Mona picks *box* and *cup*. Mom gives Mona a thin piece of paper to put on top of the card and has Mona trace the letters. When Mona gets the hang of "writing" letters this way, Mom can then provide lined paper.

Sit down with your child and have her help you make the shopping list. This activity will support literacy development through writing. It will also get her more involved in making healthful food choices!

Sight Words

Sight words are very important on the path of teaching your child to read. This is a perfect time for parents to learn more about Dolch sight words. Dolch sight words are words that have been identified as high frequency words that will be used starting at the age of four and carry through to seven or eight years of age. These words occur in about 75% of the books and materials children see and need to be learned by memory, regardless of where the child is in phonetical learning. Some of these common sight words include:

**all   and   hot   how   let   not   man   may   dry   eat
fly   off   our   put   red   sit   some   the   mom**

You can find more sight words below specific to this age and create a sight word wall in your home. Once a week together pick a sight word, tape it on your refrigerator, and try to work on using the word in conversations you have with each other at home.

not   one   and   can   for   see   big   red   you   the   run

One thing you may have noticed is that all of these words consist of three letters. Four-letter sight words can be learned after your child masters three-letter sight words. This does not mean your child can only learn to read three-letter words, but it is easier to start off small and build up in complexity.

These words are also good to start with when your child is learning to write. When you use sight words combined with writing, you can also teach the sounds that are associated with each letter. This will support reading and writing development.

Practice reading and writing skills by making a name card for your child. Place it next to things that belong just to your child (e.g. her coat or lunchbox). Make the card colorful and clear. Show your child that the letters spell an important word: her own name.

Teaching Your Child to Read

Many parents are very excited to start teaching their children to read, but some groundwork must first be laid. Your child needs to know the differences between pictures and print, understand how books are read (from left to right), and see the differences between uppercase and lowercase letters.

Your child can start identifying most letters between the ages of four and five, so now is a great time to start teaching her the alphabet and letter sounds. Parents can then start teaching their children how to pick out and differentiate between individual letter sounds, which is called **phoneme isolation**. Children who are exposed to more print and text at home tend to make these connections sooner.

There are a number of different ways you can teach your child letter sounds. Start with the your child's name and sound out each letter by having her clap her hands as she says her name. This can be done with any word; over time, children will grasp this concept of words being broken down into separate sounds and syllables. Once she learns her name phonetically and by spelling it out, go back to the alphabet.

Introduce two letters a week. Pick letters that are important to your child. If she is focused on space, use the letters S and P. Introduce one letter at a time by pointing out things in the house that start with that letter. Say the sound that the letter makes then say the name of the letter: PUH, P. You can even take turns going through the alphabet using the sounds of the letters instead of the names of the letters: AH, BUH, KUH, DUH, etc.

By following these steps, you will help your child start reading, which leads to writing.

Teaching your child to read will take more time for some children and less for others. Patience and practice are the keys to success!

ACTIVITY

 Mary is standing in the living room and takes a book from the shelf. It is a book that is very familiar to her, *The Little Kittens*. Mary begins to say, "One." Mary then flips to the next page and says, "A, and." As Mary looks through the book she points out familiar letters and pictures on the pages.

INSIGHT

Mary is demonstrating her ability to use her emergent literacy skills (locating letters and using pictures with print) to learn how to read. She applies letters and their sounds and plays with the sounds in words. As you teach your child to read, choose books about subjects that'll really catch her interest or make her laugh. One of the keys to improving literacy is to keep reading stories to your child; this improves concentration and imagination, particularly once you progress beyond basic picture books. Reading aloud is crucial to nurturing the love of reading.

4. Creative Development

> **The right side of the brain is best at expressive and creative tasks. Creativity is both a skillset and a distinct and individual personality system that is developed throughout a child's life and refined in adolescence and adulthood.**

Positive creative experiences are needed along your child's educational journey. When you support your child's creativity, you boost her confidence and ability to express her ideas using visual symbols, and you increase her learning potential. Creative thinking and the ability to show meaning in many ways are the keys to success in the 21st century.

Creativity experiences boost your child's learning and development in several ways. Some of the ways include cognitive problem solving, self-regulation, and the development of tools for communication and meaning making. In order to provide quality creative experiences for your child you need to give her different mediums to create art. For example, you should offer your child a brush to paint with, but also tools like rollers and sponges so she can create a contemporary painting. Children love to draw; offer your child crayons, but also colored chalks and oil pastels. Your child has ideas; continue to encourage her to be imaginative and creative!

WHOLE CHILD: AGE FOUR
Creative
Development Components

1. Music

Music, a complex blend of sounds, is created by using the voice or instruments, or a combination of both to make a melody, harmony, and rhythm. The singing voice is the primary instrument your child uses automatically. Parents support their child in music by offering instruments to be used in combination with the voice to extend learning.

2. Dance

Deliberate and intentional movements performed with awareness are what evolve into dance once your child matures. Watch her twirl, whirl, and move her hips side to side in response to music.

3. Visual Arts

Visual art forms include such activities as drawing, painting, sculpture, crafts, and photography. Visual art includes many other artistic endeavors, such as creating textile art; this is when your child creates a picture by gluing different fabric and yarn pieces onto paper or canvas.

4. Dramatic Play

Dramatic play occurs when your child represents her understanding of her experiences through role-playing and imitating, adding language to the mix.

Keeping art materials around and accesible at all times gives your child the opportunity to be creative anytime.

Remember, the Whole Child Parenting Program offers appropriate developmental products and monthly activity books that walk you through supporting your child's skills. Using these in conjunction with the recommended age-appropriate room materials ensures faster development.

Music >
Singing and Playing

It is a wonderful experience to watch your child engage in singing and "playing" an instrument.

Your child is learning music in much the same way she learned language. For example, after listening to the sounds of her native language, she began to babble, experimenting with speech sounds. Soon afterward, she imitated words and used them meaningfully in phrases and sentences.

ACTIVITY

 Sara is playing with her dolls in her bedroom; she says, "I know you're sleepy, dolly. Let's go to sleep now." Sara begins to sing her dolly a lullaby. "Hush, little baby, don't say a word. Mama's gonna buy you a mocking bird, and if that bird won't sing, Mama's gonna buy you a diamond ring. Shh!"

As Sara sings the song she speaks some of it and sings some of it; this results in her losing the pitch and tempo. When Sara places "shh" sounds at the end of the song, she is making reference to being quiet so the dolly can sleep.

INSIGHT

Sara demonstrates she is in the rhythm babble stage of music development; this is indicated by her inability to keep tempo, pitch, or rhythm. This is appropriate, however, because at this stage of development the skill reflects a simple musical experience between Sara and her dolly.

Musical sound is created to express ideas that your child has in her head. She creates music and responds to music.

Your child starts the stage with **music babble**, in which she makes sounds that do not make musical sense. She will move into **tonal babble** next, in which she sings in a speaking voice. In **rhythm babble** she will make voice sounds that are not on tempo. By the time she is four, she has started to be able to sing most of a short song correctly.

Picking up an instrument will help your child express herself and support social development. **She will love to experiment with a variety of instruments with you and other children as she learns to work with others to create sounds.** This enables her to create sound patterns with her instrument, her body, and her voice. Have you observed your child making noises with her armpits? Even though it may not sound like a musical sound, it is your child trying to make sound patterns with her body as the instrument.

This age is a great time to open up your child's musical world by having her take music lessons. You would not start vocal lessons because your child is not at that stage of development. You could start her on an instrument as she is developing fine motor (small muscle) skills at a rapid pace.

Picking an instrument for your child is exciting; often parents pick **something they wished they knew how to play; however, it is more important to pick an instrument based on your child's personality.** Below are some instruments to think about.

1. **Does your child like being the center of attention?**
   Flutes are great; many musical compositions contain flute solos.

2. **Is your child outgoing?**
   Saxophones and trumpets are good as they are lead instruments.

3. **Do you have a petite child?**
   Bassoons are ideal for small children.

4. **Does your child have large hands or long fingers?**
   Pianos are a desirable choice.

Whatever instrument you choose for your child, when you choose one that suits her personality you create a more supportive experience that is set up for long-term success.

Expose your child to different instruments and sounds by listening to music, visiting an instrument store, and watching a live ensemble performance in your community or local civic center.

Dance >
Boogie and Groove

The words *dance* and *movement* are inter-changeable when discussing creative development.

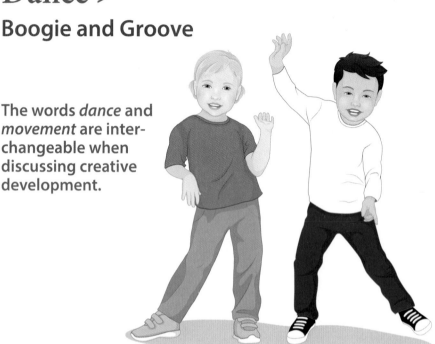

Dance is a form of art, and the human body is the canvas. It is your child's body moving in space and time with energy. Dance is a form of cultural expression; it supports the development of many other abilities.

Dance will teach your child the value of creativity, and the skills of problem solving, risk taking, and higher-order thinking.

Earlier in the book, we discussed how learning one skill leads to learning another skill and that many areas of learning have an effect on another area. This is the same for dance; it helps your child to grow physically, emotionally, socially, and cognitively. Many parents can see how dance enhances their child's physical skills but are less familiar with how dance develops other skills. Let's take a moment and visit two areas.

Social-emotional development: At this age, children want a dance partner or an audience. Dance promotes social interaction and cooperation. Your child will communicate with you through dance and the movements of his body. Dance is an excellent outlet for a four year old to express emotions and feelings. Dancing enables your child to be aware of himself in a particular music-filled space.

More importantly, dance develops the brain and teaches your child to think about the different ways he will move his body. But you have to give him tools to help him be successful with it. Tools include music to listen to and props like scarves and instruments to help support movement and music skills. If you just say to your child, "Dance," but you don't give him tools, he'll just stand there. Four year olds like to discover what their bodies can do. They delight in isolating body parts, changing directions and levels, exploring each part's range of motion, and increasing their abilities.

Dance requires your child to expand his range of motion and use every part of the body. It includes fine motor (small muscle) and gross motor (big muscle) skills, as the body parts are moved in different directions at the same time, hands included. Your child will improve his coordination skills as he learns to twirl around without falling.

A dance-infused environment will lead to new moves and new skills for your child. He will eventually feel a sense of accomplishment at conquering tasks, leading to higher levels of general self-esteem than if he was never to have dance as a part of his life.

Through dance, physical development is expanded in the following ways:

1. Flexibility—Your child can sit and touch his toes with his hands and hold his feet.

2. Stamina—When your child was a toddler he got tired after five minutes of dancing; now your child can engage in a dance experience for 30 to 45 minutes.

3. Posture—As your child learns to stretch his body and keep his shoulders back he will stand straighter and have better posture.

4. Weight—Dance can help a child who is overweight slim down.

Visual Arts >
Images

Visual arts comprise a vast category that includes drawing, craftmaking, collage, mosaic, photography, sculpture, and more.

ACTIVITY

Kayla recently received a box of pastel chalks from her mom. Kayla asks her mom if she can go outside and use her new chalk set. Kayla looks up at the sky, then looks down at the pavement and begins to draw a cloud and a sun with the chalk. She draws the lines on the sun to show that the sign is shining brightly. Kayla calls to her mom, "Look, Mom! I drew the sky!"

INSIGHT

In this experience Kayla creates a picture that is a form of realistic art. Realism has the appearance of a recognizable subject, be it an object, person, or place. When you look at Kayla's art, you can point and say, "Oh, that's a sun and a cloud." Visual art creates and strengthens the neural connections in her brain as she explores the texture of the chalk on the pavement. Kayla's parents have supported her visual art skills by simply providing her with a tool: chalk.

Visual art allows your child to explore the world without having to actually create an art piece herself; this is because visual art can be seen throughout your child's environment (e.g. a sculpture or a fountain).

When your child is able to explore visual art using a variety of different mediums—such as paint, play dough, canvas, oil pants, and watercolors—it enables her to develop both the right and left side of the brain by teaching perceptual, cognitive, and discrimination skills that will aid with reading ability and expand gross motor (large muscle) and fine motor (small muscle) skills!

Parents are role models for their children and the development of their visual art skills. Participate in art with your child and make materials readily accessible. Materials can include some of the mediums discussed above; in addition to these, set up a dedicated space within your home.

When your child creates art, take a moment to discuss her creation together. Talk about the colors that were used. This will provide a supportive environment in which your child can take a moment and reflect on her work.

Create a space to display her work. This will make her feel confident and build her self-esteem.

Engaging in visual arts when your child is young can nurture the creative spirit.

Four year olds who are exposed to a wide variety of arts and crafts are more likely to create unique inventions that are patent worthy, come up with ideas that start companies, or publish papers and books on science and technology. Many problem-solving situations require creative solutions. When you support your child in visual arts, you are supporting her ability to be creative and think "outside the box."

Engaging in creating and appreciating visual arts is both fun and educational.

Dramatic Play >
Pretend Play

Dramatic play, also known as *pretend play*, can be defined as your child using her imagination to come up with ways to role play and portray life experiences.

ACTIVITY

 Lisa is in her bedroom dressed up in her fairy costume. She has her dolls lined up. "Dolly, do you want to make a wish? Yes? Do you want to come fly with me? Okay. I will teach you. Don't be afraid. I am here." Lisa picks up the dolly and "flies" her around the room.

INSIGHT

Lisa is engaged in a dramatic play experience, which does not necessarily mimic a particular life experience, but involves her acting out a maternal role. This type of play expresses Lisa's need to show off some of the skills she has seen her parent demonstrate with her (reassuring, helping). Though no adults participate in this particular dramatic play, there are ways to engage with your child should she choose to have you there with her. Always have at ready materials for your child to use such as dress-up outfits or props like hats and wands.

Because the definition of dramatic play is so broad, we have to look at the many ways your child will participate in this experience.

Have you ever noticed your child engaged in a dramatic play experience? This is interesting to watch because you realize just how much listening your child has been doing, e.g. when speaking to her dolls she uses many of the words you use. Or perhaps she uses her transportation toys to act out a construction scene you saw while on a walk in the neighborhood.

Have you ever made the comment to someone, "All my child wants to do is play all day?" Many people have devalued the importance of dramatic play/pretend play because they think that pretending or using symbols that stand in for that which is real is not important for school readiness.

Dramatic play intertwines with all areas of your child's development, including.

Language and literacy build your child's oral skills, which are developing as she has conversations, negotiates, and takes on roles during dramatic play. You can see this as she uses vocal changes with puppetry or makes signs on poster board for her backyard construction site. Parents can support their children in language development through dramatic play by reading aloud stories and providing animation in their voices when using puppets.

Dramatic play builds science skills. Turning off all the lights in your house and making hand-shadow puppets with your child involves science and dramatic play because he is engaged in experimenting with light and shadow while he is role-playing. Using technologies such as a projector or camera to make a family movie on the computer with your child also combines dramatic play and science. Have fun with the tools at hand.

5. Physical Development

> **Physical development refers to your child's ability to use both gross (large muscle) motor skills and fine (small muscle) motor skills to move his body in different ways and patterns.**

As your child's body becomes sleeker and less top heavy, his center of gravity shifts downward. As a result, balance improves, paving the way for new motor skills involving large muscles of the body. When your child becomes steadier on his feet, his arms and body are freed to experiment with new skills: throwing and catching balls, steering tricycles, and swinging on horizontal bars and rings.

Your child is learning to move in space, move with confidence, and control all of his smaller muscles that move when he picks up something or puts it down. In physical development, children are developing body confidence, which encourages them to push their bodies to try new things, move in new ways, and even challenge themselves to see if they can jump farther or higher than they ever did before.

Physical development also supports the health of your child and helps maintain a healthy lifestyle. This includes the amount of time they spend

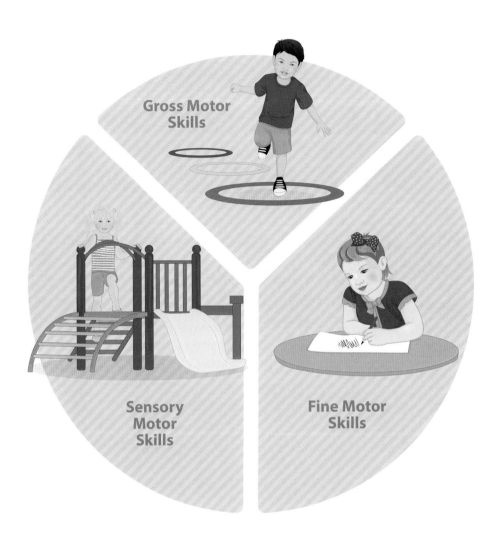

WHOLE CHILD: AGE FOUR
Physical
Development Components

moving their bodies versus sitting and watching TV or other passive activities. It includes the types of foods they put in their bodies to give them energy for movement and to gain new physical skills. Physical development also involves the ways in which your child will use a range of small and large muscles to gain new skills.

1. Gross Motor Skills

Gross motor skills are larger movements your child will make with his arms, legs, feet, or his entire body. Gross motor development started in infancy as your child began to sit up (using the torso to stabilize himself) and crawl (using the leg muscles), and it continues to grow as he matures.

2. Fine Motor Skills

Fine motor skills are small movements such as picking up small objects like a marble or toothpick. This area also started developing in infancy as your child learned to hold a spoon or a cup. Small muscles are developed in the fingers, toes, wrists, lips, and tongue.

3. Sensory Motor Skills

Sensory motor development involves children's brains receiving sensory messages and then producing a response that uses fine motor or gross motor skills. This information is received from the body and his environment through what he sees, hears, smells, tastes, and touches, as well as the **vestibular sense** (movement and balance) and **proprioception** (sense of his own body).

At about age four you can start teaching your child how to tie her shoes. Use the "bunny" ears method. And be patient!

Remember, the Whole Child Parenting Program offers appropriate developmental products and monthly activity books that walk you through supporting your child's skills. Using these in conjunction with the recommended age-appropriate room materials ensures faster development.

Gross Motor Skills >
Developing the Large Muscles

Gross motor skills are skills that involve different body parts such as your child's feet, legs, head, and arms.

Put on the sunscreen and take your child outdoors. Encourage him to run at different speeds or toss and catch balls of different sizes. By doing so you support gross motor skill development.

This is also the time when you can put your child in gymnastics, more advanced swimming classes, ballet, soccer, T-ball, or karate. These activities support his gross motor skill development, but there are things a parent can do at home as well. When you go to the park, let your child try to walk along a very low wall. He can walk a two-inch line for at least 10 feet without stepping off if you provide the experience for him to practice.

Play a game of tiptoe around the house or stomp to music. Turn on soft music first and tiptoe as softly as you can. Then play a marching band song and stomp around the house together. Four year olds can tiptoe, which encourages them to learn to balance without their hands held out for support.

Gross motor skills are important for your child to perform everyday functions, such as walking and running. These are critical for everyday self-care skills like dressing because you need to be able to stand on one leg to put on your pants without falling over. Gross motor skills impact the endurance your child needs to cope with a full day of school or home activities. In other words, **gross motor skills improve your four year old's muscular strength, endurance, posture, body awareness, balance, co-ordination, and muscle tone.** Play with your child and enjoy all the things his body can do.

ACTIVITY

 Ross is very excited because today he is going to his very first children's gym class. He sits thinking about what he will do in the class. In gym class the teacher places three hula-hoops in the middle of the floor. "Today, class, we will jump and hop in and out of the hoops. You will need to keep your hands extended at your side to give you balance. Let me show you how," says the teacher. After the teacher shows the children how to hop and jump in and out of the hoops, Ross has a turn. He starts at the nearest hoop, extends his arms, and hops from one hoop to another with alternating feet. "Good job, Ross! You made it to the other side without falling," says the teacher.

INSIGHT

This activity helps Ross develop his gross motor skills as he hops in one hula hoop and out another. Ross is not only developing his leg muscles, he is also developing his arm muscles as he keeps his arms extended for balance while he hops. Gross motor skills develop very quickly during the early years. Now that your four year old has some confidence in his gross motor abilities, this is the time when you can support him even further. In Ross' case you can support his skills by adding a tunnel at the end of the hoops. Then he works on going from a standing position to a bending and crawling position.

Fine Motor Skills >
Small Muscles

Fine motor development is defined as the development of smaller muscle movement that involves using the hands and fingers to carry out detailed tasks.

You have witnessed first hand how your child has progressed in the area of fine motor development as you watched her go from uncontrolled hand moments in infancy, then bringing objects to her midline (middle of body) and picking up smaller objects as a baby, to using a crayon to scribble and a finger to point as a toddler; and now she can tie her shoe, use scissors, write with a pencil, draw circles on a paper, and "type" on a computer. Fine motor skills enable your child to grasp, hold, and manipulate small objects.

ACTIVITY

Samantha is now four years old. Samantha walks by the office and notices her dad working at his desk writing something. "Dad, can I have a pencil and paper, please?" asks Samantha. She loves to use more refined writing tools such as pencils and pens instead of crayons or markers. Samantha then takes the items and sits at her table. She starts at the top of paper and begins to make a series of zigzag lines on the paper.

INSIGHT

In this scenario Samantha is demonstrating her ability to use her fine motor skills by pretending to write or creating a piece of art. This is a skill that is reflective of a child who is four, because it takes precision to make sharp lines. Fine motor skills play a significant role in your child's physical development because the arms, hands, and fingers work together to complete the task. Fine motor development is ongoing. It never stops. Even as an adult Samantha may continue to refine her fine motor skills by learning to play an instrument or build and paint model airplanes.

Your child was not able to progress through the timeline of fine motor development without having a strong foundation. You gave her this foundation as you provided her with learning experiences to increase hand-eye coordination skills, allowed her to have greater independence as she learned to open drawers and cabinets, and let her participate in routine tasks at home like picking up her clothes. All of these activities helped your child develop finger strength and control.

Fine motor development involves the senses. One in particular is her sense of sight and hand-eye coordination skills using her eyes to control the movements of the muscles of the hands, fingers, and wrists. Just as you supported your child in building the foundation needed to develop fine motor skills, you must continue to support her in refining her fine motor skills with specific activities provided through play experiences.

Parents can draw straight lines on paper and let their children cut along the lines or let them trace over their names if they cannot write the letters independently. Brushing teeth independently encourages fine motor development.

Activities that support small muscle development include your child buttoning her own buttons. If she is unable to do so independently, support her by starting the button and then letting her finish. Show your child how to tie her shoes by modeling side by side or by using the "bunny ear" method.

When your child serves her own food this encourages wrist development, as does pasting pictures on paper. There are many everyday experiences that can be created for your child to hone fine motor skills. Many of the skills once refined will lead to your child developing writing and articulation skills for language development. If your child does not practice her fine motor development skills, she will weaken and lose her ability to perform some tasks required by her hands (e.g. the ability to hold scissors properly or use a pencil). Have you ever heard someone say, "I used to play piano and now I can't?" When you ask what happened the response is usually, "I stopped practicing years ago." A fine motor skill is like this: Without practice and refinement you can severely limit your ability to continue performing the skill.

Fine motor development supports strong writing skills. Strong writing skills will last your child a lifetime!

Sensory Motor Skills >
Movement Makes "Sense"

Sensory motor skills involve getting stimuli from the environment through the senses, which are processed by the brain; the brain then sends the required information for action to the appropriate body part.

ACTIVITY

 Talia joins a soccer program for the summer. Today the girls are practicing kicking the ball; it is Talia's turn to practice kicking. Her coach tells her to line her body up a few feet away from the ball, to look at the ball ahead of her, then approach the ball, and kick.

INSIGHT

This process of telling Talia how to kick the ball may seem unnecessary, but it is a clear example of the steps children use with their sensory motor skills to achieve a motor task.

Early on, we defined sensory motor skills as including the senses; one of those senses is the **vestibular** (movement and balance) sense. It has a huge influence in your child's daily life.

Vestibular sense helps your child keep her balance, provides coordination for movement of her head with her eyes, gives her the ability to use both sides of her body together, and allows her to remain upright against the pull of gravity (like when a strong wind blows). It is a prerequisite skill for whole-body locomotion or movement. For example, being able to stand without falling allows for putting on pants; this motor skill also permits exploration of your child's surrounding space and the objects in it.

When the vestibular sense is working efficiently and effectively in your child, it will free up all the rest of her higher cognitive functioning and motor skills.

Maintaining balance is vitally important because it provides a base on which she can build other physical skills.

ACTIVITY

Four-year-old Matthew is in the children's book area at the library listening to story hour. The book being read is about dinosaurs, which is a topic Matthew loves. Out of the corner of his eye he sees a stuffed dinosaur toy on a display to his right. Matthew gets up during the story and goes to see what kind of dinosaur it is.

As soon as Matthew gets up and begins to walk he trips over his feet and topples onto the floor. He picks himself up and starts walking again over to the display. When Matthew makes it, he accidentally kicks it with his foot and the display falls over.

INSIGHT

This scenario demonstrates how some children at this age can have difficulty with their developing vestibular sense. We see this in the case of Matthew, specifically with his inability to pay attention to the story being read, and the difficulty he encounters with coordination, being clumsy, colliding with objects. This is why it is vitally important for you to help your child develop this sense and thus increase sensory motor abilities.

Below is an example of a specific activity you can do with your child. Start by doing the activity one time a week, then build up to two times a week; continue on a daily basis as you watch your child grow.

Eye movement control exercise
(seeing supports focus, which supports balance)

Many parents have at least one set of blocks at home. Sit with your child and create block designs. To get prepared for this activity, take five or 10 square blocks and arrange them in a shape on a piece of paper. Trace around the outside of the shape. Repeat this process four more times, creating four different block shapes on paper.

Then give your child the paper and his blocks, and ask your child to fit the blocks inside the shape by placing them on the paper. At first you will see your child putting the blocks inside the shape but not paying attention to the lines. This is why it will be important for you to demonstrate one shape and then let him do the rest himself.

It is important that parents help their children develop their use of the senses to support locomotion and navigation in the world around them by continuously providing movement experiences.

It is difficult for your child to integrate multisensory skills for balance and locomotion because his sensory and motor capabilities are still developing. Tasks such as learning to swim may take more time, but that does not mean they should not be attempted.

6. Health and Care

> **Your child's sense of independence is growing, and he is beginning to take his health and care into his own hands.**

He can now excuse himself to go to the potty without being prompted, start to brush his own teeth, and begin to wash his own hair. It is still important to monitor your child to guarantee that his body, teeth, and hair are cleaned well. You can also introduce other hygiene regimens such as flossing. If the doctor has not already, he or she will start talking to you about getting your child ready for school and all the checkpoints (hearing, vision, innoculations and a dental exam) needed for enrollment, as well as how to get your child prepared for this new routine.

Four year olds are more confident with their movement abilities, so they may test their limits more. This can result in scrapes, cuts, or bruises. Remember that the first thing you should do in these bumpy circumstances is stay calm and tend to your child.

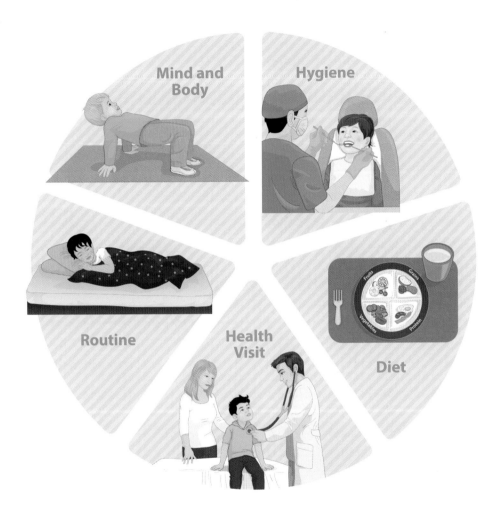

WHOLE CHILD: AGE FOUR

Health and Care

Hygiene >

Oral Care

Your child is capable of understanding not only the reasons for good hygiene, but also what happens when you don't practice good hygiene.

At this age, it is still important to help your child and make sure she washes her hands properly.

Encourage her to sing a song such as "Happy Birthday" or "Twinkle, Twinkle, Little Star" before she rinses the soap off her hands. This makes sure she is washing long enough to get the germs off her hands.

Take advantage of soaps that foam or smell to get your child excited about washing her hands. Make the sink easily accessible for your child; have a stepstool and soap readily available to make it easier for her to be more independent and productive.

Don't use rewards or punishments for your child when it comes to personal hygiene. Explain to her that these are things that are necessary to keep her healthy and safe from illness. Explain that she can't sit down and have snack until she washes her hands or that you can't read a bedtime story until she brushes her teeth.

Your child is more independent and is brushing her teeth every morning and night on her own; however, it is still important to monitor and make sure she is brushing her teeth properly. A good tool to introduce is a timer. There are a variety of digital and manual timers that can make it fun for your child as well as help her brush her teeth for the proper amount of time: two minutes.

Four years old is when your dentist will talk about thumb or finger sucking. It is important to start breaking your child of this habit now. Your pediatrician or dentist is trained to help with this problem, too, so seek advice if needed.

It is important to end this habit because it can start affecting your

child's adult teeth as well as spread germs due to your child's hands being in and out of her mouth after touching surfaces.

Your dentist will also talk to you about the correct amount of fluoride your child needs in her toothpaste at this early age. **Too much fluoride can stain your child's teeth and can also be toxic.** There are supplemental gels and special toothpastes made for children.

Milk contains sugars that are harmful to teeth. Have your child rinse with water after she drinks milk, and don't allow her to drink milk an hour to two hours before bedtime.

Now is the time to introduce floss to your child. Stop for a moment and think about your flossing practices. Do you floss regularly? Most adults do not, and if you don't floss, how can you possibly expect your child to pick up the habit?

According to dentists flossing is even more important than brushing when it comes to preventing disease and tooth decay. This is because brushing only gets the surface of your child's teeth; much food gets lodged between the teeth and decays there.

As with brushing your child will need supervision until she is about seven or eight years of age.

Flossing made simple:

1. Have your child cut off a piece of floss 18 inches long.

2. Have your child wrap the ends around her middle or index fingers on both hands.

3. Have your child gently guide the floss between her teeth, moving the floss around the tooth and under the gum line.

4. Alternatively, there are disposable flossing sticks that children can use for the same effect. They break easily so she may need to use more than one a day.

Talk to your dentist about how to maintain healthy gums and lessen the occurrence of cavities. Your doctor will talk to you about the foods your child eats and how often she rinses her mouth after eating sugary foods. Vegetables, fruits, and whole grains are highly recommended, and processed carbohydrates and foods high in sugar, such as white bread and pastries, are discouraged.

Diet >

By four years old, the dietary requirements for your child differ based on gender and activity levels. Girls between the ages of four and five need between 1,200 and 1,400 calories depending on how active they are, and boys between the ages of four and five need between 1,200 to 1,600 calories depending on their activity levels.

Dietary requirements include:

* grains: 4–5 ounces (half of all grains should be whole grains),
* vegetables: 1–1 ½ cups,
* fruits: 1 ½ cups,
* milk/dairy: 2 cups (milk should be 1% or 2% and fat-free),
* lean meat/beans: 3–4 ounces.

Sharing Reponsibility

A great way to help your child eat healthful foods is to get him involved. Talking about a healthful plate and all the healthful options can help develop cognitive skills.

To ensure diversity in his eating habits, have your child keep a tally of the different foods he has already eaten that day and what foods he still needs.

For example, if your child has cheese and crackers for snack, he can put a check under grains and dairy for the day, leaving him with three other servings of dairy and five more servings of grains for the day. This can be another opportunity to use counting skills and be more engaged in food choices.

Another example is using sorting skills when talking about different colors. Many healthful eating programs for children are encouraging a variety of colors on their plates. Many of the most colorful foods are vegetables and fruits. When at the grocery store, have your child pick fruits and vegetables of different colors or a color you have been talking about. This is a great way to have your child try new healthful foods such as red tomatoes, yellow squash, or purple eggplant. Stay away from unhealthful foods that are high in sugar, which usually come in shades of brown or white.

Cooking together is another great way to get your child involved in what he eats. Matching and gathering the materials needed to cook something and helping measure, stir, and combine ingredients can make eating his healthful creation more exciting.

Think of healthful decorating ideas for the foods you make together. You and your child can use cut up vegetables, raisins, peanut butter, cream cheese, or fruit to make your cooking creation look like a face or an animal.

High-Fiber Foods

Fruits and vegetables are excellent sources of fiber, so you should try to encourage your child to eat these foods. Other foods include beans, whole grain breads, and healthful cereals. One way to find foods that are high in fiber is to read the food labels. You can also teach your child how to read the labels by simply looking for numbers that you suggest he find.

Here is a list of other high-fiber foods that are over five grams: barley, navy beans, baked beans, split peas, lentils, wheat flour, refried beans, prunes, and spinach, just to name a few. Many of these foods may be new to your child, so show them to your child before you cook them and let your child learn a little about each food. Remember, you want to help that picky eater consume high-fiber foods.

Activity Level

It is recommended that children of this age get at least 60 minutes of structured physical activity per day, which means activities led by an adult or parent, and at least 60 minutes of unstructured physical activity such as free play each day. **Structured activities are great for working on sensory motor skills such as throwing, catching, kicking, or pedaling a bike.** Structured activities can also provide moments to practice balance and coordination through games like freeze tag, jumping, or balancing on one foot.

At age four, your child is starting to have his own interests, and this is a good time to enroll him in some extracurricular classes such as dance or team sports. He can have some structured activities planned while also socializing with other children who share the same interests.

Health Visit >

Medical professionals recommend that you bring your child in once a year around his birthday for a regular visit to keep him healthy. You can choose a primary care physician (family doctor) or a pediatrician.

Your doctor will communicate more with your child at this age and bring him into the conversation about safety and his daily routine. The doctor will ask questions about what your child likes to do, his favorite color, and how old he is. If your child is shy, try taking the lead on asking the questions after the doctor to see if your child is more comfortable telling you.

Expectations:

* Your doctor will check your child's vision with a vision test, which will focus more on sight than eye development.

* Your doctor will give your child a hearing exam.

* Your doctor will talk about your child's social and communication skills and ask him questions to hear how he answers. If your child is shy, tell your doctor so that you can ask your child the questions.

* Test your child's balance by having him walk heel to toe in a straight line and balance on one leg.

* Talk about your child's eating habits and physical movement.

* Your doctor will give any vaccines that are due. Vaccines protect your child by immunizing him against certain diseases. Many of these vaccines protect your child for life. Some are given as one shot or a series of shots. When possible your doctor will combine them.

Growing Pains

Growing pains are common among children ages four to six and again between eight and 12 years of age. Growing pains are cramping, achy muscle pains that some children feel in both legs and that keep your child awake at night because the pain usually occurs in the late afternoon or evenings.

Growing pains usually affect the muscles of your child's thighs, calves, and behind the knees. Pain varies from child to child, and most children do not have pain every day. Growing pains are not associated with bone growth but occur more often after your child has an active day of jumping or running.

Did you know that despite the name "growing pains," there is no evidence that growing pains are linked to growth spurts. In fact they simply may be due to intense childhood activities that wear out your child's muscles.

Growing Pains versus Other Pain

Growing pains are different than other medical pain because children respond differently to growing pains. They are more willing to let their parents hold them and massage the parts of their body that hurt when it comes to growing pains.

Help your child by:

*   massaging the areas that hurt,
*   stretching,
*   placing a heating pad on areas that hurt,
*   giving the proper dose of children's ibuprofen or acetaminophen.

Routine >

Building a weekly routine for your child helps establish his sleeping and eating schedule, as well as helping him build a better concept of time. Your four year old makes connections based on what he experiences. For example, if you pick up your child from school every day after lunch, that is when he will be expecting you.

Your child is building a better understanding of time. While he cannot yet tell time, he understands basic ideas such as tomorrow, yesterday, and what part of the day something will happen. You can build on these skills by having a weekly calendar for your child that shows what day it is and what is happening that day. You can have him place pictures and words on the calendar and together talk about what events and activities occur each day.

Safety

Safety is even more important for your child during this age because he has developed more gross motor skills. He is also ready and willing to challenge his gross motor abilities and this will result in frequent injuries. Your child is riding a tricycle, running, jumping, and climbing with ease.

Traffic and street safety:

Do not have your child play near streets, and talk to your child about not chasing any balls or toys if they go into the street. Your child should play in a fenced yard or playground with a barrier between him and traffic. Driveways are also dangerous. Walk behind your car before you back out of your driveway to be sure your child is not behind the car. You may not see your child in the rear view mirror. Encourage children to walk in front of the car when they get out so you can always see them.

Strangers:

Four years old is an important time to start talking about strangers. Talk to your child about what to do if someone he doesn't know approaches him. Let him know that if a stranger approaches him, he should start yelling and run, immediately tell you or his caregiver, and not take anything that a stranger gives him.

Playground equipment:

Before letting your child explore the playground, take a walk around the park and check the equipment to make sure the surface under the play equipment is soft enough to absorb a fall. Look for things like shredded rubber, sand, and woodchips or bark; loose filler should be at least nine inches deep under the play equipment. Have your child in sight so that you can monitor how high he climbs on the playground equipment.

Helmet:

Have your child wear a helmet when riding his tricycle, using a scooter, or skating. Some four year olds have transitioned out of a tricycle and can ride a bicycle. Make sure that your child is refitted for a helmet to insure that the brain is protected.

Chemicals:

Keep chemicals and cleaning solutions out of reach.

Car seats:

Four year olds still need a car seat every time they are in the car. The safest place for all children to ride is in the back seat. **At four years of age your child will likely still be in a forward-facing car seat and not yet a booster.** It is important to follow the recommended weight and height requirements for each car seat. And each state has its own age, weight, and height requirements for when it is safe to transition out of a booster into a regular seatbelt or be safe in the front seat.

Mind and Body >
Sexuality, Diversity and Differences, Difficult Conversations, Yoga

Sexuality

Around age four, your child will begin understanding what behaviors and language are used more frequently in private versus in public. **Because your child is used to exploring the world around him and learning by investigating and exploring, be prepared for him to be just as curious about behaviors such as sex and gender differences.**

Children generally don't become modest until about age six, but they will begin around age four to under-

stand that there are certain things done in private, such as going to the bathroom and dressing or undressing. Just like they have curiosity about how trees grow, they begin to exhibit curiosity by asking questions about where babies come from, attempting to see other people naked or undressed, and asking about their private parts and their bodily functions.

Don't ignore or jump to conclusions when your child asks you questions about sexuality.

You want him to feel comfortable asking you these questions. Approach the questions calmly. You do not want to embarrass your child or ignore him. Ask open-ended questions and guide your child regarding sexual behaviors you may see him engaging in.

Give your child basic information and answers to his questions.

Explain that boys and girls differ. Tell your child that girls' and boys' bodies are different and start to change more when they get older. Give simple explanations about where babies come from. Inform your child that some things are done in private.

Do not make your child feel ashamed about being curious, but it is very important to teach him about personal boundaries.

He may also pick up on "naughty" words that are not appropriate for him to use. Approach your child's use of bad words calmly. Do not laugh or ignore your child using words that are inappropriate, whether they are curse words, sexual words, or potty words. Approach the conversation in a calm manner. The more you make a big deal about it, the more he'll remember and use a word you wish he would not.

Diversity and Differences

Your child is interacting with other children and noticing more of their differences, from gender to race and different abilities. Just like they do when sorting colors and toys, children begin to make connections between people and their differences. It is important to talk to your child about similarities beyond race, such as hair color, the type of shoes people wear, or how many fingers people have, so that he is aware of cultural diversity in a broader context and understands that all people have similarities and differences beyond just culture and skin color.

Tips for helping your child be culturally aware include:

* Nurture a sense of pride in your child.

Talk to your child about differences, that differences in people do exist, and that differences are not bad. Look at the positive in some of the differences your child notices in others.

If your child is discouraged about not being able to do something as well as another child, such as running or drawing, remind him of all the things he can do well. If he is embarrassed by his own culture, talk about those differences in a positive manner. For example, say, "Our holiday has these delicious foods, and we get to spend time with our family."

* **Teach your child positive words to associate with differences.**

Instead of describing a difference in another as "not normal" say that it is "not common." Use *different abilities* instead of *disabilities*. Your child is naturally curious, so do not make him feel uncomfortable around someone new. **When you notice your child staring, ask him what he is thinking. Talk to him about the person in the wheelchair or someone of a different race or someone wearing a garment he hasn't seen before.**

If there is someone in your family or a close friend who is from a different culture, let your child ask this person questions. Instead of avoiding the person, talk to your child about being polite. He shouldn't point or stare at anyone. **Giving your child these guidelines also helps him see that everyone is different, and we should treat everyone with respect.**

* **Teach your child the golden rule.**

The golden rule is most commonly known as "treat others as you want to be treated." Talk to your child about how he would feel if he were left out of a group or were told he was not allowed to play because of the shoes he wore that day. Tell him it is okay to have friends you like to play with more than others and that sometimes it is okay to say no to someone who asks to play, but there is a nice way to say it.

Difficult Conversations

When talking to your child about some bad news (like divorce or death), or a big change (such as moving), pick a good time when he is not tired or moody. Ask him what he thinks and how he feels after hearing the news. Ask him again later after he has more time to process the news. Don't be surprised if your young child asks you about it again many days later.

If you have more than one child, make sure you take some time to talk to each child individually. Children of different ages process information in different ways.

Start your conversations with yes and no questions to get the dialogue going.

Be sure not to place blame on anyone or anything in the conversation.

Sometimes young children will change the subject to something that matters more to them at the time, such as asking what is for snack or a question about school. This is okay and is expected. Don't force him to stay on topic because it can frustrate him. Wait for another opportunity to talk about it.

Inform your child's teacher or babysitter that something is happening at home that is out of the ordinary (for example, a parent moving out, a parent traveling, or a death in the family) and ask the sitter or teacher to take some notes on your child's behavior. Your child may act out for attention at school if you are concentrating on the situation at home and not on him. Children can sense when something is wrong and may be confused and keep to themselves or act out either reaction is normal. Be sure to engage your child during times of change so that he does not withdraw emotionally or socially.

Yoga

Having your child participate in yoga gives him the ability to exercise both his body and mind.

Yoga encompasses the whole child by both strengthening children's bodies and calming their minds to shape better focus and build self-confidence. Through yoga, children are able to develop and foster more than just physical skills.

Yoga helps your child build problem-solving skills when testing his balance. Children will try to move their bodies and muscles in different ways until they find the best way to achieve the positions.

Yoga also helps his imagination and creativity skills. You can turn yoga into a story with your child and build language skills by having him name and sequence positions that go along with a storyline. Most of all enjoy your time together.

1. Seesaw

Either siblings or you and your child can practice the seesaw together to stretch the lower back, arms, shoulders, and hamstrings. To do this pose sit across from each other with legs stretched in front of you in a V shape with a tall back. The smaller member of the pair puts his or her legs on the inside of the longer-legged person's legs. Holding hands, gently rock back and forth.

2. Puppy Friends

You and your child (or siblings) should stand facing each other; slowly place your hands on one another's shoulders. Then step back and bend forward at the hips, bringing the head down to rest between the arms. Inhale and exhale several times. Puppy friends will stretch the hamstrings.

3. Holding Hands

You and your child (or siblings) should stand with your backs to each other about a foot apart from one another. Bend over and touch your toes, reach through your legs, and grab each other's hands. Hold hands together as you inhale and exhale several times.

1. Seesaw

2. Puppy Friends

3. Holding Hands

Remember, the Whole Child Parenting Program offers appropriate developmental products and monthly activity books that walk you through supporting your child's skills. Using these in conjunction with the recommended age-appropriate room materials ensures faster development.

Reaching Milestones >

Providing your child with opportunities to develop fully will be the most important gift you can give him during his fourth year. Development in all six categories, especially in the first years of your child's life, helps to maximize his likelihood of getting a good start on his future educational goals.

Monitoring your child's development in the first five years is of the utmost importance, since this is the stage of life when nerve tissue grows the fastest and matures—and is able to take in information. Development monitoring includes all activities related to the promotion of development in your child. Montoring is a flexible, ongoing process.

Use these milestones as a general guide; they are not all-inclusive. Reaching a milestone later does not mean there is a problem. It simply means he needs more time and practice to master the skills.

COGNITIVE

- Sorts objects by size, and by what kind of things they are, e.g. animals, or by color or shape. Can string large beads to make a pattern.
- Compares two weights to work out which is heavier.
- Can count to 10, recognize written numerals, and say numbers up to 20.
- Knows some variations of circle, square, triangle, and rectangle. Can copy shapes like a square, a cross, circle, and a triangle by age five.
- Understands *taller*, *smaller*, and *shorter*, but is still working on arranging a group of things in order of *smallest* to *biggest*.
- Can make observations, gather information, identify patterns, describe and discuss observations.

SOCIAL-EMOTIONAL

- Learns to understand others' feelings and needs, and shows that he can feel empathy for others. More consistently shares and takes turns.
- Learns to better manage intense emotions with coping strategies like talking it out or drawing a picture.
- Can smoothly join in a group play situation and suggest ways to resolve conflict.
- He can make friends and organize games. Sometimes behavior can be "over the top" noisy and exuberant. He may have an imaginary playmate. This is more likely if he doesn't have other children to play with.
- Sense of humor is developing, and he will laugh at a funny situation.

LANGUAGE

- Can understand two or three simple directions to do at once, e.g. "Get your sister's sippy cup, take it to her, and then bring the bowl back to the kitchen."

- Holds a pencil in a mature grip using his preferred hand and can cut on a line.

- Can tell long stories which may be partly true and partly made up. Understands adjectives, adverbs, and some prepositions; uses plurals.

- Understands that letters represent the sounds in spoken words and may associate some letters with their sounds. Recognizes some words he will see a lot, e.g. *stop* on stop signs.

- Capable of writing some legible letters and knows that writing goes from left to right and top to bottom.

CREATIVE

- Can identify changes in pitch, tempo, loudness, and musical duration. Can "sing" songs of his own creation as well as memorized ones.

- Begins to be more realistic and may incorporate letters in his art. Draws a person with identifiable parts.

- Loves to dance and is able to move rhythmically and smoothly.

- His dramatic play is highly imaginative and has the structure of specific scenarios, like going to the grocery store or rescuing a cat stuck in a tree.

PHYSICAL

- Climbs ladders and trees. Stands on tiptoes and walks and runs on tiptoe.

- Runs quite fast and jumps on one foot.

- Can walk along a line for short distances, ride bicycles with or without training wheels.

- Can hop, skip, and gallop. Stands on each foot for three seconds.

HEALTH AND CARE

- Uses a spoon and fork.

- Dresses without help, except with fasteners/buttons.

- Washes self in bathtub.

- Brushes teeth independently.

- Washes and dries hands.

Environment >
Four Year Old's Room

Your four year old is curious and inquisitive, and she wants ample opportunities to be an active participant in her own learning. Every four year old should learn through play. Natural settings like the home offer your child un-limited opportunities to explore and investigate.

A good home learning environ-ment offers a variety of play experiences as well as different types of activities that will encourage her creativity, support language skills, and inspire all of her pretend play ideas.

It is necessary to follow specific steps when setting up a home learning environment for your child.

The first way to create a flexible learning environment that ac-commodates her needs and interests is to take an inventory of your space and get organized. Remove any clutter, like old toys, from the room.

Store all learning materials in your **Six Drawer Whole Child Color-Coded Organizer.**

Then place the recommended furniture in her room for her to use in a variety of activities. She will be able to choose based on the **six areas of development: cognitive, social emotional, language, creative, physical, and health.**

The following picture gives you a glimpse of what your four year old's room will look like after you have followed the steps above.

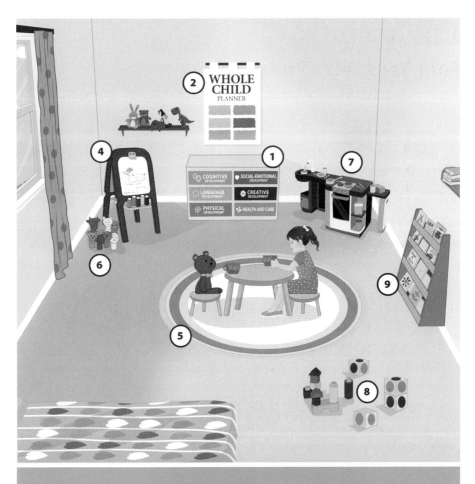

Whole Child: Four Year Old's Room

The following list contains must-have items for your four year old's room. These items will be used interchangeably with your other Whole Child Parenting materials.

1. Six Drawer Whole Child Color-Coded Organizer
2. Whole Child Wall Planner
3. Table and Chairs
4. Easel
5. Carpet
6. Puppet/Pretend Play Materials
7. Kitchen Set
8. Blocks and Manipulatives
9. Bookshelf

WHOLE CHILD

Parenting Program books and materials are available worldwide.

Also available separately

INFANT
(Birth to 12 Months)

TODDLER
(12 to 24 Months)

AGE TWO

AGE THREE

AGE FOUR

Birth to Age Five

The book that kick started the program!

Whole Child Program Activity Books

- 4 **Infant** Titles
- 6 **Toddler** Titles
- 12 **Age Two** Titles
- 12 **Age Three** Titles
- 12 **Age Four** Titles

Whole Child Program books and materials are available at special discounts when purchased in bulk for premiums and sales promotions as well as for fundraising or educational use. For details, please contact us at: sales@wholechild.co

Visit us on the web at: www.wholechild.co